D1639748

History of the
MOTOR CAR

History of the
MOTOR CAR

Peter Roberts

This edition produced exclusively for

WHSMITH

ACKNOWLEDGMENTS

The author, who owes a considerable debt of gratitude to a number of people who helped to make this book possible, wishes to thank the following individuals and organizations for valuable documentary assistance, and also to express his thanks to those who made their vehicles available for photographing.

Michael Banfield; Ken Barley, Boroughbridge; Cecil Bendall; John Bentley; John Carter of Saundersfoot, Dyfed; Jim Clark; Michael Clayton; Anthony David for vital editorial help; Susan Dell; Peter Hull of the VSCC; Joan Innes-Kerr of the VCC; Robert and Bridget Laycock; Sotheby Parke-Bernet and Michael Worthington-Williams; Stephen Manley (research); Stewart Skilbeck; Emile Snapper in association with Stephen Langton Ltd.; Johnnie Thomas of Nantgaredig, Dyfed; Wayne Warlow.

AA and RAC; Adam Opel AG; Alfa Romeo SpA; American Motors Corporation; Automobiles Citroën; Automobile Peugeot SA; Automobile Manufacturers Association, Detroit USA; BL UK Ltd.; Christie's South Kensington; Chrysler Corporation USA; Daimler-Benz AG Stuttgart; Detroit Library; Doune Motor Museum, Scotland; Falstaff Antiques (Morgan Museum) and Mr. C. M. Booth at Rolvenden, Kent; Fiat SpA; Ford Motor Company; General Motors Corporation; Heritage Motor Museum, London; Kodak Museum; Lips Autotron, Drunen, Holland; Mercedes-Benz UK Ltd.; Michelin Tyre PLC; Musée de L'Automobiles Française, St. Dizier; Norddeutches Auto Museum; Régie Renault; Rolls-Royce Motors Ltd.; VAG (UK) Ltd.; Vauxhall Motors Ltd.; Victoria & Albert Museum, Bethnal Green, London.

**This edition produced exclusively for
W H Smith**

Published by
Deans International Publishing
52–54 Southwark Street, London SE1 1UA
A division of The Hamlyn Publishing Group Limited
London·New York·Sydney·Toronto

Copyright © The Hamlyn Publishing Group Limited 1984
ISBN 0 603 03609 0

All rights reserved. No part of this publication
may be reproduced, stored in a retrieval system,
or transmitted, in any form or by any means,
electronic, mechanical, photocopying, recording
or otherwise, without the permission of The Hamlyn
Publishing Group Limited.

Printed in Italy

Contents

The Automobile Is Born: 1885-1889

Opposite top: French engineer Nicholas Cugnot's first full-sized steam fardier *of 1770. The world's first mechanically propelled vehicle was designed as a military tractor.*

The scene is an arcaded square in Paris; the time, a sunny Sunday morning in 1770. Street sellers shout their wares; ladies hold their skirts as they cross the small *place*, their escorts at their sides. Louis XV is on the throne. A son was born last year to the Corsican family of Buonaparte. The first signs of the revolution that is to devastate France are still some 18 years into the future. . . .

A clanking rumble is heard in the near distance. Through the trees at the far corner of the square a large vehicle slowly appears. No team of horses draws its wood-and-metal bulk; it progresses entirely without visible aid or command, save for one small figure standing high on the superstructure, struggling with a heavy iron handle. Plumes of steam can be seen escaping from its depths.

Before observers have time to recover from their initial shock, the gargantuan object clatters its way into the square on three titanic wheels – and out again, coming to a halt only after demolishing a high garden wall . . . .

Those French spectators had witnessed the first trial of the world's first self-propelled road vehicle – and had seen the first 'motor accident'.

Engineer Nicholas Cugnot's heavy steam-driven machine, a *fardier* or gun-towing tractor, had been ordered by the Minister of War. The French steam pioneer had produced a working model a year earlier which had interested the army. A report states: 'In the presence of General Gribeauval and many other spectators, and carrying four persons it ran on the level, and I have confirmed that it could have covered 1 800 to 2 000 toises (about 2.4 miles) an hour if it

had been run without interruption.' The full-size prototype wagon was indeed a monster, weighing about four tons and carrying an immense boiler and two bucket-sized cylinders. Since the boiler was suspended over the single front wheel and was made to swing with it, disaster was predictable.

But it *was* the first attempt at mechanically propelled travel. There had been dreamers and visionaries before. The great Leonardo himself made some very nice unworkable drawings, learned priests with a mechanical bent had made toys that moved by steam, eminent scientists had announced that man would one day be able to travel by mechanical means. But no one until Cugnot had genuinely carried anyone anywhere by such means.

Cugnot's machine has been preserved. It rests in the Conservatoire des Arts et Métiers in Paris and may be seen today.

Others were soon to follow Cugnot. Englishman Richard Trevithick made several successful steam coaches and high-pressure steam locomotives at the beginning of the 19th century; Oliver Evans of Philadelphia built his steam amphibian *Orukter Amphibolos*. By the 1830s, particularly in England where a strong interest was shown in promoting public transport, a period that could be called the Golden Age of Steam blossomed.

Notable were Goldsworthy Gurney, whose first carriage used both wheels and mechanical legs to propel it and who later set up a Glasgow 'omnibus' service, and Walter Hancock, who was perhaps the most successful with his steam coaches. His most sophisticated was *Enterprise*, a handsome bus-like

Opposite bottom: In 1805 Oliver Evans built this steam dredger, an amphibian vehicle he named Orukter Amphibolos. *Its short trip down to the river is recognized as the first successful journey by a steam road vehicle in the United States.*

Overleaf: An Early English steam carriage. Richard Trevithick of Cornwall had introduced his steam carriage in 1801. Goldsworthy Gurney's carriage shown here 'conveying the Duke of Wellington and other persons of distinction', was first seen in 1829.

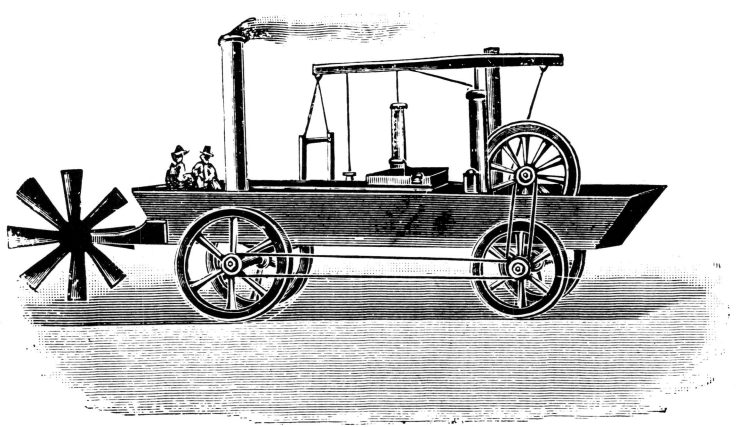

J. Doyle del.t et lithog.

A Sk

Mr. GURNEY'S NEW

As it appeared at Hounslow on the 12.th of August, with a Barouche atta

Pub.d by J. Dickins

Printed by C.Hullmandel.

1 of

TEAM CARRIAGE.

, containing the Duke of Wellington and other Persons of Distinction.

New Bond St.

9

THE "ENTERPRISE" STEAM OMNIBUS.
BUILT BY Mr Walter Hancock of Stratford, FOR THE
LONDON AND PADDINGTON STEAM CARRIAGE COMPY

The short-lived Enterprise, *one of Walter Hancock's colourful fleet of steam omnibuses, in 1833, the heyday of steam operations on British roads. By the following decade legislation had killed them off.*

vehicle that could be seen in the London area where Hancock had set up a regular passenger service. Those who put their faith in road steam transport had, however, not forseen the development of steam transport designed to run on metal rails . . . .

Railway transport and railway lines multiplied rapidly. Cheap, direct, relatively fast, this was the welcome answer to long-distance travel in early Victorian Britain – and for the rest of the world shortly afterwards. Steam road transport withered, and once more the roads of Britain were used only by the walker, the carter and the horse-drawn coach . . . .

The 1867 Paris World Fair was about to open its gates to an eager and fascinated public. The vast concourse promised to be the most colourful that Europe had yet seen, with Paris itself newly rebuilt under Napoleon III, who had ordered Baron Haussman to widen the streets into great boulevards, to lay out new parks, to erect elegant bridges and to set up international expositions to attract the

world to the French capital.

Among the technical exhibits here in the summer of 1867 was an engine from the workshop of Nicholas Otto & Company a small enterprise set up recently by Otto and his colleague, Eugen Langen, from Germany. Otto had shown a strong interest in engine mechanics as a youth, and had left the business world (he was at the time an office clerk) to devote his time to improving the crude but workable combustion engine invented by Belgian-born Etienne Lenoir.

Lenoir had already developed a stationary engine driven by lighting-gas mixed with air ignited in a cylinder at atmospheric pressure – a machine that was quiet-running, had the advantage of immediate starting, did not require large and frequent doses of water – and that gave just 1hp for a 6-litre capacity. It was, by any standards, abysmally inefficient.

However, to Lenoir must go the credit due to the producer of the world's first self-propelled vehicle – one could hardly call it a car – in 1860.

He had reduced the cumbersome engine to underseat size, fuelled it with petroleum vapour, and it would be only a slight indulgence to say that this remarkable cart had an electric ignition and a spark plug.

However, thought Otto, if the non-compressing Lenoir unit could be modified to include a compression stroke, thus concentrating the gas-mix in the cylinder, the following explosion after igniting the stuff would give the unit more powerful kick. It did, although this was not yet a four-stroke engine, as the gases were compressed *before* entering the cylinder. During these developments Otto had in fact designed a four-stroke unit, but had abandoned it in favour of his unwieldy two-stroke engine.

Gasmotoren-Fabrik Deutz, as the flourishing Otto & Langen company was called in 1872, employed a technical manager with a somewhat force-

A small gas-engine built by Nicholas Otto & Co from Germany was seen at the Paris Exposition of 1867. This is a model of his later 1876 unit, which included a fourth compression stroke, in which the gas was compressed inside the cylinder.

ful character. Although under his direction production of the engines rose to 90 a month, high success for the still-growing firm, the 38-year-old manager was to leave the company eventually and pursue his own automotive research. Gottlieb Daimler, a baker's son from Schorndorf in what was charmingly known as 'Württemberg's little Garden of Paradise', was an engineer destined to earn his place in history as one of the 'fathers of the automobile'.

Daimler engaged a new chief engineer, Franz Rings, who with Otto himself followed up the abandoned four-stroke engine of earlier years; the fiery manager had long held that the current Otto engine could be greatly improved by designing the operation to include compression. Prototypes were built and successfully tested in late 1876. The only fundamental problem was one which constantly dogged Daimler for most of his early work – ignition – which was carried out by the crude but complex business of exposing a flame to the mixture in the chamber by a slide valve and a series of labyrinthine passages to prevent the blowback of gases.

The Daimler-prompted engine from Gasmotoren Fabrik Deutz marked a major success in the development of the internal combustion reciprocating petroleum-fuelled engine, a breakthrough that separated it in history from the experimenters and the dreamers of the past whose devices either failed in practice or were never developed enough to interest the general public. And at this point in history Nicholas Otto has his niche, too, as the inventor of the four-stroke cycle, known as the Otto cycle even today. The story of the development of motor transport moves on, with Otto's one-time manager taking centre stage.

During this last quarter of the 19th century the world was ready for many changes, particularly in transportation. Railroads networked much of Europe by 1880, led by the British pioneer production, development and use of steam locomotives on land, and massive steam-driven ships plied the ocean. Steam had been used at sea since the beginning of the century and now sail was rapidly being superseded by powered vessels. Sea-travel was faster, more comfortable, less influenced by the whims of wind and weather. Engineers were looking to the air with interest, too, for even there some could see new highways now that hot-air or gas-filled balloons had proved that man could fly, though here, of course, one *was* subject to the vagaries of the elements. Gottlieb Daimler was well aware of the need for a light, reliable and simple power unit which could not only propel vehicles of various types but could accommodate the upcoming requirements for multiple power sources for the coming age of high production, to feed and clothe a world whose population had mushroomed in the past few years.

Schoolboy Engineer

Daimler's interest in fine engineering dated from his first schooldays at a Latin institution. He had quickly shown that he cared more for instruction that would gain him a sound knowledge of mechanical power than in classical languages, and became deeply involved in plane-and-solid geometry and maths.

The German states at that time were, as usual, quarrelling with neighbours and were constantly recruiting men and buying arms for local protection.

Daimler was apprenticed to the flourishing industry of small-arms making. Here he proved a first-class craftsman in metal, stayed four years, completed his pupillage – and decided that gunmaking was not his métier. He enrolled in a school of engineering and industrial arts. His evening work here

The new chief engineer at Gasmotoren Fabrik Deutz, Gottlieb Daimler. His first task was to bring the Otto atmospheric engine to its high point of design and function.

brought him, at 19, a job with a large French firm producing railway rolling stock and locomotives. He soon learned French.

Daimler's pioneering locomotive building work (the first German railway locomotive had been built only 15 years earlier) introduced him to heavy engineering – and typically he decided that his experience in this field was too slight. He must widen his knowledge.

The youthful, energetic Württem-berger also realized that steam engines and steam locomotives were not his vocation, and tried to persuade his directors that a small light engine powered by some method other than steam, an instant-starting engine which would 'cost a modest sum to run, could be used in factories that were too small to afford or need the current large engine' would, if manufactured, show a profit. He failed to convince anyone, and resigned.

Daimler's V-twin engine of 1889 had a higher speed than the single cylinder original with a maximum of 900rpm and an output of nearly 3hp in its final form.

Above: Gottlieb Daimler's original private workshop, after starting his own independent research into the internal combustion engine, was in the garden of his own home. Here, in 1883, Daimler and Maybach completed their first 4-stroke engine, seen here still on the workbench.

Opposite: Daimler's early hot-tube ignition system was basic indeed, as may be seen from this detail of his first engine. The thin-walled tube projecting into the cylinder had to be kept red-hot by a burner. Could this possibly be a 19th-century blowlamp?

By this time, 1862, Lenoir had patented his own engine. Steam experts derided its possible uses, declaring that although it needed no heating apparatus, it *would* need constant lubrication, and so on and so on – anything to confound opinion about an engine that clearly had a future.

Lenoir's atmospheric unit was described as follows in a sales sheet (a description that had, curiously, an influence on the later health and progress of the American automotive industry, but more of that later): 'The Lenoir engine uses Street's patented piston with direct and double action as developed by Lebon; the ignition is as with the Rivas engine, the cylinder is cooled by water as in Samuel Brown's engine, it can be made to run on liquid hydrocarbons as suggested by Erskine

Hazard, but in spite of all this the Lenoir engine sucks in gas and air through the action of the piston without necessitating any previous mixing, and for this reason it has a proper claim to be patented.'

A visit to Paris at the height of the Lenoir phenomenon further stimulated Daimler's wish to develop an engine independent of steam – and independent of a fixed fuel supply as provided by piped town gas.

Gottlieb Daimler, now a mature 28 years old and luckily with few financial worries, spent these years moving around Europe in search of engineering ideas. We know he spent some time in Paris, studied road traffic-flow (so say the historians) and declined to take up the offer of a post with the small woodworking machinery company of

Perrin. He could not know that this Paris firm would grow into the great Panhard and Levassor automobile company of later times.

The footloose engineer went on a peripatetic trip to England in 1861, finding Leeds' 'satanic mills' a fascinating scene and working there for a period in a machine shop, moving on to Manchester to work for the firm of Roberts & Company makers of machine tools, steam boilers and locomotives. He also made contact with firms in Coventry, a city which was later to be the home of a company bearing his own name. The industrious Gottlieb learned English.

First Engine

At Daimler's next job he met Wilhelm Maybach, 12 years his junior and a self-taught engineer of brilliance. Maybach was to play a significant part in the design of Daimler's early engines and cars, and indeed some say that modern transport owes more to him than to his master, Daimler.

In March 1872 Daimler was appointed manager of Gasmotoren-Fabrik Deutz and he took Maybach with him.

As early as 1875 Gottlieb Daimler had begun experimenting with gas engines of the atmospheric types, but with little success at first. Franz Rings now took a technical hand, designing a true four-cycle unit for the company, under Daimler's direction. The research diary entry of 9 May 1876 shows the first record of a four-stroke engine, and as the originator of the principle, the system bore Otto's name. It was the foundation of all that followed.

Daimler and Maybach decided to set up on their own – there had been disagreements at the company and Daimler's two basic precepts for engine success, a high rate of revolution and light engine weight, had been ignored. The new Otto four-stroke units were still slow-operating heavyweights. By 1882 they had set up a workshop – a greenhouse and lean-to shed – in the spacious garden of the Daimler family house in the Taubenheimstrasse of Cannstatt, near Stuttgart (the greenhouse is still there in the wooded garden, by the way, and Daimler's bench and tools, exactly as they were left a century ago, may still be seen), where together they built their first working four-stroke petrol engine.

Right: Daimler's 'single-track' machine was tested in 1885, and his 'motor coach', shown here, in 1886. Its engine turned at 650 revolutions a minute, an extremely high speed for the time (slow idling speed today) and developed just over one horsepower.

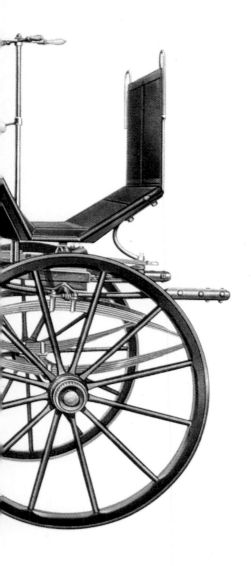

For the late 19th century, the engine was indeed high-speed, as Daimler had laid down in his prime requirements; at up to 900 revolutions per minute it was faster by far than the larger stationary engines, which were also about 10 times heavier than Daimler's small single-cylinder unit.

Two years later the two engineers and Daimler's 16-year-old son, Paul, were trundling around the garden paths at Cannstatt on the world's first petrol-engined vehicle, a crude motorcycle. Something between a hobby-horse and a wheelbarrow, this curious two-wheeler was purely an experimental essay. Daimler had no intention then of creating a road-going motorcycle, and, in fact, it was more than a decade later that the first practical motorcycle was seen. His intention had been to create an engine capable of powering either mobile or stationary machinery.

But by 1885, after two years of development — and one dead-of-night visit by the local police who thought he might have been forging coins — the now-improved engine was ready to install in a four-wheeled phaeton.

Daimler had ordered a sturdy model, saying that it was to be a birthday gift for his wife (secrecy was a feature of much technical development then, not to protect from theft but as a safeguard against unfavourable reaction from the local populace) and quietly fitted his 1-hp engine into the rear floor-well of the carriage where it sat like an oversized samovar near the rear passenger's legs. It was coupled to the rear wheels, and a steering rig directed the front wheels.

Left: A few months after Daimler had completed his first motor vehicle he could often be seen demonstrating his motored river-boat to other distinguished engineers on the River Neckar at Cannstatt.

Early the following year, 1886, Daimler's 'birthday' coach could be seen clattering through the extensive gardens of Daimler's home. Later it puttered out on occasional clandestine sorties along local roads.

Now Gottlieb Daimler saw his life-long aspirations in tangible form. His engine would propel everything on wheels and every craft that plied the ocean routes, but first a motor-powered boat for the local river, the Neckar. Not six months after the first engine was built he had installed another in a small river boat and was soon sitting at the tiller, silently propelling it up and down the Neckar to the complete astonishment of the people of Cannstatt. Said the local newspaper of 5 November 1886: 'Recently a boat has been seen circulating on the Neckar with about eight persons aboard. It appears to be propelled by some unseen power up and down-stream with great speed.... The first run was made in August and many outstanding engineers have been on these trips . . . .'

Daimler went on to power a fire engine, a small airship, a tram, a railroad car and other vehicles – all within a couple of years. His immediate success, however, came from his engined boats – people seemed less apprehensive of this nasty 'explosion' engine when it was surrounded by water – and he built several for German royalty and other eminent people.

This railroad car propelled by a Daimler belt-driven single cylinder unit was in operation by 1887, just a year after the engineer's first motor carriage.

Meanwhile at Mannheim . . .

At this point in history one had to take a day's carriage-ride down the road to Mannheim to meet another German engineer who was working on an almost identical project and who, in fact, produced the world's first practical motor car – just after Daimler had built his motorcycle, but before he had

publicly exhibited his first four-wheel vehicle.

Karl Benz's background was in many ways similar to that of Daimler, with the exception of the financial support that Daimler could command. Physics and chemistry were his subjects and his hobby was photography, then in its early form. A period at the Karlsruhe Polytechnic, arguably the finest institute of its kind then in Europe, taught Benz, like Daimler, to search for a more efficient engine than the ponderous steam giants of the day.

By an odd coincidence Daimler had earlier been taught during his first working post by a former teacher at the Karlsruhe Polythechnic, philosopher-

The power department of Herr Wolfert's new airship of 1888. Once a free balloon, the craft could now be driven directionally and made to change its altitude. Daimler's engine drove two propellers.

Karl Benz, maker of the first petrol-fuelled motor car. This formal picture of him was taken while he was a student at Karlsruhe Polytechnic, aged 20.

The improved version of the first Benz three-wheeler with Karl Benz's daughters aboard. A family picture taken about 1889.

engineer Ferdinand Redtenbacher. Still revered for his advanced technical thought, Redtenbacher's advice to Benz, 10 years Daimler's junior, that he concentrate on a new form of engine, proved a major influence. 'The worthwhile thing to spend time on,' Redtenbacher told Benz, 'is getting to the bottom of the problem of heat .... then we can throw out these steam engines for good .... The key invention must be made first, so that engines can be kept down to a reasonable size.'

'The key invention' was to be the internal combustion engine, and several minds were directed to this end during the 1860s.

Karl Benz also found work in a locomotive-building factory at Karlsruhe, the very company that appointed Gottlieb Daimler as its chief engineer just three years after Benz had left. Benz was also to come into contact with Otto's atmospheric engine — which also fired him with a desire to improve it.

Fraulein Bertha Ringer, daughter of a prominent builder in Pforzheim was also 20 years old when she married Karl Benz to become his lifelong inspiration.

Benz and his pretty wife, Bertha, who became his lifelong inspiration, set up a tiny machine shop in Mannheim in 1872. Their main assets were faith, hope and energy, and to augment their meagre living, Karl took orders for making clamps and pipes for the building industry, and even took on the hydraulic pressing of tobacco into plug. Occasionally a court order to repossess their goods threatened total ruin.

With what tools he had left after yet another domestic financial disaster Karl Benz turned to his long-term goal, the small high-speed engine. He knew that only some dramatic achievement could save them from catastrophy, and Karl worked feverishly on improving a two-stroke engine half-developed by Scotsman Dugald Clerk. Otto had recently patented his four-cycle engine, and thus anyone else who wished to pursue the development of the internal combustion motor was forced to do all his experimenting with the two-stroke (or two-cycle) process. The trouble, as in all these early engines, was ignition – the fuel mix would often ignite outside the cylinder and cause havoc. Benz managed to overcome this danger and also arranged that hot exhaust gas was expelled before the fresh mixture was introduced.

New Year Bells

Karl Benz's two-stroke engine design took it far into technical *terra incognita,* where it remained stubbornly silent.

The project was life-or-death to 35-year-old Benz and his family. For them the New Year's Eve that heralded 1880 was grim. Towards midnight Bertha suggested that they go out again to the garden workshop and try to start the thing just once more.

In his later memoirs Karl Benz wrote of that moment in moving terms: 'So there we were, standing in front of the engine as if it were a great mystery . . . my heart was pounding. I turned the crank . . . the engine started to go put-put-put, and the music of the future sounded . . . If sorrow had been our companion on the way over there, joy walked beside us on the way back . . . Suddenly the bells started to ring – New Year's Eve Bells. We felt they were not only ringing in a new year, but a new era for us . . .'.

This must be considered the first practical modern engine, sounding out its single note to the world some three years before Daimler's first power unit.

Court photographer Emil Bühler saw Benz's machine – and immediately lent funds for development, giving the penniless couple a brief breathing space. But after three months of altercation Benz resigned from the newly formed company. Now fundless again and with four children, Benz doggedly went back to his engine development. By 1883 he had set up business once again – Benz et Cie – 'To build combustion engines to the design of Karl Benz' as the company articles stated.

Benz, with partners Rose and Esslinger, made engines to the Benz pattern for static uses, but Karl was

still preoccupied with making a motor vehicle driven by his own engine, an aim which was not shared by his colleagues. 'When the company is making enough profit, then we can think about taking a jump into the future' argued the partners who held the purse-strings. And anyway, the firm was producing Benz's new four-stroke engine to capacity.

His power units were so successful – they won Benz an award at the *Exposition Universelle* in 1885 – that the company was under pressure to expand into larger premises. This success hardened Benz's resolve to start work on his engined carriage. He eventually obtained his partners' unenthusiastic agreement and began building his engine and vehicle at almost exactly the same time as Daimler was putting together his single-cylinder en-

gine down the road at Cannstatt. One may be excused for assuming that they knew of each other's work and indeed possibly knew each other, as their lives and careers, in retrospect, seem so entwined. However, the fact that they never met, even though their two companies later became one, is one of those odd quirks of history.

Unlike Daimler, Benz was concerned only with a motored road vehicle. His engine was an integral part of a complete design that was new from tiller to tyres. His designs were formalized in German Patent No. 37435 of 29 January 1886, but the car was built and running during late 1885. Meanwhile Benz was improving the ignition, the carburetion and throttle control, until in July 1886 he held a public demonstration of the car.

The water-cooled cast-iron single-

Karl Benz' first 'Patent Motor Wagen' was completed towards the end of 1885. The water-cooled one-cylinder unit developed about 0.8 hp and used electrical ignition.

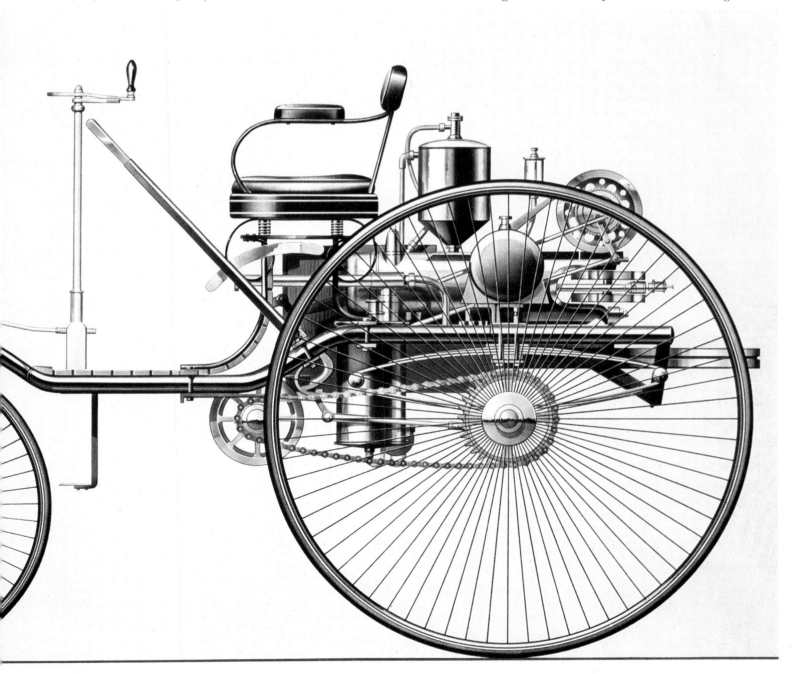

The first advertisement for Karl Benz's Patent Motor Wagen, dated 1888. Selling at 2 000 marks this machine, we are told in the ad, runs on paraffin, petrol, or naptha, and 'is an agreeable vehicle as well as a mountain-climber'.

cylinder engine with horizontal flywheel (Benz thought that a vertical one would interfere gyroscopically with the steering) developed about 0.8 hp at 400 rpm – an extremely high rate of rotation for any power-machine of the day. The car (short for carriage) had a lone front wheel which coped well enough with the steering for several years, until Benz solved the geometric problems associated with steering two front wheels.

Belts connected to a countershaft and chain drive to the rear wheels provided forward movement and Benz had also given the little car a 'neutral' so that the engine could be left running when the car was stationary. But perhaps the most astonishing innovation was the ignition. Benz had overcome the hazardous ignition problem with 'a Ruhmkorff trembler coil with a buzzer interrupter', a spark plug

(made by himself) and a chromic-acid battery, a far more sophisticated system than Daimler's uncertain hot-tube ignition. The steel-framed three-wheelers top speed was about 9 mph, and its local-journey reliability was good.

The world's first long-distance motoring 'joyride' reads like something from a Disney Story – almost too good to be true – and for many years was doubted as historic fact for this reason. However, research has confirmed that Bertha Benz and two of her children, Richard and Eugen, did indeed prove the car in no small way one Sunday in 1888. They had, by then, often been out for an evening spin along the road from Mannheim to Weinheim – about 6 kilometres (4 miles) but had never tested the car over a longer route.

Secretly mother and sons set off early, while father Benz was away, and headed for the neighbouring town of Pforzheim. Their journey had its problems: replenishing water, finding an apothecary for petroleum fuel, pushing the car up the hills of the region, persuading a cobbler to make a new leather brakeblock, using Frau Benz's garter as a replacement rubber insulator. All were overcome and they sighted the lights of Pforzheim at dusk. They had travelled about 100 km (60 miles), the first-ever long-distance day-trip in a motor car. Curiously this epic journey was never reported in the German press, although today it is recognized as a historic watershed in the chronicle of the automobile.

Twin-chains, wooden-spoked artillery wheels and fully elliptical leaf springs comprises final drive and suspension on this early Benz, Dos-à-Dos.

The Postmaster's Opinion

A letter to Karl Benz making some useful comments on his horseless carriage was probably in answer to a suggestion that the local mail service should use his vehicle for deliveries. It gives us an insight into a personal view of the future of the motor car. Dated January 1890 it is from the postmaster in the town of Speyer, a few kilometres from Benz's workshop at Mannheim. It is slightly abridged here:

'Since you mentioned that up till next spring you expected to attack this problem (of automotive transport) with greater energy, I would like to allow myself to call your attention to certain points as follows:

The steering mechanism of the vehicle is inside the chaise, in your new four-wheeled model (not yet built) could you not have a sort of coachman's seat up in front so that the enclosed space could all be at the disposal of the passengers?

Why are there no controls for going backwards? The fact that you cannot go backwards is something to puzzle at.

Should you not employ a more powerful engine, so that swampy sections of the road and deep snow could more easily be traversed? ... If you are to include these improvements in your car, indispensable for a safe and sure road performance, I am positive that your ingenious and most practical invention will be crowned with great success. I am not only thinking of its usefulness to the postal services, but am convinced that it would be most excellent for a country doctor. Not every doctor in a small village has box stalls, horses, and a farm to maintain them .... Before he has roused the sleep-drunk peasant out of his bed and got him to put bridle and harness on the horse, a lot of valuable time has been lost.

Another (good) thing about your vehicle: it comes to a stop and turns off and that's it. It does not need any feed or any groom, no blacksmith, no danger of having a horse shy; it just moves along as if a ghostly hand were pushing it, and one stroke of the brake and it stops .... That is what makes it so inexpensive to operate.

Even the stupidest blockhead must be able to see such an immense advantage as this.

The vehicle in motion *does* have something comical in its appearance from the aesthetic point of view, and someone who did not know what it was might think it was a runaway chaise (light carriage) he was looking at. But here also a lot of minor changes and adjustments can be artfully made to improve its appearance without in any way losing sight of the characteristics that serve its purpose.

If this were done, the lack of an animal in front to pull it would not be so striking to the beholder.

You must, Herr Benz, forgive me for making known my views at such length, but I know that men in special fields often wish to know how a layman feels. I am very curious to see how the first four-wheeled vehicle works out, and I wish you success with your most excellent invention, which cannot be wanting once you get it started.'

Postmaster Kugler's lucid and constructive letter was indeed a help to Benz at the time, and must have influenced his next move, the development of his first four-wheel vehicle, the Viktoria, although, as a two-seater, it was more of an owner-driver's car, with little accommodation for coachmen. The Viktoria was the Benz family's favourite transport for several years.

The news of the new transportation crossed the Atlantic rapidly. Here the Scientific American *magazine of 5 January 1889, under the heading 'A complete Substitute for Carriage with Horses' extols the Benz car, now sporting a new cover for the rear-located engine.*

France Takes the Lead: 1890-1899

Designed in 1888–89 by Wilhelm Maybach, Daimler's close friend and valued assistant, the new Stahlradwagen – the steel-wheeled car – was a four-wheeled light car using the Daimler V-twin engine.

A brief five years after Benz and Daimler had built their first motor vehicles, the cradle of motoring had moved to France.

Perhaps it was the volatile and imaginative French temperament, or the country's good road network which cried out for fast long-distance transport, or the large areas of France that were not accessible by railway. Whatever the reasons, the French were ready for the automobile from the time they first laid eyes on it. German industry of the type that could have taken up car-making in the late 19th century was hesitant – it was geared for the production of sewing machines or bicycles and was not yet eager to risk

its reputation and funds on a new and untried engineering development. Not a single customer could be found in Germany. France, on the other hand, had experienced mechanical road transport and, indeed, Paris was accustomed to seeing steam vehicles on its boulevards and avenues. Both Benz and Daimler in Germany were promoting their products both in their own country and in France and had been developing the cars to appeal to buyers anywhere.

Benz had improved his three-wheeler considerably by 1889, raising the power of the tiny horizontal engine by stages from under a single horsepower to over 2 hp. He had issued a prospectus in several languages and was in business as the first 'motor-maker'. Little real progress had been made, however, and the main profit-earner of the Benz company was still the stationary engine. Parisian agent Emile Roger began to boost his sales a little about this time, and was now building some parts of his machines – identical to the Benz model – in France. Benz, however, was far from satisfied with this very limited market.

Gottlieb Daimler, on the other hand, did not pursue the road transport theme fully until around 1889. His visionary essays into rail, air, and marine transport clearly indicated that he saw his engine, more sophisticated

in some ways (ignition excepted) than that of Benz, as a universal magic carpet. But when he developed his *Stahlradwagen* – the steel-wheeled car – he returned to road vehicles and subsequently paid more attention to that form of transport, while selling 'loose' engines which were by then twin-cylinder. At this time Daimler was also licencing other manufacturers to build his units.

At the Paris World Fair

In 1889 a great World's Fair was held in Paris. Eiffel had built his fantastic tower to mark the site and the occasion, and the wealth of France was gathered there. This was the centenary of the French Revolution. For motor transport it heralded the new technological revolution.

About 60 gas engines were exhibited, most atmospheric. Daimler showed his new steel-wheeler and Benz his three-wheeler 'Patent Motor Car', in the company of several steam cars – a De Dion Bouton, an experimental Peugeot with a Serpollet engine and a Brazier. The public, however, took little notice of the machines that were to change their lifestyles so radically during the next generation.

Both Karl Benz and Gottlieb Daimler were at the Paris Exposition, and both had high hopes of selling their

Both Benz and Daimler had improved their machines by the early 1890s – although until the beginning of the decade Benz's main business had been in stationary engines, and Daimler's in engines for general use. This is Benz's first 4-wheel vehicle, the Viktoria of 1893.

By 1894 Karl Benz had built his first machine for series production – the light and simple Velo. He produced 62 in the first year. Benz is seen here with his children, Richard, Thilde, Ellen, Clara and Eugen.

vehicles and engines. Benz had already made several demonstration runs for Emile Levassor of the Panhard and Levassor Company in nearby Paris streets. But Madame Sarazin, a lady of some business acumen and the recent widow of Daimler's intended agent in France, took over the sole French rights of the Cannstatt-built engine, married Emile Levassor and saw to it that the Daimler unit was installed in the first genuine French automobiles.

This pivotal move in the advancement of the motor car was of interest to very few in the days when Van Gogh still painted the leafy gardens of Paris and Lautrec still haunted the Moulin Rouge, for automotive transport and its enormous (or monstrous) influence on the human condition was far from the minds of the peoples of Europe.

Both Daimler and Levassor wished to promote engine sales for static and mobile uses. To this purpose they visited Le Fils de Peugeot Fréres, the important French cycle manufacturers

at Valentigny. They both knew that young Armand Peugeot, scion of a family who had amassed its first fortune in the days of Empress Eugène by making supple steel stays for crinolines (saving the ladies of society the discomfort of whalebone), was fascinated by the new mode of wheeled transport. The company had long ago moved from corsetry to umbrella ribs, thence to cycle spokes and later to the complete cycle, and young Armand had constructed a steam car in collaboration with Leon Serpollet.

Rigoulet, the chief engineer at Peugeot, had ridden on the Daimler steel-wheeler and by 1889 was designing a car for Armand, who was by now disenchanted with his steam car. Panhard and Levassor, the latter whose marriage now entitled him to distribute Daimler engines throughout France, suggested the new V-twin unit recently built at Cannstatt.

Levassor discussed with Peugeot the location of the engine in the new car.

Armand argued that the engine's place was at the front to counter the weight of the passengers, while Emile Levassor advocated rear-mounting where its noxious odours would be wafted away from the passengers. It must have been quite an argument, for when Peugeot built its first car the engine was placed at the rear – and when Panhard and Levassor went into production theirs was front-mounted.

Panhard and Levassor had, at this point, no great interest in using their engine in a vehicle of their own design; they were satisfied that their home-produced Daimler V-twin should be employed in industry and sold to prospective horseless-carriage builders. Armand Peugeot, on the other hand, just could not wait to get his first unit into a vehicle and on the road. Sometime in 1890 Peugeot built a sophisticated quadricycle, a light car based on cycle-type tubular frame construction. A tiller-steered two-seater, it was powered by the Daimler 2-hp unit

Son of a master baker, Gottlieb Daimler was born in 1834 in this house in Schorndorf near Stuttgart (top left). In 1883 he developed the first light high speed internal combustion engine in his workshop at Cannstatt (bottom right). An improved version was patented in 1885 (top right) and used to drive the world's first motor cycle (bottom left) in the same year.

placed at the rear. Cruising speed was 18 km/h (11 mph) says the official company record, but one must take that with a pinch of *sel de mer*.

There is some doubt about whether Panhard or Peugeot produced the first French car but the fact is that someone at the woodworking firm must have

Armand Peugeot's first machine, built in 1890. In it he followed a 680-mile cycle race from Paris to Brest and back. Using a Daimler V-twin engine of 8 hp this light car could reach 15 mph 'on a level run'.

days later Levassor *'pousse avec succès jusqu'à Versailles* which we must assume does not mean he pushed it there. Four weeks later he drove it to Boulogne and back, a long and testing voyage. Thus Levassor established his position as a pioneer in the motor industry. However, he was not

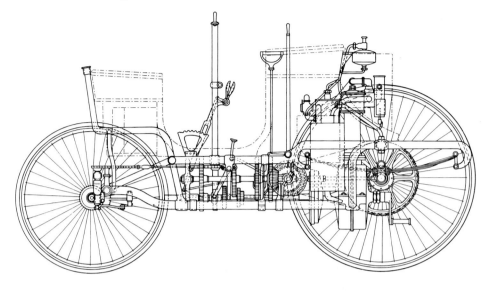

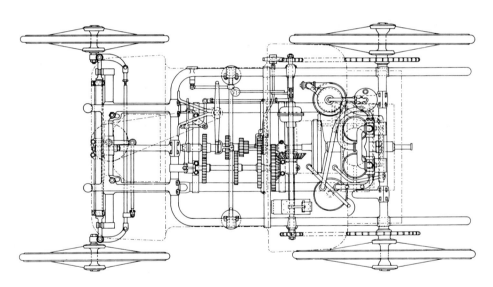

changed his mind, for Panhard came up with a road vehicle just a little before Peugeot showed his first automotive product to the public, although both vehicles were probably built about the same time.

Levassor's first car (he was the technical mainspring of the company) was painstakingly built by eight men in the Ivry factory at Paris. Sometime in 1890 it was tested on the road. The heavily built car, whose natal history is somewhat uncertain due to lack of documentation, broke down continually, and it was not until February of the following year that its first 'official' journey was undertaken, from Ivry to Point du Jour 'without incident'. Five

completely satisfied with the car's engineering layout. The midships engine, hot, smoky and smelly, was right under the passengers' seat. It also put too much of the total weight over the rear wheels (Peugeot had been right first time) reducing the efficiency of the steering wheels at the front.

By June 1891 Levassor's second vehicle was ready for testing. The motor was now at the front, its crankshaft aligned longitudinally under a bonnet that looked like a small teachest. Behind it followed the clutch, then the open-to-the-elements 'gearbox' with its mainshaft, layshaft and sliding gears and then the drive to the rear wheels by chain, completing the power train—the classic drive-sequence for most automobiles to be made for many years.

But it was a blacksmith's job, that first P & L, roughly built and rough to conduct, in spite of its fully elliptical leaf springs, over the unforgiving *pavé* of the French roads. Its large gear-change lever selected the different gear ratios with reluctance and its neutral position was as often as not undiscoverable. However, as Levassor ruefully stated: '*C'est grossier mais ça marche!*' (It's rough but it goes!).

It 'marched' straight into the records as the first French-built car to be sold,

A smart tiller-steered Panhard, circa 1894, seen taking a morning promenade in the Bois under the firm control of its lady driver.

The ubiquitous De Dion engine designed by Georges Bouton. From around 1895 De Dions equipped with this little high-speed unit swarmed like bees over the roads of France.

as the first development of an industry in France that was to take the automotive lead for a number of years and as the first product from a vigorous company (soon to have competition from compatriots) that forged well ahead of

the hesitant Benz and Daimler concerns in Germany, was years ahead of the American entry into motoring and was just as far ahead of the abortive efforts of Britain to unharness the horse age. P & L and Peugeot, De

Dion, Bollée and others in France took that country so far and so fast into the motoring age that, just as the language of music is Italian and the language of psychology German, the language of motoring is French.

The Comte de Dion and his brothers-in-law, Bouton and Trepardoux, had joined forces nearly 20 years before the turn of the century to make light steam road vehicles. Trepardoux had left the firm when the Comte and George Bouton decided to change over to petrol engines, and from then on the Paris company knew great success. The lightweight ¾-hp single-cylinder air-cooled engine buzzed happily away at the rear end of De Dion tricycles, quads and voiturettes – all light vehicles – and to everyone's surprise, including that of its designer, Georges Bouton, the toy-like 137-cc unit could run at up to 3 000 rpm, due to the electrical ignition system that George had invented. By 1900, when Henry Ford in the U.S.A. was trying hard to interest backers in a popular car with no success at all, De Dion were selling over 200 light cars a month, and the high-revving miniature engine was being used in at least 140 other makes of road vehicle.

Harnessed to the Horse Age

Where was Great Britain in this eager race to begin a transport revolution that even in the 1890s many could see would shortly change the life-style of the civilized world? Britain's horse breeders, tack and feed suppliers, cab companies and, of course, horse owners were still firmly in the saddle and all that most Britons knew about acceleration and braking was giddy-up and whoa. The powerful railway companies had the long-distance transport monopoly, and neither horse nor rail faction was anxious to see an upstart motor industry whittle away profits. However, the rest of the world was moving in a certain direction and, willy nilly, everyone must follow or be lost.

There were engineers in Britain who may, if they had been encouraged, have been hard on the heels of the German pair, Benz and Daimler, in their engineering developments. Pre-

Daimler, too, had built his vehicles on similar lines to his Mannheim neighbour Karl Benz, although more heavily constructed. The rear engine of this 1040cc 2 cylinder Vis-à-Vis of 1894 was belt driven, its chief advantage quiet running and reliability.

An early Daimler in Britain, 1898. This 'Coventry' Daimler was probably an import from Cannstatt, sold under either Panhard or Daimler licence. Its great height is emphasized here by the standing figure.

vious pioneers of the internal combustion engine had paved the way; engineering techniques now allowed cylinders to be bored and pistons to be made with the accuracy needed to manufacture a high-speed lightweight power unit. The exhibitions in Paris and other European venues had been visited by British engineers.

But the law actively discouraged the development of a modern motor industry in England. The maximum speed limit was indicative of the mood – 4 mph in the countryside and 2 mph through towns, quite fast enough for the nasty explosion engine. There were, however, already other forces at work.

The law regulating the use of motor cars on the roads of Britain had been formulated and enacted to drive heavyweight steam omnibuses off the roads some 60 years earlier. It was clearly unjust. A small group of influential people, some no doubt with an eye to getting in on the ground floor of a new and potentially fast-growing industry, decided to use their persuasive powers both in society and in Parliament.

The British motoring lobby had a perfect ally. H.R.H. The Prince of Wales, later to be King Edward VII, had already had a spin or two in a car and had been impressed. F. R. Simms, an Englishman resident in Germany, had purchased the rights to sell Daimler engines in Britain and had, by 1895, imported the first German-built Daimler into the country. Interest was naturally slight at the time but Frederick Simms, looking ahead, formed the Daimler Motor Syndicate to handle Daimler products and rented an office in a London suburb.

A curious group, headed by entrepreneur Harry Lawson, a bicycle-boom fund raiser of doubtful background, bought-out Simms, acquiring the patent rights for more or less all of the British and Continental developments.

However, it is primarily to Lawson that we owe the birth of the motor industry in England. Whatever his motives, he lobbied Parliament aggressively to bring in a new Act allowing motor carriages to travel at speeds up to 12 mph. On 14 November 1896, the legal shackles were struck off and mad-

In the Metropolitan Police District.

To *Walter C. Bersey*
of *39 Victoria Street, Westminster*

INFORMATION ———————————————————————— has been laid
this day by *George Dixon*
for that you, on the *20th* Day of *October*
in the Year One Thousand Eight Hundred and Ninety *six*
at *a certain public highway, to wit Parliament Street*

within the District aforesaid, ~~did~~ *being the owner and having the charge of a locomotive propelled by other than animal power, to wit; a motor car, did unlawfully neglect to have such locomotive whilst in motion preceded by at least 20 yards by a person on foot*

Contrary to the Statute etc

You ARE THEREFORE hereby summoned to appear before the Court of
Summary Jurisdiction, sitting at the *Bow Street* Police Court
on *Satur* day the *31st* day of *October*
at the hour of *two* in the *after* noon, to answer to the
said *information.*

Dated the *23d* day of *October*
One Thousand Eight Hundred and Ninety *six*

H. Lushington

One of the Magistrates of the Police Courts of the Metropolis.

SCH. I.—2.

SUMMONS.

GENERAL FORM SUMMARY
CASES.

S. J. A. Rules, 1886—2.

W B & L (484v)—64151—10000-6-96

cap autocarists were permitted to scorch down the road from London to Brighton on the south coast at breathtaking speeds. And make no mistake, they *were* breathtaking – anyone who rides in an ancient Benz or a tall Panhard or a spindly, only slightly controllable Peugeot at 12 mph, will soon find his breath whipped away by wind or fright.

The 'Emancipation Run' to Brighton on that raw November day in

Just a month before the Locomotive on Highways' law was changed. This summons to appear in court was written in October 1896, when the law still demanded that the vehicle be preceded by a man on foot.

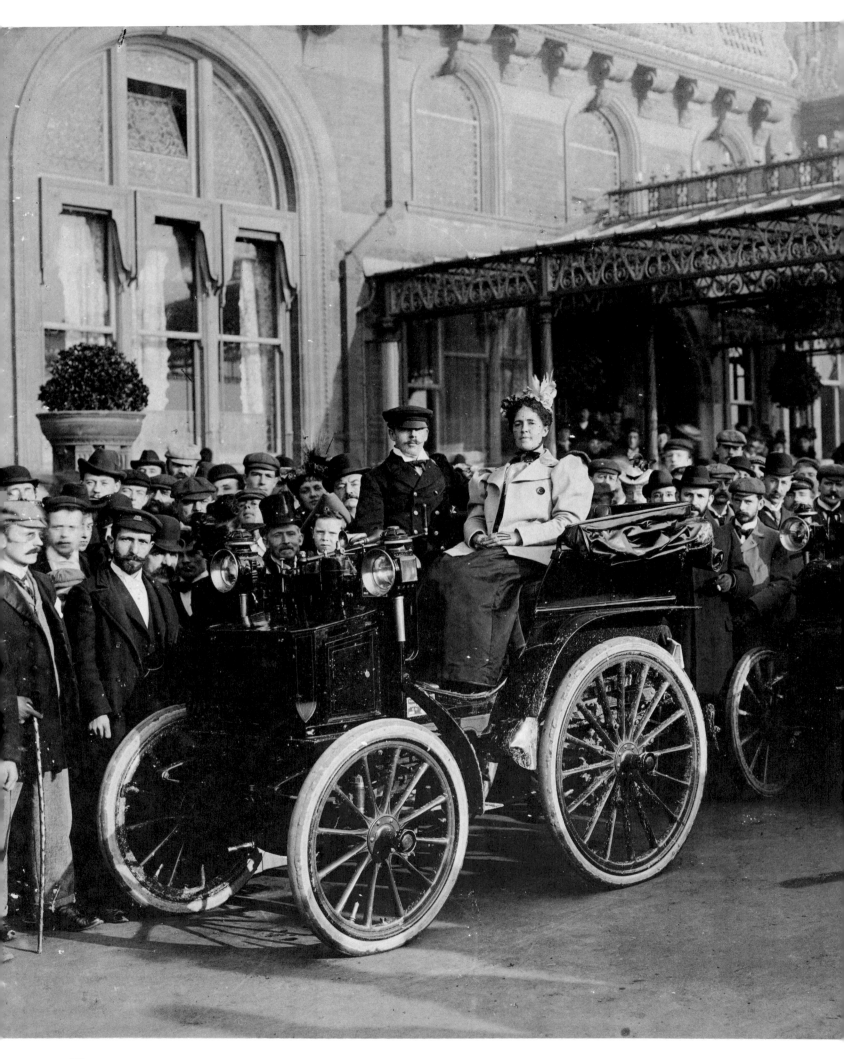

1896 attracted motor cars from several countries, including the United States of America. Among the 32 participants were two brand new Duryeas, about a dozen Panhards or Daimlers from France (the writer of the report did not appear to know which), including 'Old No. 5' Panhard in which Emile Levassor had won the Paris-Bordeaux race of the previous year, but which now carried Harry Lawson. Gottlieb Daimler himself travelled down to the coast through the rain and mist in a barouche of his own marque. In the distinguished parade was a delivery van which was soon to pioneer parcels delivery in Britain, five French Bollée's ('fast and troublesome' said a report), a British Beeston tricycle built on De Dion lines, a handful of electrics, a Pennington, some Roger machines identical to the Benz product of the time, and an electric bathchair complete with indigenous occupant.

Spectators were thrilled. This was the first procession of horseless carriages they had ever seen and they were delirious with excitement. Police control was impossible. The press of the crowds slowed down the cars until well past Brixton in south London. Then the Frenchmen, so it is reported, began to make a race of it, drawing some of the more hot-headed drivers after them. Wrote a scribe from *The Automotor Journal* passionately: 'To rush through the air with the speed of a torpedo boat destroyer down a narrow curving road enclosed with hedges and without being able to see what was to the front of us was novel, a thrilling experience ... all the while our motor was actively impelling us onwards, adding to the velocity which had already been imparted to the vehicle by the momentum.'

Said England's premier motor magazine, *The Autocar*, already at issue No. 55 by the great day, 14 November 1896 ... 'Yesterday we were criminals if we ventured upon the Queen's highway, and our journeys were either taken surreptitiously, in fear and trembling, as trespassers upon forbidden ground, at the mercy of every officious country bumpkin in the uniform of the police force who sought to score points for promotion .... Today the users of the autocar enjoy the rights of free British citizenship restricted in such points only as are necessary for the comfort and safety of other liege subjects of the Queen ...'.

Pioneers' great day, 14 November 1896. The 'Emancipation' run to Brighton to celebrate the raising of the speed limit to 12 mph finished here at Brighton's Metropole Hotel. The car in the foreground is the very same Panhard which Emile Levassor had won the Paris-Bordeaux-Paris the previous year. Harry Lawson and his wife are seated on the machine.

Above: This two-cylinder 10hp Wolseley tonneau breezes down the London-to-Brighton Road on an Emancipation Day Commemoration Run.

Opposite: An early Decauville advertisement. Another light car made in France, this is an 1898 3½hp 'voiturelle', the company's first model, unique in that it had independent front suspension, the first production vehicle to be so equipped.

A little theatrical perhaps, but who could blame Harry Lawson's journal for blazoning its success in helping to change the antiquated regulations.

A Thousand Miles Around Britain

That event, and two earlier small but important 'motor shows', brought Britain into the automotive age. Progress, as usual in Britain, was slow however, and it took an event in 1900 to introduce and promote the motor car to the ever-reluctant British public.

At the turn of the century there were perhaps 400 self-propelled road vehicles in Britain. People living in the Home Counties around London would certainly have seen a motor car, but those in more provincial regions would probably not yet have encountered one – and if they had, would undoubtedly have considered it a device of the devil. In those villages remote from the metropolis little boys threw stones at it, horses plunged and kicked at the sight of it, elderly pedestrians contrived not to notice it, young women were seen fleeing from it and innkeepers would not have it anywhere near their premises. What was it? No one quite knew, so the proud owners would hang a sign on it in an effort to divert a thousand questions:

L'AUTOMOBILE
DECAUVILLE

'It is an autocar,
Some people call it motor car,
It is worked by a petroleum motor,
The motor is of four horse power,
It will run sixty miles on one change of oil,
No, it can't explode, there is no boiler,
It can travel at fourteen miles an hour,
Ten to eleven is its average pace,
It can be started in two minutes,
There are eight ways of stopping it, so it can't run away,
It has to be steered with one hand,
The speed is mainly controlled by the foot,
It can be stopped in ten feet when travelling at full speed,
It carries four gallons of oil and sixteen gallons of water,
The water is to keep the engine cool,
It costs less than three farthings a mile to run,
The car can carry five people,
It can get up any ordinary hill,
It was built by the Daimler Motor Company in Coventry and costs £370,
We have come from John o' Groat's House,
We are going to Land's End,
We are not record breaking but touring for pleasure.'

A page of the London-based Automotor Journal *of January 1902 illustrates the awakening interest in the new world of motor cars. Amongst the sales ads were offers of chauffeurs, mechanics, car parts and other paraphernalia familiar even today.*

'YOUNG Man Wants Job in motor shop, handy chap for repairing shop; good references. A.M. 1 Frederick Place, Ampton St, King's Cross, London.'

'Thoroughly Practical ENGINEER and DRAFTSMAN experienced and capable designer of high speed steam, gas, and oil engines and general work of the highest class. Box 65.'

'ADVERTISER (21) seeks situation as DRIVER. Can do own small repairs. A. H. Beaurepaire, Basingstoke.'

'PRACTICAL OPINION on any make of car, also intending purchasers met by appointment in London with car, and driven round to inspect cars of various makers, good terms obtained, trials and instruction free. E. J. Coles Motor Expert (8 club awards), 2 St John's Villas, Upper Holloway, London N.'

... or similar information sheet from which today's reader will understand that technical terms were not yet stabilized (oil motors were petrol engines; 'petrol' was not a generally recognized term until about 1903). Those small boys who did not use cars for target practice would swarm around the vehicle, as apparently did the girls, to examine the irresistible brass levers, knobs, ratchets, wheels, plungers, dials and so on.

The Thousand Miles Trial introduced the new transport to the country. Its daunting route encompassed most of England and some of Scotland; 65 starters set out and (officially) 23 returned to Marble Arch in London. Perhaps the most trouble-free run was enjoyed by a small two-seater of 3½ hp, designed and built in 1899 by Mr. Herbert Austin of the Wolseley Sheep Shearing Company. The tiller-steered light car had a single cylinder, fintube-cooled horizontal engine and was Austin's third attempt at a prototype. Similar production Wolseleys were to come from the Birmingham factory in 1901. This little car, kept now in London's Heritage Museum, did the 1 000-mile trip again a few years ago quite successfully, and often takes part in the annual London-Brighton Commemoration Run held every November.

A number of other pioneering makes took part in this marathon run; Coventry-built Daimlers, Panhards, MMC cars, an 8-hp Napier made at Lambeth in London, a Brown-Whitney, a Locomobile steamer from the United States, the uniquely unconventional Lanchester, and sundry cars from De Dion, Benz and other German makers.

The Automobile Club of Great Britain (later to be elevated to the title of Royal Automobile Club) must have handled the advance publicity for this event well, for 'at every cross road in the country there were knots of onlookers' reported one newspaper, 'the parson and his daughter on bicycles, the country squire on his horse, the old dowager safely escorted in her landau, and cyclists in legions.' Towns were packed to see the cavalcade pass through, schools were shut for the great day, and the crowds were so dense 'that only the narrowist passage remained through which the motor vehicles had to pass.' 'If you broke down on a remote moor,' recounted one of the participants, 'a group of watchers would appear like Bedouins in the desert to gather round you closely.' The public – millions of them – turned out, full of curiosity, cheering on the cars, inciting them to go at a full 30 mph and chastizing those who failed to put up a turn of speed. Repairs were done on the move, using corks, coins and even leather boot-soles as brakes. Buckets of water, balanced on the laps of co-drivers to be sloshed over hot brake shoes and engines, were often the most effective cooling methods.

Eventually the tired, exhausted drivers and their dirty dented cars arrived back at London. A previously uninformed public had now seen at least one autocar on the move. Small boys would now nurture distant ambitions of becoming a racing driver and grown men would make plans to purchase their first motor car. First to see the tangible benefits was the medical profession, who could squeeze more patients into their daily rounds with a car than with their poor plodding horses, just as Benz's postmaster friend had prophesied. Thus it was that the automobile moved into the second stage of its history, as a useful tool of society, firstly in the form of a 'doctor's coupé'. But that was still a handful of years ahead.

This Stephens prototype used a similar system of i.f.s. as the 1898 Decauville in the same year. This product of the infant British automotive industry (made in Somerset) may still be seen today putting up a good turn of speed at veteran car rallies.

A page of the London-based *Automotor Journal* of January 1902 illustrates awakening interest in the new world of motor cars; among others were advertisements for chauffeurs, mechanics, car parts. A sales ad from 'The largest Motor Works in London' offers Panhard, Daimler, Mors, De Dion, Renault, Darracq, Benz, Delahaye, Peugeot, and steam cars from Serpollet and Locomobile. When one considers that Louis Renault, for instance, had opened for business just two years earlier, and that Darracq, Delahaye and others were only six-year-old infants, one begins to appreciate the incredible spread of motoring interest and the rapid rise of motoring empires in those early days of the automobile.

The American Buggynaut

North America, too, suffered at the beginning of the new age of the automobile from a number of restrictions to the progress of its development.

The American continent had no roads. Outside city limits, the paved highways quickly degenerated to cart trails, hard-rutted and dusty in summer weather, and muddy enough to swallow up small animals in winter rainstorms. When the California Gold Rush got under way in 1848, people soon discovered that the continent was almost impossible to cross overland (three months was the estimated wagon journey time from the Eastern States to the West). The new railroads came to provide the sole lines of communication to the western regions of the continent. As a countrywide rail network spread, most rural tracks were used only for driving cattle to the nearest railroad depot.

The first practical motor vehicles to be built in the United States, therefore, were designed for local farm work or short urban journeys, not for the sporting and luxury travel uses to which Europeans had put them.

Several attempts at motorized road transport had been made in the United States back in the beginning of the 19th century. Probably the earliest self-propelled vehicle in North America was an amphibian steam cart which was built by Oliver Evans, a mechanic

Opposite: Within a year of the first sporting event in 1894 motor clubs began to spring up. In 1895 the Automobile Club de France was formed and shortly afterwards, the Automobile Club de Belgique.

The final year of the last century – and the lady driver arrives. A fashionable female conducts an 1899 MMC (Motor Manufacturing Co Ltd) of Coventry.

The first practical gasoline engined automobile in the United States, the Duryea, built by two brothers of that name in 1892–93. It was a powered buggy in the traditional American idiom with a single-cylinder 4 hp motor.

from Newport, Delaware, and was first seen by open-mouthed locals in 1805, about the same time as Englishman Richard Trevithick was building his steam coaches and rail locomotive. Evans's waddling wooden dredger apparently made just one short journey through the streets of Philadelphia and into the Schuykill River.

Others followed Evans, although there is something of a gap in American records. The next documented attempt was made by Sylvester Roper, who in 1869 could be seen hissing gently along – at 30 mph no less – on his steam velocipede, spell-binding the good people of New England at their country fairs.

A little later came the Shrank tricycle with 'an engine as big as a kitchen stove' and another tricycle built by Lucius D. Copeland in 1884 on more refined and delicate lines; its steam unit was small and unobstrusive and its lightweight wheels and sun canopy gave it a swan-like air.

However, it is generally agreed that the two young Duryea brothers from Springfield, Massachusetts, blacksmithed up the first marketable gasoline-engined automobile to be made in the United States. The first Duryea was something between an early Benz and a high-wheeled buggy. Tested in 1893, it hopped a few yards before becoming a piece of roadside furniture. Later tests proved more successful and the 'Buggynaut' (their own name for it!), now with spray carburettor and electric ignition designed by Frank Duryea, was entered in a race for motor vehicles sponsored by the *Times Herald* of Chicago. It won the event, run after some delay, over slithery drifting snow on Thanksgiving Day, 28 November 1895. Thus the United States entered the motor-manufacturing world.

A report in the November 1895 issue of *The Horseless Age*, a U.S. journal that was in the van of the automotive movement, says of the Duryea: 'In appearance the vehicle does not differ materially from an ordinary heavy built buggy. It weighs about 700 pounds and has ball bearing and rubber tired wheels, the tires also being Mr. Duryea's invention (?). The variable speed ranges from three to sixteen miles an hour . . . and to obtain greater speed than ten miles an hour the pressing of a button at the front of the seat will increase the speed of the motor. A brake drum of peculiar construction placed under the seat is connected with a thumb button located at the front corner of the seat and by pressing the thumb upon this button the carriage if running at twelve miles an hour can be stopped within a distance of twelve feet.' Some button, some thumb!

The Selden Battle

Lawyer George Selden had made an application to the U.S. Patent Office for what he termed 'a reliable road locomotive, simple, cheap, lightweight, easy to control and powerful enough to climb any ordinary hill.'

Selden had studied an earlier two-cycle motor built by G. B. Brayton, an Englishman living in the U.S.A. and applied his considerable talents to designing a lighter three-cylinder unit. Tested (one cylinder of it) in 1878, Selden found he had, in theory at least, an engine that could be fitted into a buggy. He filed a patent application on 8 May 1879, which included his own motor and many of the fundamental elements of the internal combustion engine operation, including their working combination with each other. Yet Selden had never built a car to his or to anyone else's design.

Selden's broad patent description also encompassed the specifications of a legion of backyard engineers in the United States, who were to be faced with a claim for royalties on their one-off steering systems, clutch

Brayton motor c1878. This is reputed to be the first earliest American internal combustion engine still preserved – and the first commercially made engine in the country. It developed 2hp at 250 rpm from its bucket-sized single cylinder. George Selden's engine design was based on this two-cycle unit.

NOTICE

To Manufacturers, Dealers, Importers, Agents and Users of

Gasoline Automobiles

United States Letters Patent No. 549,160, granted to George B. Selden, November 5th, 1895, controls broadly all gasoline automobiles which are accepted as commercially practical. Licenses under this patent have been secured from the owners by the following named manufacturers and importers

Electric Vehicle Co.
The Winton Motor Carriage Co.
Packard Motor Car Co.
Olds Motor Works.
Knox Automobile Co.
The Haynes-Apperson Co.
The Autocar Co.
The George N. Pierce Co.
Apperson Bros. Automobile Co.
Searchmont Automobile Co.
Locomobile Company of America.
The Peerless Motor Car Co.
U. S. Long Distance Auto. Co.
Waltham Manufacturing Co.
Buffalo Gasolene Motor Co.

Pope Motor Car Co.
The J. Stevens Arms and Tool Co.
H. H. Franklin Mfg. Co.
Charron, Giradot & Voigt
    Company of America.
       (Smith & Mabley)
The Commerial Motor Co.
Berg Automobile Co.
Cadillac Automobile Co.
Northern Manufacturing Co.
Pope-Robinson Co.
The Kirk Manufacturing Co.
Elmore Mfg. Co.
E. R. Thomas Motor Co.
The F. B. Stearns Company.

These manufacturers
pioneers in this industry, and have commerci
by many years of development, and at a g
owners of upwards of four hundred United
many of the most important improvements an
Both the basic Selden patent and all other
    will be enforced against all i
No other manufacturers or importers are a
gasoline automobiles, and any person makii
machines made or sold by any unlicensed m
    will be liable to prosecution for

Association of
Automobile Man

No. 7 EAST 42nd STREET

N O T I C E

To Dealers, Importers, Agents and Users of Our

Gasoline Automobiles

WE will protect you against any prosecution for alleged infringements of patents. Regarding alleged infringement of the Selden patent we beg to quote the well-known Patent Attorneys, Messrs. Parker and Burton: "The Selden patent is not a broad one, and if it was it is anticipated. It does not cover a practicable machine, no practicable machine can be made from it and never was so far as we can ascertain. It relates to that form of carriage called a FORE CARRIAGE. None of that type has ever been in use, all have been failures. No court in the United States has ever decided in favor of the patent on the merits of the case, all it has ever done was to record a prior agreement between parties."

We are pioneers of the GASOLINE AUTOMOBILE. Our Mr. Ford made the first Gasoline Automobile in Detroit and the third in the United States. His machine made in 1893 (two years previous to the granting of the Selden patent, Nov. 5, 1895) is still in use. Our Mr. Ford also built the famous "999" Gasoline Automobile, which was driven by Barney Oldfield in New York on July 25th, 1903, a mile in 55 4-5 seconds on a circular track, which is the world's record.

Mr. Ford, driving his own machine, beat Mr. Winton at Grosse Pointe track in 1901. We have always been winners

Write for Catalogue.

FORD MOTOR COMPANY

688-692 Mack Avenue, - - - DETROIT, MICH.

48

arrangements, gearboxes, carburettors, fuel tanks containing liquid hydrocarbon and so on. By the time his patent was issued in 1895 the Rochester lawyer had effectively tied up almost every facet of car-making in a patent that was to prove the most serious stumbling block to early American automotive progress. He had assigned the patent to the Electric Vehicle Company, part of the later Association of Licenced Automobile Manufacturers who claimed royalties · from anyone building a gasoline car.

This was precisely the time when investment cash, previously withheld, began to pour into the budding gas-auto industry.

The A.L.A.M. lawyers moved in. 'Our client informs us that you are manufacturing and advertising for sale vehicles which embody the scope of the Selden Patent. We . . . request that you desist from the same and make suitable compensation to the owner of the patent therefore.'

Court cases followed. The Buffalo Gasoline Motor Company was sued, and the Winton Motor Carriage Company and many others, right down to little shanty firms run by a couple of teenagers. U.S. importers were sued for the Peugeots, Renaults, Fiats, or whatever that they brought into the country and which, the lawyers stated, were all infringing the Selden Patents. Some paid up, some baulked at the arrogance of the demands, and in 1902 a band of manufacturers decided to fight for a reduction in royalty payments.

Enter Farm Boy Ford

But they all reckoned without 'a jumped-up farm boy' who in 1903 was just starting his own business. Henry Ford had applied for a licence to build within the now malodorous patents, but must have changed his mind before finally agreeing to the terms, and backed out. 'Selden made no discovery and gave none to the world,' said an irate Ford, pointing out that he had studied Lenoir's automotive principles, not Selden's and that Lenoir had borrowed from half a dozen sources. Eight years and two lengthy legal trials later Ford won his case against the Selden Patents and the auto industry heard no more of them. But the U.S. motor manufacturers had been just a sliver away from permanent damage; such a restrictive monopoly could have

changed the course of industrial North America.

George Selden returned to obscurity, still maintaining that he was the true 'father of the automobile'. And if he had actually *built* and demonstrated his car in 1879, one could have agreed. For the car built to his 1879 specifications in 1905 in order to prove his case, actually worked, predating Benz's and Daimler's vehicles by seven years.

Henry Ford, just 40 years old when he finally opened up for business in 1903, had first appeared on the automotive scene at about the same time as the earliest American woodshed motor pioneers. He had built a steam unit when he was 15 and had patched up his first gasoline engine in 1893, bolting it to the kitchen sink and connecting the ignition to the domestic circuit.

Three years later at his modest home at Bagley Avenue, Detroit, he began to construct his first vehicle. Unusually low-slung for the period (high-wheeled buggies that kept the running gear clear of the bumps and mud were the norm), it was a four-cycle-wheel two-seater, and took shape in a shared storeshed at the bottom of the garden. Neighbour Felix Julien had been so fascinated with Henry's work that he insisted on moving his coal and wood to allow the 35-year-old engineer more room to work.

The little box-like car had two cylinders, two belts giving a choice of forward speeds, and a tiller. Brakes and reverse gear were luxuries Ford could not at that time accommodate. In true pioneer tradition Henry had to axe down the shed doorway to get the thing out on to the road.

His employer, Thomas Edison, talked to Ford about the car later that year. Said the great inventor: 'You have it – keep at it.' Ford's answer was to leave Edison's employ and set up his own company, the Detroit Automobile Company. It rapidly failed. Ford, nothing daunted, entered the speed-record-breaking field, first building his '999' and later, his Arrow. The former car is described as having 'a giant grease-spewing engine and a 230-pound flywheel, a Stone-Age crown wheel and pinion, the whole bolted to a wooden frame'. The car may· have been crude – but the land speed records of 1904 includes the name of H. Ford, who is credited with a speed of 91.27 mph. This type of publicity kept Henry's name in the front of the car-

Opposite: When the Selden patents threatened the whole of the American automotive industry, Henry Ford was the leader in the fight to retain freedom from the payment of royalties. This is the notice of patent rights and Ford's defiant answer.

Bagley Avenue Ford, 1896. A two-cylinder engine, a belt system giving two speeds, four cycle wheels, a boxwood flitch-plate, a minimal body and tiller steering completed fundamentals of the car. It had no brakes and no reverse gear.

buying public, and persuaded several people to invest in his new company.

The Henry Ford Company, his second attempt at setting up in business was something of a mystery, but by 1902 it, also, was ailing. It was taken over by the former gunmaker Henry Leland, who changed its name to that of the Founder of the city of Detroit, Antoine de la Mothe Cadillac.

Meanwhile, Henry, now at an age at which most men of that time began to consider occupying a rocking chair on the veranda after a lifetime of hard work, started yet another company, the Ford Motor Company.

He invited a few friends to invest some cash in this new venture. Alex Dow, his old chief at the Edison Plant, declined with thanks, as did many others. 'I didn't know then of course,' Dow later remarked ruefully, 'that he was going to make a million out of the blamed things!' The blamed things made more millions that could be written on this page.

Modest sums were contributed. Two lawyer friends put in $5 000. In 1919 when Ford bought them out, they received $12 500 000 each.

After a few false starts and one or two cars that were too upmarket for some of his customers, Ford's business eventually flourished. Later, when he had several factories running at full production, a humorist was to write: 'Two flies can breed 48 876 million new flies in six months – but they haven't got anything on two Ford plants.' Such pieces of wit were to build up over the years into a veritable tome of folklore and legends about Ford and his car-making empire.

Other U.S. tyro carbuilders were running parallel to Ford – some with more initial success before the end of the 19th century. Nobody took much notice of them; few writers were perceptive enough to remark that 1895 represented a watershed in the history of transport in the U.S.A.; most historians, if they mentioned motor buggies at all, considered them a whim, a passing fancy, an inventor's abberation. Barnum and Bailey, the great circus company, put 'the famous Duryea motor-wagon' at the top of the bill in 1896 along with the fat lady, the clowns, the giants, and the headless dwarfs. It was a measure of the attitude of most of the world to the automobile's future.

Before the new century opened up with the so-called Edwardian period,

50

several new makes had appeared on the limited market. *The Horseless Age*, a magazine launched in 1895 and calling itself boldly 'A Journal published in the interests of the Motor Vehicle Industry', displayed advertisements for several motored vehicles, and printed editorials about products of this almost non-existent 'industry'.

The Racine Motor Vehicle Company is mentioned, as is the Duryea Motor Wagon Company of Springfield, Massachusetts, and a number of gas-engine firms offered their units for static or mobile operation. The 'latest model' Daimler phaeton is shown and a 'motor drag' by the De La Vergne Refrigeration Company of New York.

Hiram Percy Maxim, 'son of the well-known inventor of the Maxim machine gun and the flying machine', offered a motor tricycle so unstable that it looked as though it would do a 'wheelie' if the rider were an ounce or two heavier. Stephen H. Roper's steam-vehicles were also on the mar-

ket; the fascinating Buckeye Gasoline Buggy was illustrated; and a D. Lybe of Sidney, Iowa, revealed his 'spring motored' two wheeler which 'stored up power when the vehicle was going downhill, price $120'.

There were, in fact, half a dozen spring-motored light vehicles optimistically on offer in the magazine; unfortunately many of them fitted Dr. Johnson's opinion of a mechanically propelled road vehicle. The English philosopher was told in 1769 of a newly invented machine which went without horses, contained a man who sat in it and turned a handle, which worked a spring that drove it forward. 'Then, Sir,' said Johnson, 'What is gained is, the man has the choice whether he will move himself alone, or himself and the machine too.' Johnson's comment was justified, and these latter-day 'springers' came to nothing.

Elwood Haynes of Indiana, on the other hand, showed his carriage in *The Horseless Age* – and went on to become

Henry Ford in his one-off car built in 1907 to Lenoir principles of 1861 as a weapon in his fight against the so-called Selden patents.

Rural America 1902. An Autocar Type 8 crosses a ford. Made at Ardmore, Pennsylvania, it sported a two-cylinder 3½hp motor with shaft drive.

an important founder member of North America's motor industry, producing cars until 1925. Riker from Brooklyn had made an electric car which enjoyed popularity in those early days and Alex Winton of Cleveland built his first two-seater in 1896; Ransom Eli Olds drove his first high-wheeled car and, of course, Henry Ford of Detroit hacked his way out of the woodshed to test his 4-hp quadricycle. The Stanley brothers started their steam car business in 1897, and the Packard brothers made their first 12-hp car in 1899.

There was, unknown to an uncaring general public, much stirring in this new and boundless field of automotive manufacturing and within a year or two some 109 different makes of car were being produced in the United States.

Hiram Maxim, who had already produced his first electric carriage, the Columbia, for the Pope Manufacturing Company which normally made bicycles at Hartford, Connecticut, had an interesting comment to make on the reasons for this sudden and fervent activity in the new industry during those years at the turn of the century.

'It has been the habit to give the gasoline engine all the credit for bringing the automobile – in my opinion this is the wrong explanation,' he writes. 'We have had the steam engine for over a century. We could have built steam vehicles in 1880, or indeed in 1870. But we did not. We waited until 1895.'

'The reason why we did not build road vehicles before this, in my opinion, was because the bicycle had not yet come in numbers and had not directed men's minds to the possibilities of independent long-distance travel over the ordinary highway. We thought the railroad was good enough. The bicycle created a new demand which was beyond the ability of the railroad to supply. Then it came about that the bicycle could not satisfy the demand which it had created. A mechanically propelled vehicle was wanted instead of a foot-propelled one, and we now know that the automobile was the answer.'

That may be an American answer, it was certainly not the European one. It well illustrates the completely separate development for completely different purposes that took place on the North American continent. In Europe the car replaced the carriage, and motor trade succeeded carriage trade. The large cycling population, particularly in Britain, was a manifestation of the newly liberated working classes who could not have hoped to purchase a motor car in these early days. In Europe, too, technical progress was responsible for the appearance of the motor car; knowledge of metals, of electricity, and of the necessary techniques that would enable accurate boring and milling had reached the sophisticated point at which the internal combustion engine could be fabricated. Lenoir pointed the way, Otto furnished the means, and Benz and Daimler put the accumulated knowledge into practice. In the United States similar early development, some ten years behind that of Europe, was inevitable, but the automobile would seem at first have been more of a replacement for the farm wagon or one-horse buggy than a cycle.

Let's Race!

Young and eager French *automobilists* clamoured for contest. They were to be offered it in 1894 by a distinguished French publication, *Le Petit Journal*. Its dynamic *Chef des Information*, Pierre Giffard, had organized a cycle

Overleaf: An elegant Landaulet for 'carriage folk' from Benz, 1897–9. After 12 years of steady improvement Benz still used his rear-engined unit, which by this time was becoming somewhat dated. The competition – Panhard Peugeot, Daimler with Renault soon to open for business, had all opted for front-engined vehicles.

An early American gets a family washdown. This two seater of 1898 with a twin-cylinder horizontal motor was the first automobile made by the Winton Motor Carriage Co of Cleveland Ohio.

Above: Paris-Rouen Trial: the steam wagon of the Comte de Dion.

race back in 1891, a real marathon from Paris to Brest and back (which Armand Peugeot had followed all the way – some 1 500 miles in his Daimler-engined light carriage, a notable feat for those days and for some years to come) and had now decided to sponsor a contest of motor carriages. Giffard had had a few earlier brushes with *les nouvelles inventions* as he called them, and his opinion of the motor-carriage as a reliable form of getting from A to B was low. A reliability trial might, he thought, with suitable rewards encourage makers or owners to improve their vehicles a little.

From Paris to Rouen was a distance of 126 kilometres (78 miles) and with a top speed of around 15 mph the cars would present an intensely exciting event. It would be the first contest of its kind, pitting skill against skill in a way never before considered.

This historic Paris-to-Rouen Trial of 1894 attracted large crowds, and some 102 prospective contestants – only 21 of whom actually managed to get their vehicles to the start-line at Paris.

Competitors were to conduct their cars to Rouen, the winner to be '*le*

Voiture sans Chevaux remplissant les conditions:-
–d'être sans danger (without danger)
–aisement maniable par les voyageurs (easily manageable by the voyageurs)
–de ne coûter trop cher sur la route (doesn't cost too much to run).'

A great deal of fun was had by all, including the spectators, who could be seen wandering in and out of the traffic, most of which shuffled along at perhaps 10 mph. A heavy steam wagon-and-trailer entered by Comte de Dion arrived first, but as it needed two people to operate it (not so *maniable*) it was a bit heavy on coke (*trop cher*) so the joint first prize of Fr 12 000 went, predictably, to M. Emile Levassor driving a Panhard & Levassor, and a Peugeot from Valentigny; average speeds were about 11.5 mph.

The lessons learned were many. Perhaps the most significant was illustrated by the fact that all 13 *voitures a pétrole* actually arrived at Rouen, while the steam-car contingent behaved very poorly.

The swing away from steam and electric to petroleum fuel was inevitable after this first public demonstra-

Opposite: Motor sport's first-ever event, the 1894 Paris-Rouen Reliability Trial. Although contemporary reports say that the trial turned into a race as soon as the starting judges were out of sight, this picture shows that two of the concurrents passing through a small town on the route exerted only a minimal effect on its strolling populace!

Opposite: Rudolf Egg of Zurich had made his first experimental car five years earlier than this 1898 vis-à-vis model. Of conventional appearance it departed from tradition by using a variable belt transmission rather like the Dutch DAF of over half a century later.

Below: History in ceramic. A tiled mural of the race from Marseilles to Nice and La Turbie. This event was the first to attract interest in motor sport from fashionable society. The Comte Chasseloup-Laubat (later to become the first Land Speed Record holder) won in this De Dion Brake.

tion of the internal combustion engine's reliability.

The open arrow-straight roads of France were ideal for long-distance speed competitions, and by 1895 the first had taken place – from Paris to Bordeaux and back, an impressive distance of 732 miles. The victor was, once again, a Panhard driven by the ubiquitous Emile Levassor. His average speed of about 15 mph is misleadingly modest. Considering the appalling road surfaces, the long unbroken hours at the tiller and the fact that Levassor scorned a relief driver, his twice-round-the-clock drive was a magnificent feat of endurance. He rested only to take a single cat-nap and to take water and fuel; at the halfway point in Bordeaux he made an about turn in eight minutes taking only a glass of champagne as refreshment. His time of 48 hours, 48 minutes established his car and its Daimler engine as foremost in the French automotive field.

The Michelin brothers, well established in the bicycle field, had been experimenting with pneumatic tyres and had fitted them for the first time on a competing Peugeot. This Peugeot was later given the curious name of *Éclair* (lightning) by the public – not, it seems, because of its high velocity, but because of the erratic course it took on its new tyres which, it is said, resembled zig-zag forked lightning!

City-to-city races became the prime motoring attractions of the years between 1895 and 1903. The Paris-Bordeaux-Paris race was followed later in 1895 by the Paris-Marseilles-Paris race of over a thousand miles. The social and motoring event of 1898 was the Paris-Amsterdam-Paris race, the first speed competition to cross international borders. This race was won by a Panhard driven by Fernand Charron, one of the first of the new breed of racing 'heroes' that today includes such names as Fangio, Moss, Hill, Hunt and Piquet. Speed had almost doubled in those few years – the Amsterdam race was won at 42.29 km/h (26.9 mph), and the 1903 Paris-Madrid event saw speeds of up to 80 mph.

MARSEILLE-NICE
1896

BREAK DE DION   PAR

The Motoring Edwardians: 1900-1909

Louis Renault, engineer, captain of industry, builder of the greatest motor company in France. He had the face of a poet and the mind of a dunce, said his teachers.

Twenty-one-year-old Louis was down at the bottom of the garden as usual. His continual hammering annoyed the neighbours in the quiet Paris suburb of Billancourt, and the acrid smoke that rose regularly from the garden-shed forge drew strong comment. For much of the autumn of 1898 young Louis had closeted himself in his workshop, and those who took the trouble to visit him would find him there with smudged face and greasy hands, working frantically at a jigsaw of metal shafts, gearwheels, rods and bolts. An evening out in Montmartre, Louis? A few drinks up on the Butte? They usually failed to prise him from his small forge and workbench.

Louis Renault's parents, stolid bourgeois drapers, were driven to despair. Their youngest son had been one of his school's incorrigibles, a regular truant (he was found one day by the driver of the Paris-Rouen train hiding in the coal tender) who had shown no aptitude for academic education or for the family business. He just wanted to potter about in the shed at home.

Louis Renault pottered to some effect as France, and history, now knows, but there were few at the end of the last century who would have given much for his future. No great interest was shown in the work of a man who was to found a company that grew so large that it would finally become part of the industrial fabric of France itself.

Renault was in the grip of motor fever. He was determined to make a trip in a vehicle of his own design before he relaxed over another glass of *vin rouge*.

France was on the brink of the Motor Age then. German and French manufacturers were turning out motored carriages and enthusiasm – albeit in a very limited section of society – was growing for motor travel. Louis Renault, even then a perceptive, self-taught mechanic, could see that most of the so-called 'automobiles' (the word was beginning to be used in France) were still, with some exceptions, light carriages with the equine equipment removed and an engine – either a Daimler or De Dion – slotted in somewhere. He had several new engineering ideas that would do away with some of the clanking mechanics of then-current motor vehicles.

Louis had already travelled in a steam car. Eminent steam pioneer Leon Serpollet had given him a short ride after seeing the 15-year-old lad hanging around the factory gates at the Rue Des Cloys – the boy, it seemed, was determined to discover the secrets of conducting a self-propelled vehicle – which, although it ended in a minor accident, in no way deflected Louis from his avowed goal, that of building and driving his own car.

Renault had bought a 1¾-hp 273-cc air-cooled De Dion three-wheeler, dismantled it and had added a fourth wheel. He designed a new transmission system (to replace the unreliable tangle of belts and chains that were used in most of the machines of the time) by building a gearbox which gave three forward speeds and a reverse; the top speed was a direct drive to the rear roadwheels via a short shaft and differential. Renault's shaft drive was one of the most significant advances in the development of the automobile, and was the foundation of his immediate success. For the first time

one could buy a car without side-chains or belts. Louis was persuaded by his brothers not to sell the rights of his new system to the industry but to form a company and build a car around it.

The first Renault prototype was the modified De Dion: a simple tubular frame, four wheels with Ackerman steering, an open body providing side-by-side seating for two. The tiny engine was hidden under a bonnet [hood] the size of a hatbox.

Commercial success came unexpectedly on Christmas Eve 1898. Renault decided to drive his home-produced car to a festive meeting in a café on the Butte Montmartre, the

only hill in Paris. A dozen people were there including an old friend of Renault père, the *avocat* Maître Viot. Viot asked Louis if he could have a ride in his gimcrack vehicle, and was taken up and down the steep Rue Lepic. Pedestrians stopped to stare, children ran alongside, dogs barked, and the car worked perfectly.

Back at the café-cabaret in the Rue de Helder, Maître Viot slapped down 40 gold Louis on the table, the first Renault customer.

Now everyone else present at the café was captivated with the new machine. That evening Louis Renault took 11 other friends up and down the Rue Lepic – and received a total of a

First Renault, 1899, with 1¾ hp De Dion single-cylinder engine, three forward speeds and reverse, shaft drive, tiller steering.

Three bowler-hatted Charlie Chaplins in Paris. Renaults 1,2, and 3, and the world's first saloon car on the left of the picture. The front end of the 1900 car (centre) had already been changed from a hatbox shape to an elemental coal scuttle.

dozen orders for the little car. His pockets were heavy with coin. His car, and more specifically his new drive system, had sealed his fate. He *had* to become a motor manufacturer. That Christmas party had spawned an industrial empire . . . .

Building the cars in the garden shed was obviously out of the question. Brothers Marcel and Fernand threw in their lot with Louis and staked their own savings on the future. The three formed a company with its head office

at Billancourt, near the old home.

Screw-cutting lathes, grinders and a small steam engine were bought and in six short months no less than 60 little Renault cars were made, all tested by the company's directors who were to be seen in the early mornings puttering about the Paris suburb, three bowler-hatted Charlie Chaplins. One of the cars was a closed version, *à conduite intérieure,* a 'drive-from-the-inside', still the French term for a closed car. It was in fact the world's first saloon

(sedan), taller than it was long and designed to accommodate passengers in top hats.

Exactly 179 units were built at the Billancourt works that year by 110 workers, using single-cylinder De Dion engines. Renault also exported his cars to Britain, where they sold under the name M.C.C. Triumph.

By 1903 France was by far the most advanced motoring nation, producing over 60 000 vehicles that year, a figure which represented half the world's to-tal output. Peugeot, Panhard, Dar-racq, De Dion, Renault, Delahaye, De Dietrich, Mors and so on, all had long waiting lists. Motoring had become a fashionable occupation and it was *très chic* for madame to be seen in the *bois* of a morning, driven around by a liveried chauffeur or using an auto-mobile to get from her residence to a dinner party. A Renault publicity poster of the time depicts a scene which includes a motorboat, a flying machine and a Renault car entitled

Overleaf: A turn in the Bois. Anyone who was anyone considered it de rigueur *to take their morning exercise this way. The vehicle in the foreground is a Peugeot phaeton, followed by a five-seater omnibus and a two-seater, circa 1896.*

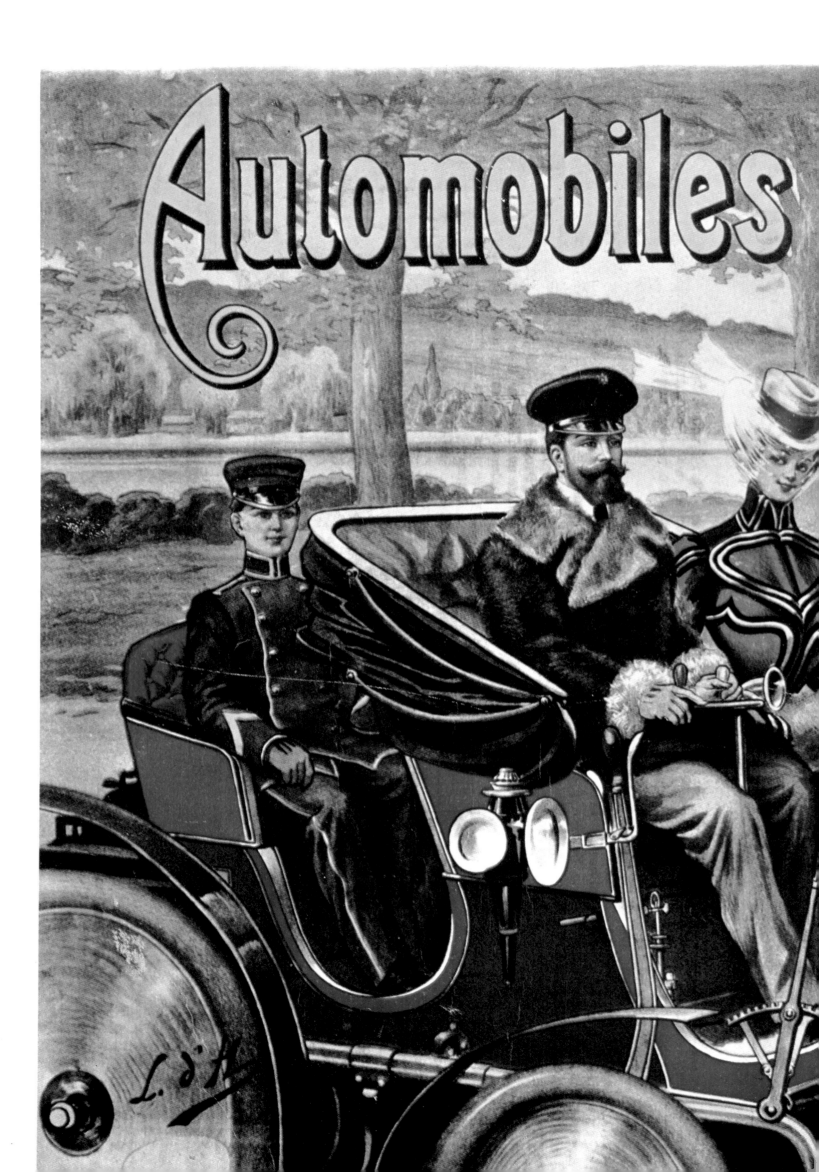

PEUGEOT

PARIS
83, Boul. Gouvion St. Cyr

IMP. DU GRIFFON
10, RUE DE BUCI, PARIS

The 'society fad' of the day on land, sea and in the air. A Renault poster of about 1905 in which, predictably, all the transport is powered by engines from Billancourt.

'Les Grands Sports' – all society 'fads' of the period.

There was in France, however, the feeling from the very earliest days of the automobile, that it was to be a servant of business as well as an instrument of amusement, and indeed some 25 per cent of cars on the roads of France were registered for business use in 1903.

Taking a car to the Continent was an adventure at the turn of the century. Nevertheless many English car-owners shipped their cars over the Channel in pursuit of pleasure. King Edward had motored into Europe several times – to take the waters at Marienbad or sample the tables at Biarritz, and where he went others rapidly followed.

Monsieur Mercedes

Many enthusiasts from the motoring countries were staying at hotels in Nice on the French Riviera during March 1901, to witness the exciting Sports Week which was to open with a parade of flower-decorated cars, the *Corso Automobile Fleuri*.

The first race for 'speed and touring cars' was to be over a long course from Nice to Aix, Senas, Salon and back.

Panhards, Rochet-Schneiders, Mors, Audibert-Lavirottes (and a Gladiator tricycle) churned down the road to the west, led most of the way by a new car called in the programme 'Mercédès', owned by Baron de Rothschild and driven by his *mechanicien*, Werner. The car completed the course to win the race in six hours 46 minutes – an impressively high speed on poor roads in bad weather.

The mystery 'Mercédès' from the Daimler stable at Cannstatt, received the prizes and the plaudits that day – and in the rest of the week's events. The Mercedes team won everything from speed events to the daunting hillclimb up to La Turbie, the village which hangs on the edge of the mountain above Monte Carlo, a steep snaking climb that had already claimed the life of one Daimler driver two years previously – and which was to claim the life of Monaco's Princess Grace 81 years later.

Said *The Automotor Journal* in its next issue: 'The performance of the German Daimler-Mercedes [already the new and as yet unofficial name was being used by the press] was a source of bitter disappointment to the French champions who, up to the present time, have practically carried everything before them ... their *amour propre* was evidently greatly hurt.' And Britain's premier automotive journal, *The Autocar*, reported that 'The entire workmanship, design, and performance of this car have stuck terror into the heart of a capable critic like Paul Meyan [doyen of French motoring writers] who warns the French manufacturers that the pride of place in autocar building is about to be wrested from them by the Germans. He quotes the remark made to him by Monsieur Mercedes (whose identity was still a mystery to many) the day after his triumph, which ran as follows: "That car will be nothing beside what you will see next year," and then asks if M. Mercedes could have been joking.'

Monsieur Mercedes was not. The 1902 car from Cannstatt was indeed a marked improvement; it developed 40 hp compared with the 35 hp of the first model, and was lighter and faster – and indeed wrested pride of place from absolutely everyone.

But let us look for a moment at the original Mercedes of 1901. Mercédès, by the way, was simply the name of the 11-year-old daughter of the local diplomat (and agent for Daimler), Emile Jellinek, who wished to conceal the Daimler car's German identity for a while, and who later had the names of

This 35/40 hp Mercedes from Cannstatt was built in 1904 – and may still be seen taking a lively part in Veteran car rallies, often travelling at speeds comparable to modern transport.

the imported cars officially changed to Mercedes as a sales aid. Jellinek himself also took his daughter's name as a personal pseudonym for this purpose and for sporting events.

After an accident during the 1900 Nice week, Jellinek, an influential figure on the Côte d'Azur, had suggested to Willi Maybach, Daimler's brilliant engineer, that a new and better balanced vehicle should be designed and built. The result was the Mercedes.

The new car had a longer wheelbase, lower centre of gravity, and a higher engine output than anything yet produced at Cannstatt. Jellinek had already contracted to buy the first 36 examples, so sure was he of sales to his friends.

Contrary to the current practice of building larger and ever more powerful engines, Maybach had produced a relatively small four-cylinder unit of 5.9 litres (other vehicles housed engines of up to three times that figure) with mechanically operated inlet valves, which opened and shut positively and accurately, where others relied on the suction created by the descending piston to open the inlet valves. The use of mechanically operated valves was a vital step in engine progress, allowing the use of a throttle with the carburettor; thus an engine could operate readily at widely differing speeds. Its Bosch low-tension mag-

neto ignition could be advanced or retarded at will.

The car's 'honeycomb' radiator (with 8 070 separate cooling tubes) was another leap forward. Coupled with a water-tank, it was far more efficient than the serpentine finned-tube arrangements which needed regular topping-up. A newly designed spring-clutch encouraged smooth operation, and a gate system of gear-change in which the lever could be shifted through two dimensions instead of being limited to the fore-and-aft movement as on the standard quadrant change, brought modern motoring a tangible step nearer. The new pressed-steel chassis frame placed the armoured-wood frames of the competition of 1901 in the farm-cart class.

These technical innovations caused rival manufacturers much gnashing of teeth. Not that they were all new – the honeycomb had been used before by Daimler, low-tension magneto ignition had been seen earlier, the gate-change had been used on a previous car. But seen under one cover like this, coupled with the general appearance of the long low car and its relatively silent operation, the technical advances of the new Mercedes were recognized immediately as the necessary qualities of a new generation of motor vehicles.

And when the speed-conscious onlookers at Nice saw its pace and handling, they clamoured to buy.

Opposite: Early 20th century – fresh-air motoring as depicted in an advertisement.

Below: Fresh-air motoring in reality. A single-cylinder 6hp De Dion Bouton of 1904. By 1902 De Dions had achieved a front engine with an under-slung radiator.

Racing in the herioc period. For sheer suicidal bravery these splendid long-moustached gentlemen of Edwardian times had no peers.

Other manufacturers scuttled back to the drawing board and very soon were offering near-copies of the great new Mercedes. Undoubtedly the greatest single influence of automobile design in the first 50 years of motoring, the 1901 Mercedes set standards of motoring that have been maintained by the makers (now Daimler-Benz in Germany and Mercedes-Benz elsewhere) to this day.

Racing for Heroes

A great race had been organized from Paris to Vienna, and the whole motorsporting world was to attend.

Levassor, de Knyff, Charron, Giradot, Fournier and Zbrowski, household sporting names of the day, with their gigantic 40-hp Mercedes, 70-hp Panhards or Mors, were to compete. Renaults with their smaller cars had taken part in earlier events – in the Paris-Bordeaux of 1900 and the Paris-Berlin of 1901 ('the madmen's race', the French press dubbed it), but this

745-mile contest was to be the most dramatic, the most heroic of them all, routing the contestants through the mountainous Vorarlberg region.

The roads over the first sections to the Swiss frontier at Belfort were reasonably good but British driver Jarrot was careful. 'I had decided that in no circumstances would I be bustled over the first 80 kilometres [50 miles] to Provins,' he said. Nevertheless, several of the larger cars covered that part at around 70 mph, Henri Fournier's Panhard actually overtaking the spectators' 'express' train running parallel to the route, proving again that for sheer suicidal bravery those long-moustached Edwardian gentlemen drivers had no peers. First to arrive at the Swiss border was the Chevalier de Knyff who had covered the 253 miles in just over seven hours, followed by two French-driven 70-hp Panhards and ex-racing cyclist Jarrot, also in a big Panhard.

The second part of the event was

run through Switzerland – strictly at touring speeds, for the Swiss authorities would have none of this crazy racing over *their* peaceful countryside. The last section was to be run over the Austrian Alps, including the precipitous Arlberg Pass, then along the Inn Valley to Salzburg, and on to Vienna.

The race over the appalling mountain-goat-track roads was made more hazardous by the regulations of the time, which imposed a weight limit of 1 000 kilos (2 200 lb) on the unladen cars. This had been a genuine attempt to divert the dangerous trend to larger and more powerful engines. Manufacturers accepted this new regulation – and kept their cars' weight down by drilling holes through every piece of support metal in sight until the cars looked like Gruyere cheese, and by throwing overboard everything that could be unscrewed without crippling the car. The result, said a motoring journalist of the time, was that 'The chassis of these racing cars is now a mere skeleton, but the engine a raging lion, immense in size and power although exceedingly light … the ingenuity displayed in reducing the weight of this year's racing models, while at the same time greatly increasing their power, is such as to reflect the great credit on the designers …' – a somewhat back-to-front logic it proved, as a large number of competitors bent their vehicles at weak spots. 'All muscle and no bone' was a more apt description given at the time.

Marcel Renault's little car – 4.5 litres and Lilliputian compared with some of the giants – proved the quality of the modest Billancourt cars very nicely, thank you. Marcel arrived at the Vienna finishing line so far ahead of the estimated arrival time that officials had to be persuaded that he *was* Marcel Renault, the competitor … who had

Arrival at the Prater, Vienna, 1902. Marcel Renault reached the finishing post so far ahead of other competitors in his little 30hp car that he had to persuade officials that he was indeed Marcel Renault from France and the victor of the 1902 race from Paris to Vienna.

The Paris-Vienna marathon sharply increased the reputation of the four-cylinder French Darracq – four of them arrived in the first nine. This is a 1907 16–18hp touring Darracq, a direct development of the Paris-Vienna cars of five years earlier.

preceded the leader of the rest of the field by some 35 minutes.

Almost equally astonishing was the performance put up by the Darracq entry. No less than four of these French light cars finished in the first nine. The lesson of that day was clear: speed and reliability did not necessarily increase in proportion to engine size. It took several years, however, for some manufacturers to appreciate this and start scaling down their huge engines.

The following year tragedy hit the sport when an accident during the Paris-Madrid event killed a number of people. Open road racing was abandoned. The Gordon Bennett Cup, the first real international series of races which had been run on public roads since 1900, and had been part of the longer Paris races, was held on a closed circuit in Ireland in 1903.

By 1906 the Automobile Club de France, exasperated by some of the regulations of the Gordon Bennett series, dreamed up a new international race to be run on its own country's soil.

It was to be called the Grand Prix, a term borrowed from horse-racing circles. The first Grand Prix (more accurately *Le Grand Prix de l'Automobile Club de France*) was run at a closed road circuit near the Sarthe town of Le Mans, although not on the same circuit on which today's endurance races are run.

Although he had vowed never to race again after the Madrid disaster in which his brother Marcel had been tragically killed, Louis Renault could not resist this new-style motoring challenge, and decided to enter his cars.

In the event, a Renault was victorious. With Hungarian *pilote* Ferenc Szisz at the wheel, the 90-hp car's speed during the two tropical days in June 1906 often exceeded 90 mph.

Chased for the first day by a gargantuan 16.5-litre 100-hp Fiat driven by Nazzaro, and hounded by De Dietriches, Darracqs, Mercedes, Italas and Panhards – the latter housing engines with jumbo-size cylinders of 18 litres – the Renault's win was one of the most exciting spectacles of the new racing period. The next year the position was reversed, with Fiat leading the field.

Fiat, the company that was, within a decade, to become the largest industrial organization of any kind in Italy, was well established by 1906. The Torinese firm (that had started business in an old bicycle factory making a carriage which was somewhat dated even for the last days of the 19th century) flourished by producing vehicles which were at first modestly furnished with 1-litre engines, but soon climbed the capacity scale to 3, 6, 7, 10 and 14 litres, offering the new car-buying public a wide range of models. They adapted many of them for competition. The Fiat Corsa (racing) models soon found fame with Nazzaro, Vincenzo Lancia and others at the wheel, and consolidated their sporting reputation in 1907, when Fiats won everything in the racing calendar including the German Kaiserpreis, the Targa Florio and the French Grand Prix. That year was to be the *annus mirabilis* for the Fiat sports team, a pinnacle of achievement never again to be reached.

However, Fiat the manufacturer continued to grow. Like most others it had copied much from the design of the 1901 miracle car, the new Daimler

The first major Grand Prix motor race was held on a closed road circuit at Le Mans in the Sarthe region of France in 1906. Open road races had already taken a heavy toll of lives. Here the winning car, a Renault, passes through a village on the circuit. From a water colour by Michael Wright.

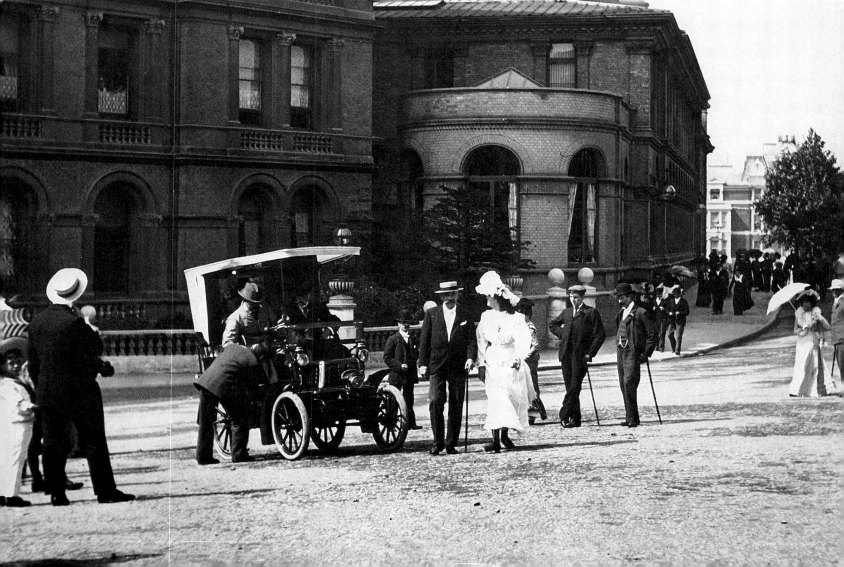

called 'Mercedes', and had reaped the benefits in healthy sales of its 1903 –1908 models. Fiat (*Fabbrica Italiana Automobili Torino*) was making commercial vehicles by 1903, opened a ball-bearing plant in 1905 and began to build ships the same year.

Hazards of the Road

Great Britain was still struggling forward, half-in half-out of the horse age and, as in the United States, much advice was given on how to accustom the horse to the occasional car. 'Drive the vehicle around it, in gradually decreasing circles,' says one equestrian scribe, going on to advocate a soothing chat with the animal, which he assures readers will follow the movements of the vehicle with his eyes, in time allowing it to be driven close without signs of fear. Less sympathetic was the mandatory American notice to automobilists, stating that when they encountered a horse in the countryside they must dismantle their vehicle and hide it in the hedge! Another advised the firing of hand-rockets into the air on approaching a town.

However, the days of motoring merely as an eccentric amusement were over. Journeying by motor car was no longer considered just 'good sport', but was beginning to take its place, by mid-Edwardian times, as a serious, if cripplingly expensive, mode of long-distance travelling, both socially and professionally. Sufficient technical progress had been made for transcontinental tours to be essayed. The pioneering adventure was still to be had, but with a servant to precede the family conveyance reserving hotel accommodation for the main party, European travel was not now considered a grave hazard.

Roads, dust, police, weather, breakdowns and roadhogs were the hazards of the mid-Edwardian motorist in his newly acquired Alldays or Wolseley, his Vauxhall, Thornycroft or six-cylinder Napier.

Opposite top: This De Dietrich of 1906 was built in the sporting idiom of the day. Its 5.4 litre engine with four pair-cast cylinders, four-speed gate change and twin final drive chains can still take it, some 80 years later, to an invigorating 55 mph.

Opposite bottom: In Britain motor cars were still objects of interest and curiosity in 1902. Sunday strollers at Richmond, Surrey found time to stand and stare at this vehicle which the slight uphill gradient seems to have halted.

Below: Another English aristocrat, the Alldays made by Alldays & Onions Ltd of Birmingham, a conservative design originally using a vertical twin-cylinder unit of 1.6 litres, and a four from 1906. This is a 1909 model.

A very real nuisance in Britain was the vacuum-cleaner effect of rapidly moving cars on the unmetalled roads. Loose stones, bound with mud or at best a sprinkling of tar, would accumulate a thick layer of white dust which, in the days of walking-pace horse transport, would remain where rain and wear deposited it. But the speed limit for motor vehicles in Britain had been raised to 20 mph in 1903, effectively doubling the pace of traffic. The increased speed's effect, apart from breaking the road surface up more rapidly, was to create a low-pressure area at the back of the car, drawing up thick choking clouds of dust which billowed out behind and tended to follow the car in an ever-increasing cloud. Urban householders were not amused. Complaints were made about increased throat infections, damage to crops and to the Monday wash. The police, under the direction – and the thumb – of the local Bench, were instructed to deter speed as much to reduce dust as to reduce danger.

Sadly their task became obsessive, prosecution turned into what looked very much like persecution, and a spin in the country became something of a roulette game with the odds loaded against the car owner. 'Trapping' was naturally distasteful for the well-heeled motoring coterie. Privately hired squads of cyclists patrolled certain main routes – the London to Brighton road was one of the earliest to be

One of the first AA telephone kiosks that were to become a familiar sight on British roadsides.

patrolled – to warn drivers of lurking police activity. By 1905 they had formed themselves into the 'Automobile Mutual Association'.

The AA, as it was soon called, began to employ its patrolmen to observe police activity near roads on which speed traps were frequently set up. The AA patrolman would cycle through a known stretch of road, note the three policed points (needed to mount a speed trap), cycle back to a point outside the trap and warn motorists whose cars displayed the Association badge of the danger. Such action was soon interpreted as 'obstructing the due process of the law', and before long an AA man had been thrown into gaol for perjury for confirming in court

that a motorist had been travelling at a mere 15 mph, after the police patrol had accused him of speeding above the limit of 20 mph. It was then that the increasingly powerful AA opened its own legal department for the defence of staff and members.

There was an element of sport in the whole ludicrous trap-dodging business however. The AA devised several ways of warning their members without breaking the law and finally settled on negative or 'non' action should there be any 'interesting activity' in the vicinity. 'If your AA patrolman does *not* salute an approaching member,' advised the Association, 'Stop and ask him the reason why.'

Even in England, last bastion of

*'She acted like a charm all the way ...
taking hills like level ground.' So wrote a
delighted customer of his new Vauxhall in
1905, similar to the one pictured here. This
year the cars were equipped with a new
three-cylinder engine of 9 hp, replacing the
earlier one-pot 6 hp. A four, wearing the
distinctive bonnet flutes, appeared in 1906.*

four-footed transport, many were aware by 1905 of the impending change in travelling habits. Commented a young Member of Parliament, Winston Churchill, 'Five years ago, a motor car was an object of derision if it stopped for one moment; now the horses have got used to them, the asses [on the other side of the house?] have got used to them, and we see them on every road.'

There was, however, still some way to go before the law recognized the right of the car to move faster than the 20 mph of the cyclist.

Best of British

The rich were playing at carnivals or gymkhanas, manoeuvring their mounts around in fair imitation of the cavalry, or racing down to the Hotel Hermitage at fashionable Monte Carlo, while others were reading all about fast travel in the flood of new romantic novels and children's adventures that were appearing on the sixpenny shelves in the bookstalls. And when the world's first purpose-built motor-racing circuit was opened at Brooklands, near London, the public flocked to see the first motor races and record-breaking attempts.

The increase in motor traffic was measurable by 1907, and the difference in the speed of horsed and motor traffic was, in the more crowded urban areas, beginning to cause some delays. A census of the traffic situation taken at a point on the Great North Road in North London illustrates the changing scene. The date, 1905; the timespan, 10 a.m. to 6.30 p.m.:

Motor cars	43
Motor cycles	8
Motor lorries	1
Cycles	99
Total	151
Heavy horse-drawn vehicles	63
Tradesmen's carts	35
Private carriages	33
Total	131

British industry was developing rapidly. Sickly infants in their first days, by 1905 several firms had plunged into motor-making production.

'Aug. 4th 1905. Dear Sirs, You will be wondering how I got along with my little Car. Well, she acted like a charm all the way ... taking hills like level ground. I took her across London Bridge and drove all through Borough Market, where the traffic kept two policemen as busy as they could be.' (From a new owner to the manufacturer).

And in *The Western Times*, this editorial comment is typical of the carefree innocence of the day: 'Messrs. Gould have acquired the sole agency in Devon and Cornwall, for the supply of the popular "Vauxhall" petrol car, which has largely "taken on" – one having recently been acquired by a well-known City M.M. The Vauxhall is a masterpiece in simplicity of construction, easily controlled and carries sufficient petrol for a run of 100 miles. Mr. Gould who brought one of them by road from London, did the journey comfortably in 12 hours. About 40 miles can be run with one gallon of petrol.'

Vauxhall Iron Works Limited, the old marine-engine company at Lambeth on the banks of the Thames, had made its first car in 1903, a tiller-steered one-cylinder 6-hp runabout. By 1905 business was so brisk that the company decided to move into the country where there would be more room for expansion. Vauxhall chose Luton, in Bedfordshire.

The company employed engineer Laurence Pomeroy to design one of the first true British sports cars, later

The first real British sports car, the 'Prince Henry' Vauxhall of 1911 was also the first 20hp car of any make to exceed 100mph. The 20hp unit was replaced by a 25hp engine in 1913.

dubbed the 'Prince Henry', which took the company to several sporting successes just before World War One, and was developed into the even-more-renowned Vauxhall 30/98 sports car. Just as the early version of the Prince Henry Vauxhall had been the first 20-hp car of any make to exceed 100 mph, so the 30/98, built between 1913 and 1926, achieved the highest number of sporting 'firsts' (75 in Britain) in the days immediately after the war, taking its place as one of the world's classic cars. Curiously this car was neither 30 hp nor 98 hp, nor did it have any other specifications of either figure. Nobody to this day knows the origin of its name.

Wolseley, Vauxhall, Lanchester, Napier and Austin were also producing cars, if not in quantity at least with enthusiasm, in 1906. Firms like Hor-bick had turned from textile machinery to the lucky dip of the new industry; Swift of Coventry had moved from sewing machines to bicycles and then to cars (first car 1900); John Marston's tinplate and japanning company of Birmingham had shown its first Sunbeam car in 1899, and had by now stopped making the bizarre diamond-shaped Sunbeam Mabley, and was making a conventional 12 hp; the Riley Cycle Company was now making Riley motor cars; Napier & Son Limited was producing luxury six-cylinder cars.

Henry Royce had bought his De-cauville from France, examined it with some disdain, and had built his own far-superior Royce car in 1904. The Honourable Charles Rolls, car salesman and son of a noble house, joined forces with the fastidious cranemaker

Opposite: A Napier by any other name ... This one, built by the British company in 1908, was called a Hutton, a name used to enable the four-cylinder cars to be manufactured by Napier who were then promoting their six-cylinder models.

Below: The ubiquitous De Dion. This 1904 rear-entrance 8hp tonneau was popular when it first appeared in France, sold well on the British market – and is still the marque with the greatest number of survivors in the entire range of veteran vehicles today.

81

from Manchester in 1905 and formed Rolls-Royce Limited a few months later. Their eventual one-model policy was to result in the Rolls-Royce 40/50, the illustrious 7-litre six-cylinder Silver Ghost of 1906.

Royce's first car of 1904 was 'favourable compared with the competition' reported a newsman, 'which sounded like an avalanche of tea-trays when matched against the silence of the Royce progression!' The 10-hp two-cylinder model, first of the Royce series production cars, sold for just £395.

By 1907 the Rolls-Royce Silver Ghost was in demand by heads of state, monarchs and managing directors throughout the motoring world. For 19 years it held the title of 'Best in the World' (rivalled for a time only by the distinguished French-made Hispano-Suiza) and when the Silver Ghost was followed by the Phantom I in 1925, it retained the crown. Rolls-Royce Limited of Manchester and later of Derby, by combining the Honourable Charles Rolls's sales abilities and social connections with the work of perfectionist Henry Royce, had created such a demand for the car that during the halcyon days before World War One they could not be produced fast enough to clear the order books.

Sadly, tragedy dissolved the partnership. Charles Rolls, a restless spirit always seeking fresh experiences, found a new enthusiasm, powered flight. He purchased one of the first French-built Wright biplanes and competed in a pioneer race over the English Channel in 1910. A few weeks later, he was killed when his frail aircraft crashed during a minor competition.

However, the company continued to flourish. Testimonials were received from many owners, particularly from Indian princes who were enchanted by the ability of coachbuilders to equip their cars for safari conditions. American newspapers eulogized. Said *The New York Times*, 'We were amazed at the smoothness of running, the easy steering and simplicity of control,' and *The New York Herald* burst into song with, 'The wonder is a Rolls-Royce . . . it is so silent that it has been necessary to place a glass "tell tale" on the dashboard in order that the driver may know whether or not the motor is in operation'.

A pioneer on the automotive scene was the Wolseley Sheep Shearing

Opposite: Glimpse of a Ghost. The 1906 7-litre Rolls-Royce unit with pressure lubrication was conventional even then but soon proved that it was superior to all others. A 15,000 miles marathon trial in 1907 confirmed this – and this one built in early 1907 is still in fine running order after over half-a-million miles of travelling.

Below: From heavy steam engines and ship's boilers to car engines. Maudslay had a high reputation when they moved into the automotive field in 1902, the round radiator (introduced in 1905) shows their steam tradition and the cars were offered in 20/30 and 35/45 hp forms. Circa 1908.

Machine Company. Its manager, Bert Austin, who had been an engineer in Australia and knew something of the difficulties of using machinery in the backwoods, was more interested in motor vehicles than sheep – in fact he considered motoring *was* the use of machinery in the backwoods and his designs reflected this. In 1895 he cunningly made an early move in the right direction by adding cycle-making to his fleece-cutter production. He built an experimental car on Bollée principles, but went on rapidly to make a 3½-hp four-wheeled model which was tried out in Britain's great show rally, the Thousand Miles Trial of 1900. Production followed, but by 1905 Herbert Austin had quarrelled with his directors who had considered that a 'vertical' engine (early Wolseleys had horizontal cylinders) would be more efficient than his own design. Austin left the company.

The normally single-minded Herbert must have had a change of heart, for when the Austin Motor Company of Longbridge, Birmingham, opened its doors in 1906, it built cars housing sidevalve, T-head *vertical* engines. The Wolseley Tool and Motor Car Company, as the ex-sheepshearing-machine company was now called, had already commenced making vertical engines for J.D. Siddeley, who sold his cars (in reality only thinly disguised light Wolseleys) as Siddeleys, which, ironically, soon began to outsell the Wolseley itself. Wolseley bought out Mr. Siddeley and wisely appointed him general manager.

Every Man His Own Mechanic

A day's spin over the country roads of England was a day's experience to be remembered in those years before road surfaces had been stabilized by asphalt or tarmac, a gradual change that began in about 1905.

Few motor cars had more than primitive weather protection. This was accepted by the pioneers of the new travel. Comfort was not expected. Garment manufacturers offered a wide range of clothing for the motorist, ranging from protective face masks for both sexes, to all-enveloping dust coats (at 19/6 a pair). Ladies' and Gents' hats took on a new look. Men had, at first, worn yachting caps and blazers, along with much else that had been borrowed from marine usage. But before long it was realized that when

motoring the only place for the peak of a hat was at the back of the neck and so drivers took to wearing flat caps, turned about. Ladies' hats often incorporated the veil-and-mask element, and some were so thorough in their efforts to keep their wearers' delicate complexion unblemished that it looked as though the female passengers' heads had been sewn up in sacks. For cold weather there were foot-warmers (with coals) and hand warmers (of fur) and vast fleece-lined tents that wrapped round everyone. Rain brought out heavy rubber storm garments, spring-fastened horrors that streamed water directly into one's boots. It must have been fun.

'Every motorist his own mechanic' was naturally the rule, except for the most wealthy. There was no chance at all of surviving a morning's drive without a puncture, and the damaged tyre would have to be 'spooned' off, the tube examined (in a basin of water, for smaller injuries) and patched with a complex vulcanizing apparatus or sticky patch. Liberal powders would be applied and the whole mess returned to the flimsy cover. Around 1906 a makeshift godsend was the Stepney wheel which one carried as a spare and which could be clamped on to the damaged wheel, thus allowing the vehicle to be driven carefully home. In fact most breakdowns were trivial – dirt in the carburettor jets or an electric disconnection caused by constant vibration. The trouble was raised to disaster level only because most motorists had never before tackled anything more complicated than a bicycle.

The automobile was about to introduce a new way of life to the entire world. Manufacturers of a dozen different products, unconnected with transport, changed direction and entered the automotive industry. In a handful of seasons, advertisements in the social, yachting or motoring journals had changed from tentatively introducing readers to the motoring world with ads such as this in *The Motor-Car Journal* in 1902: 'Careless Capel & Leonard of Hackney Wick London, specially distil petrol, the spirit best adapted for motors . . . . Maximum of efficiency and perfect combustion . . . no deposit in cylinder. No smell, no dirt, no trouble' to this in *The Autocar* of April 1906 (which could be last week's insertion): 'Lease

Opposite: The Wolseley firm bade farewell to Herbert Austin in 1905, when designer J.D. Siddeley (later Lord Kenilworth) took over. Wolseley-Siddeleys were all vertical-engined by 1906 and dominated the firm's range. This distinguished model, a 1906 25hp Landaulette is the sole survivor of its type.

A Dutch Spyker, 1904 (2.8 litres, four cylinders), one of the famous pair of veteran cars used in the 1950s film Genevieve, *a comedy feature that gave the interest in old cars an immense boost. Seen in Lips Autotron, Drunen, Holland.*

of premises for Disposal with possession, now occupied as motor car showroom, workshops, and garage ... situated in important London thoroughfare'.

By 1910 the larger cities of Europe and North America were fully accustomed to the world of motoring – at least vicariously – and little boys in London's suburbs no longer ran to the front gate at the sound of a passing motor car. A motor-show poster of the time illustrated the newly acquired sophistication; it depicts a little girl leaning out of an open car in a city saying, 'Mama, look there's a *horse*!'

The fundamental engineering layout and the general appearance of the motor car had long since settled down to what had now become accepted as conventional. A vertical engine mounted at the front of the structure was by now a four- or even six-cylinder unit, and the drive train to the rear road wheels was through shaft rather than chains. By the end of Edward's reign in 1910, many larger vehicles were clothed in luxury and gave total weather protection. Sedan (saloon) bodies were tall, rectangular (one could actually *walk through* a motor car), and surrounded by bevelled glass

bodymaker's terms remind us:

Brougham: a squarish saloon-type vehicle (a term still used in the U.S.A.).

Landaulet: a limousine, the roof of which was flexible at the rear, folding down if desired.

Coupé de ville: a saloon-type car, the passenger compartment of which was enclosed, leaving the chauffeur exposed.

Voiturette, voiturelle: early terms for a light car.

Buggy: American lightweight high-wheeler, patterned on the horse-drawn buggy.

Runabout: a light car, e.g. Olds Curved Dash; a cyclecar, e.g. Morgan.

Wagonette: a vehicle for large families, with inward facing seats at the rear also known as a brake (or break).

Roi des Belges: a large open car with two luxurious rear 'wrapround' seats. Also called a tulip phaeton.

Limousine: a closed motor car with a glass partition between the rear compartment and the driver.

Tourer: an open four-seater.

Torpedo: an open four-seater with an almost unbroken line from the front of the bonnet to the rear end of the vehicle, with seat backs the same height as the body sides.

The changing face of America. In 1900 children stared in wonder at the automobile. Ten years later they looked with affection at the slowly disappearing horse.

"LOOK MAMMA, THERE'S A HORSE!"

through which the occupants could be admired. Cape Cart hoods were still seen with their leather straps attached to for'ard ironwork, which turned a car into a sort of parachute. Landaulet bodies with their downward folding rear top for city promenading were popular, and *coupés des villes* and other 'sun-parlour' arrangements were *de rigueur* for leisured society. By this time phaetons, tonneaux and Victorias were old hat; the apron-strings attaching the motor coachbuilding industry to the horse age were quickly being loosened. However, some of the nomenclature remained, as these

Above: An Opel Torpedo of 1920.

The latest in body-line development in 1910-13 was the torpedo with its smart front-to-rear continuous line along the shoulder of the car. Still a leisure vehicle in concept, the tourer belongs more, perhaps, to the 1920s rather than to the late Edwardian days in England, but the first of this design, with its scuttle shape now also moulded into the bonnet-line protecting the driver's legs from the elements, was typical of the new functional attitude to motoring. Gone were the wrought-iron filigrees and brass knick-knacks; the torpedo was a 20th-century contour – forceful and unadorned. It was just the thing for the war games that the sabre-rattlers of Europe were mounting in those increasingly uneasy years towards the end of the first decade of the century.

Separate Development in the U.S.A.

By the turn of the century the one-time backyard 'blacksmith' car-builders were applying themselves seriously to the business of manufacturing genuine American automobiles.

In 1900 some 4 000 cars were made in the U.S.A., mostly high-wheelers with their buggy ancestry grinning through. Ransom Olds was one of the

first and, like the firms of International, Anderson of Indiana, Holsman, Walker of Detroit, and a dozen others, hung on to the horizontally opposed twin surrey-with-a-fringe-on-top style for several years after most of the world had settled for 'real' motor cars.

Olds built 2 000 pramlike Curved-Dash Runabouts in 1902 and increased his sales during the following years. His slow-revving single-cylinder 'one-chug-per-telegraph-pole' buggies were cheap to buy and simple to run. The former quality was due to Ohio-born Olds's clever new idea of 'stage' production. Said the American journal *Automobile* in 1904, when some 5 000 tiller-steered Curved-Dash cars were produced (three times as many vehicles as the large firm of Peugeot) in the Detroit works, 'The motors are passed, step by step, down the assembling bench towards the testing department which is in the next room, a new piece being added at every move with clock-like regularity.' That report with the now-familiar ring told a largely unheeding world that mass production was here. It took Henry Ford to develop it to quantity production with his Model-T moving assembly lines, but Olds had blazed the trail well ahead of him.

Opposite: American rural scene, West Virginia 1906. Climbing up a steep hill at Harper's Ferry is a 1904 Pope-Toledo.

Henry Leland's first Cadillac of 1903 was a modest enough affair. With one underfloor cylinder, two-speed transmission and a single chain-drive it looked remarkably similar to Henry Ford's model of the same year.

By 1903 engineer and gunsmith Henry Leland (he had earlier made rifles for the Union Army) had taken over the failing Henry Ford Company after Henry Ford had left, and renamed it Cadillac. With his precision-tool background and meticulous engineering methods he guided his new company into the top-quality bracket, where it has firmly resided ever since.

Other companies great and small flourished in the first years of the 20th century, but precious few are still with us. Most of them managed to turn down a blind technological alley, make

The Pierce Arrow

Prestige automobile, U.S.A. circa 1910. Together with Packard and Peerless the Pierce Arrow, (formerly the Great Arrow) was one of the three early aristocrats of U.S. production.

a fundamental marketing misjudgement or an irreversible financial error, and foundered. Over 2 000 one-time auto-manufacturing companies in the U.S.A. are now only nostalgic echoes.

It needs no written record to tell us that Henry Ford was an exception. In spite of producing several early models which proved to be unremarkable, with consequent financial problems, his luck held. The Ford Model K, a large six-cylinder model offered in 1906, did nothing to stimulate his fortunes (he had not been enthusiastic about its production but was overruled), neither did the $500 Model N which also appeared during 1906, although its price undercut the comparable Oldsmobile of that year.

But the Model N had some of the features that were to become widely known in Ford's car of the following year – the homely, the ubiquitous, the best-selling Model T. 'The automobile of the past,' said Henry, explaining why the world needed his Model T so badly, 'attained success in spite of its price. The automobile of the future must be enough better than the present car to beget confidence in the man of limited means, and enough lower in price to insure sale for the enormously increased output. In the low-priced car dwells the future success of the automobile.' He was right at the time: his witness, the sales of 15 007 033 Model T examples.

The October 1908 issue of the U.S. magazine *Motor* carried a huge advertisement introducing the new Ford

Above: America's general dogsbody – the famous, the everlasting, Model T Ford. This is a 1910 example, a year in which over 100,000 Model T's were made at Ford's Highland Park plant.

Opposite top: Mercedes marches on – in 1906 the company installed six-cylinder 120hp engines for the first time. This 1907 two-seater is a 10.18 litre 70hp version.

Opposite bottom: The scorcher, circa 1905. Unlike today's learner drivers, there was no expert tutor to teach newcomers to motoring in the early part of the 20th century.

Model T to the American public. It stated 'The cars have been run under every conceivable condition. Last winter they were tried on snow-and-slush-covered country roads – all summer they have run on hills, on sand and mud roads in good and bad weather. While we do not know how many of these cars we will build the next 12 months, the price is based on building 25 000 cars.' By 1912 no less than 200 000 cars rolled off his lines in 12 months and at one point in the 1920s *half the entire world's automobiles* were Model T Fords.

Propelling this gawky maid-of-all-work was a 20-hp four-cylinder 2.9-litre (3¾ × 4 inches) unit, cast in a single block with a removable water-jacketed cylinder head. The gearbox, which needed some understanding before it responded to reason, was a pedal-operated two-speed epicyclic arrangement. To be fair, it was simple enough to use, even though it gave the

car an occasional tendency to run down its owner as he swung the starting handle. Transverse springs, front and rear, proved the simplest and most durable suspension system. The Model T could travel 45 miles to a (U.S.) gallon of gasoline.

Ford sold the first Model Ts for $850. By 1917 he had progressively reduced its price (he had promised that the car should be sold within the reach of a man of limited means) right down to $360. War then forced prices up again, but when it was over, Ford dropped his prices again, until by 1924 the Model T rolled off the floor of the huge Highland Park factory near Detroit at a rock-bottom $290.

If the 1901 Mercedes had presented the world with its first great step forward into modern motoring, then Henry Ford's Model T must be given the credit as the car that most influenced the pattern of social history in the Western world.

Mercedes Production 1901-1912

Daimler-Benz production of Mercedes cars has continued unbroken since the first of the line was seen at Nice during the Spring Meeting in which it won almost all the trophies and prizes on offer. That occasion is generally accepted as the debut of the original 35-hp car, although they had in fact been seen a month earlier at Pau in France by a small number of spectators at a try-out appearance. The 35-hp with its low centre of gravity, its pressed steel frame, honeycomb radiator, gate-change and mechanical inlet valves, was copied by numbers of established manufacturers. This list shows the Mercedes development in its first decade.

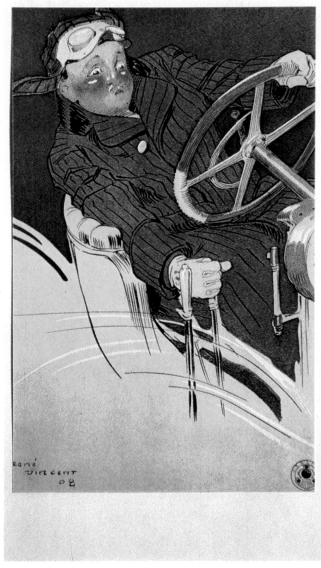

Date of Manufacture	hp	Cylinders	Model
1900/1	35	4	First Mercedes car
1900/1	35	4	First Mercedes racing car
1902/03	8/11, 12/16	4	Mercedes tourer
1902/06	18/22, 28/32, 40/45, 60/70	4	Mercedes Simplex car
1903/4	60 and 90	4	Mercedes Simplex racing car
1904/5	80 and 100	4	Mercedes racing car
1905	26/45, 31/55, 36/65	4	Mercedes tourer
1906	37/70	6	Mercedes tourer
1906	120	6	Mercedes racing car
1907	39/80	6	Mercedes tourer
1908	135	4	Grand Prix racing car
1908/13	8/18, 10/20 14/35, 21/35 22/40, 28/60	4	Mercedes shaft driven (poppet valve engine)
1910/13	10/30, 16/40 16/45, 25/65	4	Mercedes Knight car (sleeve valve engine)
1910/13	22/50, 28/50 38/80, 37/90	4	Mercedes chain driven car (poppet valve engine)

The Detroit Self-starter: 1910-1919

'Oh, the car! the taximeter car!
It's better than taking a trip to Spain,
Or having your honeymoon over again;
If you're out with your sweetheart,
Your mater or papa
Do it in style for eighteen pence a mile
In the taximeter car.'

The first personal motoring experience for the majority of people before World War One would have been as passengers in a taxi. The taxicab was the inevitable development of the hired hansom cab or the growler and had been in use since Daimler set up a hire company in the late 1880s.

By 1912 motored cabs had almost completely taken over from horse-drawn hire vehicles. They had originally appeared on the streets of Paris when Renault first produced a little two-cylinder 8-hp car. In 1905 the Paris Hackney Carriage Company had ordered 1 500. From that time both Renault and another French make, Unic, flooded the cities of Europe with fleets of taxis so effectively that at one time – before the *Entente Cordiale* had been generally accepted – it was considered unpatriotic in London to use a taxi, which was seen as taking work from the British cabby and his four-footed 'Dobbin'.

The eternal argument between

The legendary Renault Taxi de la Marne. It was one of the 'Deux Pattes' (twin cylinder) taxis that ferried troops to the front line as German forces approached Paris in 1914.

driver and driven was solved by the invention of a new fare-metering device, the taximeter, which was attached to the cab. It, in turn, created its own 'haggle' in which the passenger accused the driver of having switched it on before he entered.

This description of a taxi-driver (admittedly a Parisian) is an evocation of the period, and is not all that inaccurate today . . . written by essayist E.V. Lucas in 1912:

'The cabmen! Our London chauffeurs are sufficiently implacable, blunt and churlish, but the Parisian chauffeur is like fate. There is no escape if you enter his car: he lights his cigarette, sinks back into his seat, and his shoulders into his back, and his head into his shoulders, and drives like the devil. He seems to have no life of his own at all: he merely exists to urge his car wherever he is told. The foreigner has no hold whatever upon the chauffeur; he arranges the meter to whatever tariff he pleases, and before you can examine the dial at the end of

the journey he has jerked up the flag . . . . Always terrible, he is worst in winter, when he is dressed entirely in hearthrugs.'

As for the privately employed chauffeur, he too was sometimes a doubtful asset to the motoring family of pre-World War One days. His three-week motor-mechanic training course would have given him airs above his station and he invariably considered himself superior to the other servants of the house. His master (who knew abysmally little about his motor car) would learn to be suspicious of the mechanic-driver and would advise his friends 'to employ in preference a young coachman, who may be trained in the ways of the motor car. He will have at least a modicum of road habits, and have proper respect for the wishes of the household. Some young chauffeurs, on the other hand, have never been on anything but an omnibus since they were born. A coachman knows what another coachman is going to do . . .' and so on.

Above: The privately employed chauffeur was 'sometimes a doubtful asset to the motoring family . . .' wrote one owner. On this visit to the battlefields of Waterloo the chauffeur looks like the one he was writing about. The car is a 1903 De Dietrich 24/30.

The first taxicab – a Daimler of the end of the last century.

There were no doubt many 'cowboys' offering their semi-skilled services to the motor owner, with dire results. Knowing little of the rules and courtesies of the road after their brief training they would 'come over from France with a bundle of certificates,' said one unhappy owner, 'each one forged to the last line.' The coachman turned chauffeur was not always the answer either. His former four-legged charge would have taught him to rely somewhat on horse-sense but not necessarily on mechanical or technical logic. But of course for every villain there were a hundred conscientious fellows whose praise was never sung outside the servants hall or the master's club.

Some masters laid down strict rules of conduct for the chauffeur and notices like this were posted on the motor-house door:

1. The car to be hosed on return from any journey.
2. Engine, paintwork and brass to be cleaned every day.
3. All tools to be kept either on the car or in their proper drawers . . .
4. The car to be covered when not in use.
5. No racing of the engine under the pretence of adjustment.
6. No tinkering with the engine when running well.
7. In cold weather water to be drawn off every night.
8. Cleanliness the supreme rule of both car and the motor-house.

Those who may have attended the course at the Royal Automobile Club School or the London Motor Academy at Notting Hill would have seen such instructions before, but one may imagine the reactions of less responsible employees.

Kipperbox Cars

The yearning to own a motor car was not confined to the rich, and the industry – or at least a section of it – made an effort to offer the less wealthy a chance to buy a car – or, to be precise, a cyclecar, a term which was all too self-explanatory.

Due to emphases on ultra-lightness of weight, economy of operation, simplicity of control, minimum price and other corner cutting qualities, cyclecars naturally attracted the impecunious. But these factors cannot explain the cyclecar fever that swept Britain, Europe and even the United States during the four years before World War One.

It was perhaps an almost unconscious para-political left-wing movement, its adherents impervious to criticism, persuasion or even plain logic. It was an automatic reaction to a decade of 'gilded youths driving snorting Mercedes' and interminable reports of 'the idle rich in their juggernauts'. Cyclecars were to be the new 'gondolas of the people', a title once held by electric tramcars. Thus, those who could least afford to waste their frugal fortunes were supplied with much sub-standard – even dangerous – machinery.

Combining the worst features of the motorcycle and the more suspect qualities of the small motor car, cyclecars, with some notable exceptions, were wire-and-bobbin affairs of little substance, less endurance and almost no safety at all. Steering was often by centre-pivot, similar to carriages of 50 years earlier; engines were usually air-cooled singles or twins of elfin capacity; and coachwork was as sophisticated as a Grimsby kipperbox. In the French Bedelia, a coffin-shaped affair with seating in tandem that sold in amazing numbers from 1910 to 1914 (and even immediately after the war), the passenger in the rear seat at first steered and changed gear, then later only changed gear while the front man steered. Nor was this confection the only curiosity; such respected companies as Humber, AC and Armstrong Siddeley joined the rest to manufacture these undersized but strikingly saleable cyclecars. Thus three or four wheelers with, perhaps, some rudimentary weather protection, and a flimsiness that lent them wings (and sometimes gave the owners a pair) flooded the lower end of the market.

One or two were worthy of better report. In France (where there was a Cyclecar Grand Prix!) some of the better engineered ones – Salmson, Senechal, Amilcar – matured into a new breed of small car, and Britain's more enduring examples such as G.N. and Morgan became highly respected light vehicles.

The Morgan three-wheeler cyclecar of 1913 was only just a little more than a motorcycle. But it was one of the few that grew into a highly respected sports/touring vehicle, offering a fourth wheel in 1935. The model shown has an air-cooled 954cc JAP unit.

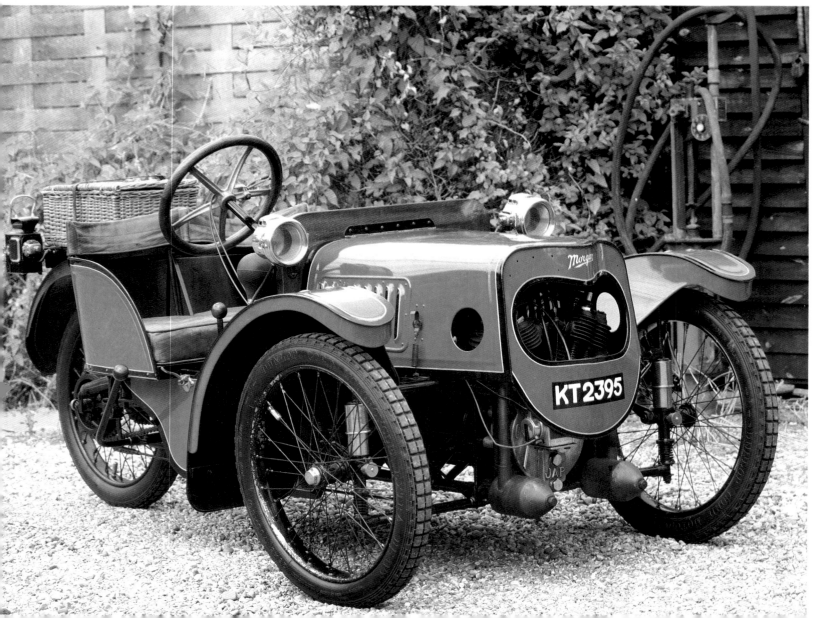

After a modest start, G.N. produced (1910–1925) a small cyclecar designed by H.R. Godfrey and Archie Frazer Nash (who knocked one up in 1910 in the stable of the latter's maternal home in Hendon near London) which became a lusty 1100-cc V-twin, capable of running at incredible speeds. G.N. production models gathered a dedicated following that is still in evidence at vintage race meetings in Britain.

The Morgan produced a similar story. Built in the workshops of Malvern College in 1909, the prototype, a three wheeler (two of them forward), sported a V-twin 1100-cc JAP motorcycle engine, giving it a respectable power and reasonable performance.

The Morgan is still with us, now as a four-wheeled vehicle – almost the only one in the world that still looks like a traditional open sportscar. It is a highly sophisticated model with engines ranging from 1.6 litres to the Morgan Plus 8s, 3.5-litre V-8s, capable of 125 mph. Not many would have dared forecast that the little Morgan Runabout with its cramped seating, too few wheels and overbusy engine would have survived the motor industry's vascillating fortunes up to the present day. Its parent company is still not much larger than it was in 1910, and still produces carefully built motor cars in the classic idiom at Malvern in the heart of Worcestershire.

The 'New Motoring', as the cyclecar craze was called, certainly introduced a new class of motorist to the mysteries and joys of the internal combustion engine and the open road, but perhaps the single event that changed the fundamental attitude to the proper uses of

Opposite top: G.N. supplied basic motoring from around 1911. After 1918 the featherweight car rapidly matured into a tough little vehicle sporting an 1100cc JAP unit. This is a 1922 car.

Opposite bottom: Morgan success story: Harry Morgan made his first experimental three wheeler in 1910, at a time when light inexpensive cars were preferred to the less stable motorcycle-and-sidecar. By 1913 the Morgan (seen here) was a success – and by 1914 had been entered in the French Cyclecar Grand Prix.

Below: A 1927 Morgan Standard with 980cc JAP side valve aircooled engine, two forward speeds and no reverse. This was the cheapest of the range, priced at £89.

Overleaf: Still in the 1920s, this is a more advanced Morgan 1096 racing Super Sport Aero KMB Blackburne. It competed at Brooklands in the last of the Vintage years.

In 1909 a rail strike stimulated a universal desire to travel privately, though this painting shows young people on a continental tour that would have been too costly for most.

the car occurred in 1911 – the great Railway Strike.

In 1909 the British government's budget had set up a Road Fund and a Road Board, neither of which had yet much benefited the motorist or the dust-smothered urban resident. Motoring still retained something of its aura as a leisure activity, although owner-driving was on the increase particularly in Europe and in North America where higher wages increasingly precluded the employment of a paid driver. Occurring just before holidaytime, the railway workers' strike in England came at an opportune moment to stimulate motoring – if increased motoring could be considered a virtue (which indeed it was at the time, as a source of employment and national wealth). With the railways out of commission, car owners, who had previously used cars only for local journeys, piled the family and the dog into the car and set out for Bournemouth or Blackpool on their vacations. For the first time their cars were being used for their own personal transport. The rail strike proved a watershed. Motoring holidays were to become increasingly common thereafter, and the railways were no longer to be the undisputed masters of long-distance travel.

Starting from the Driver's Seat

The other enormously significant event that influenced the condition and usage of the automobile was, at the time, just a small incident in the advancing automotive technology of the U.S.A.

It too was engendered by high wages and the consequent higher ratio of owner-drivers. As engines became larger and more powerful, even the huskiest of American motorists suffered sprained wrists from the kickback of starting handles attached to maladjusted engines.

Delco engineer Charles Kettering had been working on cash-register machines and had turned his hand to automobile-engine ignition problems. Henry Leland of Cadillac asked him to develop an electric starter for the automobile. 'What was needed,' said Kettering 'was a small motor that could give a big spurt of power for a short time (just like a cash-register) and a generator to charge the battery between spurts.' He fixed it to a Cadillac – and by 1912 all new Cadillacs had electric self-starters operated by the seated driver.

Kettering commented later on the surprisingly far-reaching effect of his invention: 'I believe people are stretching things a little when they said the self-starter was responsible for women taking their places behind the steering wheel and as a consequence ... adopted more suitable attire such as short skirts, and discarded such things as bustles, layers of petticoats and towering coiffeurs.' Kettering continues, 'However, since today nearly all women drive, maybe I should take the blame for some of that!' A glance at the change in women's dress before and after the 1914–1918 war confirms Kettering's statement. Its logical progression, a radical change in women's attitudes to the assumption that mechanical skills are an exclusively male province, soon followed. This small electrical gadget produced a giant step in the change in relations between the sexes. U.S. car registrations grew from half a million in 1910 to nine million in 1920, a startling growth in which Kettering's starter played its part.

Not altogether unconnected with that automotive hurdle was the arrival of Louis Chevrolet, a swashbuckling Swiss racing driver-engineer whose first car, a six-cylinder, 9-litre tourer, was seen in 1911. The new Chevrolet Company on Grand River Avenue in Detroit was backed by W.C. Durant.

Durant had already bought up and reorganized the Buick Motor Car Company and had formed the General Motors Company, buying Cadillac, Olds, Oakland, Carter, Ewing and lesser companies. He had then been forced out of the organization through financial difficulties. However, Durant's huge success with Chevrolet's four-cylinder overhead-valve series of 1914 – the Royal Mail and the Baby Grand – brought him back into the field again. He went to Wall Street, asked the vast Du Pont concern to back him, picked up a cool $20 million, made Chevrolet a holding company – and bought up as many General Motors shares as he could. One morning in 1915, Billy Durant walked back into the GM headquarters with a basketful of stock certificates and took over the company (it became a Corporation in 1918). The little Chevrolet Company had swallowed up the giant, General Motors.

Several other very sophisticated cars were made in the United States in the late Edwardian period (or more accurately during the Wilson Presidency). Outstanding examples of fine engineering were the 1913 Cadillac, now billed as the 'Self-starting, Self-

American engineer Charles Kettering changed the image of motoring in 1912 – by developing the electric self-starter. It was not the first self-starter – just the only one that really worked. This is an earlier attempt that looks fairly impossible!

THE BALL SEAT STARTING DEVICE

Patents pending in the United States and Europe.

"This starts so easily that I love it." "This is what I hate about driving a car."

Many progressive builders are arranging to use our device and dispense with the starting crank on their new models. Don't buy a car with a starting crank, for next year it will be a worse back number than the rear entrance car.

If you are tired of standing in the mud and cranking the engine of your old car, give us a description of it and we will see if it cannot be brought up to date in the matter of easy seat starting.

F. H. & F. O. BALL   **Plainfield, N. J.**

Above: The self-starter introduced women into a male preserve – the driver's seat. It rapidly changed female attitudes to the motor car, changed their mode of dress – soon changed the relations between sexes. The car is a Citroen B2, 1921–25.

igniting, Self-lighting Cadillac'; the quietly established six-cylinder Packard '48', which by 1913 had been fitted with the now-obligatory dashboard-operated electric starter; and the Pierce Arrow from Buffalo, a car with the famous fender lights. To complete the American trio of classics, 'The Three Ps', there was the Cleveland-made Peerless, a six-cylinder that was about to be developed into a V-8 – a move which was promptly trumped in 1915 by Packard's 'Double Six', the world's first series-production V-12. To these distinguished marques should be added such names as Chadwick, Oldsmobile, Studebaker, Haynes, Kissel, Franklin, the General Motors pack (which included Cadillac), Stutz and Mercer for the race-about fans – it may be seen that the United States of America had pulled itself into the mainstream of auto production in little more than a single hard-slogging decade.

The World's First Racetracks

Brooklands in England had opened in 1907, quickening the interest in speed contests and enabling the home industry to develop and test cars with high-speed and endurance capabilities. Two years later, American businessman Carl Fisher had completed his 2.5-mile racing basin at Indianapolis, later covering its surface with some three million paving bricks.

Long-distance racing at 'Indy' started in 1911 with the now-classic Indianapolis 500 which was im-

Opposite: Mother steps down from a new twin-six Packard tourer of 1915. The Packard unit was the world's first series production 12 cylinder engine.

Start and Fi[NISH]

mediately won by a home team in a home car, the six-cylinder Marmon. The race, limited to cars under 10 litres, was held again the following year with a king's ransom purse. This time the race was won by an Indianapolis-made National. In the years up until the war, however, U.S. feelings were somewhat bruised by the victories (at other venues) of Peugeots (twice), a Delage and a Mercedes.

In 1908 the American Automobile Association had mounted another classic race – the American Grand Prize – which was designed to compete for popularity with the Vanderbilt Cup which had been run since 1904 and which had become the social event of the season for New Yorkers.

The 400-mile 'American GP', run under European regulations, had captured the imagination since it was first run near Savannah, Georgia, over 402 miles of a twisting road circuit with the cream of European and American drivers competing. By 1910, already considered a classic, it was won by brilliant

American driver David Bruce-Brown (whose mother had arrived at the circuit to prevent him taking part just before the start, and who ended up cheerleading his fans when it was apparent that his 120-hp Benz was going to win!) from the great French *pilote*, Hémery.

Those three early race series, the Vanderbilt Cup, the American Grand Prize and the Indianapolis 500, brought the U.S. into the sporting world and speeded the progress of her engineering technology. Locomobile, Buick 16, Lozier, Duesenberg and later, Chevrolet, were all names that benefitted from their racing appearance at Indianapolis and the forced development that competition demanded.

Britain Catches Up

Transcontinental safaris, lengthy drives of extreme discomfort over exotic terrain, were other means, together with racing, of attracting the attention of the public. In these modern times,

Above: The first American Grand Prize race took place in 1908, and in 1912 when this photograph was taken had moved to a circuit at Milwaukee, Wisconsin. Almost hidden by smoke is Fiat No 20, the eventual winner piloted by Teddy Tetzlaff.

Opposite: Indianapolis opened in 1909 and held its first long-distance race in 1911. The first 500-mile race was won by Ray Harroun in a Marmon.

107

it was no good telling the public merely that 'the Mugmobile is a car that really *goes*' as earlier ads would have stated. Now you had to be able to announce with suitable documentation that the Mugmobile had travelled a distance equivalent to a trip to the moon and back for the weekend, or that it had won somebody's Grand Prix at an astounding velocity, or that the vehicle had broken a world speed record in its class. Only then would the manufacturer get the message over and reap his reward.

Everyone had done it; even Rolls-Royce had driven from London to Glasgow using only the top two gears

skid-proof treads were developed more rapidly than they would have been in normal road use.

The automobile had, in fact, advanced in both engineering, handling and appearance enormously between 1909 and 1912. In Britain there were no fewer than 72 000 registered private cars in use in 1911 – 10 times the number of seven years earlier – not all of them 'wandering machines, racing with incredible velocity and no apparent aim, over the roads of England' as one critic sourly wrote. Motoring costs were coming down with a vengeance, encouraging the less wealthy to purchase a car and by 1912–13 many

By 1911 there were some 72 000 motor cars on the roads on the British Isles – one to every 560 of the population. This is an early traffic jam at Epsom, England. The car is a W&G Du Cros taxicab.

(and to Edinburgh in top only) and had accepted several Brooklands challenges. Privately owned Hispano-Suizas and Mercedes and Napiers were seen madly racing each other down to the Riviera, and American cars frequently and heroically crossed the impossible roads of the American continent or bounced down the steps of the Capitol, in an effort to obtain publicity.

There is no doubt that these early racing and endurance events also improved the breed, searching out weaknesses that would have passed unnoticed for much longer without such stresses. Items such as four-wheel brakes, better springing and shock absorbers, more reliable tyres and

motor showrooms had a bookful of orders for up to a year ahead. The motor trade was desperate for young men to support the growing business of car maintenance, and a new generation of craftsmen were needed for bodywork repairs. Several training schemes were organized to recruit and train future motor engineers and mechanics.

It was a period of political unease as well as one of new developments. The approach of a war in Europe was apparent to many and this, plus the fact that demands were being made on the automotive industry to produce lighter and more efficient engines for the new aircraft industry, lent an urgency to the industry's research programmes

that increased as time ran out.

But rumours of wars apart, new manufacturers were multiplying. One, a small cycle repairer, had gone into business straight from school, starting in a shed at the back of his parent's house in James Street, in the university city of Oxford. In 1905, by the time he was 27 years old, William Richard Morris, son of a mail-coach driver, held the agencies for a string of cars – Arrol-Johnston, Belsize, Humber, Singer, the Standard and Wolseley companies, the American Hupmobile, and a number of motorcycle makes. His talent lay not in promoting the sales of these cars but in the skilful repair and maintenance work he could carry out at his shop.

Morris Garages (the initials were used later for M.G.) bought half a dozen Daimler buses in 1912, and Bill Morris began to operate them on city routes, deeply offending the council-run horse-bus-and-tram concerns. However Bill's buses were an immediate success with the people of Oxford, and Morris swept away in one night

Above: The year is 1911, the car a Mercedes with a sleeve-valve engine designed by American Charles Knight; the central figure is the Czar of Russia who is with two of his daughters. The occasion, a visit to Germany to observe military manoeuvres.

Below: Worcester-born cycle-mechanic Bill Morris started work in a shed at Oxford and by 1905 was agent for a string of motor manufacturers. This is his workshop in 1907, where his main business was repair work.

the out-dated and inefficient transport of a town that he considered should be in the forefront of technical as well as academic achievement.

Young Bill – he was still only 36 – marketed his first Morris Oxford light car in 1913. Some of the credit for its success must go to the Coventry-based company, White & Poppe, famous for their carburettors and engines, who designed and made an efficient 10-hp unit for Morris and who also planned the original chassis frame for W.R.M. Motors Limited, the new name of Morris's firm.

The Morris Oxford was a winner, if a little tight under the armpits for the fuller figure. At a modest £175 each, over 1 300 were sold by the end of 1914, by which time the terrier-like William Morris had opened agencies as far away as Italy and Uganda.

The following year saw the larger Cowley, assembled mainly from American parts, as Britain was working to capacity on war materiel. On an earlier visit to the U.S. he had managed to find an engine that would cost him a give-away £25, an opportunity he had grabbed with both hands. He ordered three thousand 1 495-cc Continental units from Detroit (half of which were later sunk by U-boats on their Atlantic crossing) and offered his Cowley in two- and four-seater form. The story of this dynamic little man

and his cars continues right through the rest of automotive history, until Morris, long elevated to the peerage, died in 1963 aged 86, one of the world's greatest philanthropists. He had built an Empire which was finally fused into what is now BL (British Leyland); he gave huge sums to Oxford colleges and lavishly endowed hospitals all over the world. As Lord Nuffield he gave away millions in his lifetime – yet remained just Bill Morris in his manner to all.

The Silver Lady

Firmly entrenched at the other end of the market, the already legendary Rolls-Royce had long captured the title of 'Best in the World' from the earlier Mercedes (which had worn it with credit from 1901 to 1906 until the Rolls-Royce 40/50 appeared at London's Motor Show). However, Rolls-Royce was being strongly challenged by the six-cylinder Napiers, and indeed still received the strong competition from the very fine 'Mercs' from Daimler in Germany – products such as the 75-hp Six of 1908 and, perhaps the most impressive, from Unterturkheim (near Cannstatt), the top-of-the-range Mercedes 90, first seen in 1911 with its new poppet-valve power unit of 9 570 cc and a powerful 90 hp at 1 300 rpm.

The Rolls-Royce company's sole

Opposite: Morris Oxford, 1913. A little tight under the arms for large passengers (William Morris was a small man) it housed a 1 litre engine, cost £175 and was a 'real' car in the time of the flimsy cyclecar boom.

Below: The company flagship, the Mercedes (not yet Mercedes-Benz) 90 was a leviathan; a poppet-valve four cylinder unit of 9½ litres developed a puissant 90 hp. This example is a roomy tourer that has been painstakingly brought back to its former glory by its present British owner Robert Laycock.

The Rolls-Royce Silver Ghost had long captured the accolade 'Best in the World' and in 1911 the Derby company succumbed to confirming the fact with a trip from London to Edinburgh and back in top gear only. This is a 1911 SG.

model, the 40/50-hp six-cylinder, some time ago dubbed the 'Silver Ghost', was still the goal of a long queue of crowned heads and other personages. In mid-1909 the Ghost's engine had been enlarged to 7.4 litres and its suspension improved. Bodied by Barker or Mulliner or other respected coachbuilders – one still bought the chassis and ordered highly individual coachwork – the car's basic chassis price was £985 as early as 1908. One had to have a deep pocket.

Around 1910 there had been a craze for mounting somewhat trivial mascots on the radiators of cars – comic policemen, donkeys, cats, birds and so on. The directors of Rolls-Royce were distressed when they saw their elegant products arrayed with these fripperies, and commissioned artist Charles Sykes to sculpture a suitable mascot for the car's Parthenon radiator. Miss Eleanor Thornton who was, it is believed, chosen to model for the 'Spirit of Ecstasy', the Silver Lady mascot, worked as editorial assistant to John Scott-Montagu (Lord Montagu from 1905), editor of the magazine *Car Illustrated*.

Here lies a personal tragedy with nightmare overtones, one that has little to do with motoring history but lends a sad poignancy to the Silver Lady we still see on Rolls-Royce cars today. Montagu and his Eleanor embarked on the P & O liner *Persia* in December 1915 for Port Said in Egypt. The ship was torpedoed by a U-boat in the Mediterranean, and began to sink rapidly. Little remains of the detail of the story, but apparently Montagu and Eleanor clambered up the sloping deck to the starboard side. As they reached the rail the *Persia* dived stern-first into the sea. A wall of water engulfed them, and hand in hand they went down with the stricken ship. Some freak of underwater current wrenched them apart, carrying Montagu to the surface and survival. Eleanor Thornton's body was never found. . . .

By 1912 the day of the monsters with their many-litred engines was well over. Peugeot, for instance, used a comparatively modest 7.6-litre engine in the Grand Prix held at Dieppe, a race that was run concurrently with the newer Coupe de L'Auto for light cars (a highly dangerous practice) which had been so successful the previous year. By 1913 Grand Prix regulations demanded a fuel consumption minimum of 14.2 miles per gallon, changed the following year to an engine-size restriction of 4.5 litres unsupercharged, the first time maximum engine-size limits had been spelled-out in the regulations.

Since the days of multi-litre machinery, pressure had been put on the designers to produce smaller engines. The whole concept of the power unit up to 1908, the last successful year of the giants, had been based on the principle of 'more litres equals more power' but now after nearly 30 years of the internal combustion engine, lessons about the properties of metals and castings, about gas-flow and lubrication, cooling and carburetion, had been digested and new designs and techniques had rapidly brought the size and weight of each unit down, concurrently increasing efficiency. Where in 1900 an engine would develop about 5 hp per litre, by 1914 the figure had soared: the Grand Prix Mercedes of that year represented the best in automotive engineering with a claimed 115 hp from 4.5 litres – 25.5 hp per litre.

Not the least important factor influencing increased efficiency, reduced size and weight, had been the new aircraft industry. Early motor builders had happily added weight to their engines, but now that heavier-than-air flight was far more than just an eccentric hobby, the need for lightweight engines was pressing. The first whispers of air warfare were also to be heard.

The quality motor car of the last years before the Edwardian age was swept away forever by war, had full electric equipment (which was now almost universal), and front-wheel brakes and self-starters were increasingly seen. The 'average' engine in a car designed for the professional classes was a four-cylinder sidevalve with a fairly long stroke and (usually) pressure lubrication. Chain-drive had vanished, and armoured wood frames had given way to pressed steel. Fundamental engineering was to remain much the same for the next 15 years – and in the case of the run-of-the-mill engine very much the same until just after World War Two! With the general increase of comfort and refinement it is a little odd to note that Rolls-Royce in 1913 had no self-starter – until one realizes that owners of such cars kept one living above the motor-house!

Following pages. The Manchester company of Crossley Motors produced this elegant 20/25 H.P. Tourer in 1914. It gained its spurs during World War I as a reliable staff car for the Royal Flying Corps, and also served as a small truck and an ambulance.

Middle-of-the-road British, 1914. A four-cylinder 14.3hp Alldays from Birmingham. Owned by the Alldays family until recently, this solidly built two-seater is still highly active today in the North of England.

End of an era. The French Grand Prix held at a circuit near Lyons; one of history's great races it ended in a victory for the German Mercedes team. Here the French favourite Georges Boillot takes a bend near Givors in his Peugeot.

End of an Era

On 4 July 1914 the French Grand Prix took place on a 23.5-mile circuit just outside Lyons. By early morning thirty thousand spectators were jostling for a good position in the stands, down the long straights and at the notorious Piège de la Mort hairpin bend.

Favourite for this one, and 'representing the spirit of France in motor racing' as one breathless report put it, was Georges Boillot, small, fiery, very Gallic and a wizard at the wheel of his new Peugeot. He had won the 1912 and 1913 Grands Prix driving a Peugeot designed by Swiss engineer Ernest Henry whose design had put the top-heavy monsters of a few years earlier out of the game. Henry's engine was a four-cylinder unit with four valves per cylinder and twin overhead camshafts. He had built two, one of 3 litres for the light car Coupe de l'Auto and a 7.7-litre Grand Prix engine with which Boillot had won the 1912 Grand Prix.

The Grand Prix of 1913 had been run on the Circuit de Picardy near Amiens; this, too, had been won by the indomitable Boillot who covered the 29 laps (579 miles) well ahead of competitors in a Peugeot now reduced to a mere 5.6 litres. This Henry-designed unit was, in fact, the true progenitor of the modern racing engine and was to influence the design of racing and sports cars everywhere for many years; its twin overhead camshafts and valve arrangement, ball-bearing crankshafts and dry-sump lubrication made it the most advanced unit of its time.

But it is the 1914 French Grand Prix (Grand Prix de l'A.C.F., not to be confused with the less important Grand Prix de France) that lives in motor-racing history. The regulations restricted engine size this year to 4.5 litres, the smallest-ever, and the international entry was crowded with Europe's most impressive machinery. Daimler of Stuttgart had entered a team of five Mercedes cars, their engines very similar to those being developed for use in aeroplanes (as later events confirmed) and Opel, earlier the leading German team, was also there. Two French équipes, Peugeot and Delage, were to appear and Fiat had entered its new car, the S57/14B, now a formidable streamlined bolide whittled down to 'modern' capacity, with four-wheel brakes and an inside gear lever. Others were Sunbeam, Schneider, Vauxhall and Alda, all conducted by the world's most celebrated racing drivers.

The cars set off at 8 a.m. in pairs at 30-second intervals, with the partisan crown cheering for the hot favourite, Georges Boillot. His blue Peugeot was sighted approaching the stands within about 10 minutes of the last competitor getting away, and the packed stands went wild when they saw his lap time of 21 minutes 29 seconds on the scoreboard. As his exhaust note growled away into the distance their mood was somewhat dampened to observe that Mercedes driver, Seiler, who had started 90 seconds later, had clocked up the even better time of 21 minutes 11 seconds.

That fierce first lap by the German driver indicated to the *cognoscenti* that some ruthless team tactics had been planned by the Mercedes stable and that in this race victory or defeat would not depend on the merits of one car or one driver alone.

Seiler continued to hound the Peugeot. His first lap established a lead of 18 seconds (although he was physically behind Boillot on the circuit) and he increased this to 45 seconds on the second long lap. The German team had guessed that the little French hero would never allow anyone to nose past him. The honour of Peugeot—of France—was involved in this race. As the wasptail Peugeot came whipping down the shallow hill toward Les Sept Chemins and the stands on lap three, Boillot was still in front, but with Seiler now on the slim blue car's tail.

Boillot was stung into even wilder efforts. He took corners faster, it seemed, than centrifugal forces could allow, his car screaming down into corners at a shattering speed using all the advantages given to him by his four-wheel brakes. The No. 14 Mercedes, with rear brakes only, slid into the corners 'like a duck sitting on water' as one scribe reported.

At lap five the Mercedes was still hanging on to the Frenchman. Then the German car was seen to grind to a halt. The crankshaft had broken and Seiler was out of the race, much to the relief of the French crowd, who decided that Boillot was now in an unassailable lead.

Lautenschlager, victor of the 19th French Grand Prix.

Opposite: André Citroen had opened his gear-making plant in 1913 and turned to war work for France. When peace returned he put his knowledge of U.S. production methods to good use, with his first Model A, a 1.3 litre four-cylinder car built for popular sale.

However, not only were there three other healthy cars in the Mercedes team, but one of them was now creeping up to the still flat-out Boillot whose undoubted skills and energies had by now been heavily taxed, having been used to their limits for several laps.

The Peugeot continued to dive into corners on its four brakes, faster than anyone thought possible. Lautenschlager, Mercedes number two driver, peeled off the Mercedes convoy and began to harass Boillot. The result was predictable. The French car entered another duel at speed. For Boillot it was no longer a motor race, but Peugeot versus Mercedes, a battle between France and Germany. But the previous joust had taken its toll. On the last lap Boillot's Peugeot began to slow down. His lead fell to a few metres . . . then Christian Lautenschlager was past and in the lead. Boillot stopped forlornly at the side of the track, just 12 miles from the finish. His differential had shattered. A few minutes later the Mercedes driver passed the winning flag – without realizing that he had won.

A sad footnote to that lesson in team tactics is that just a few months after the race, George Boillot, now a flyer in the French Air Force, saw a German *Jagdstaffel*, a hunter squadron, approaching. Discretion should have told him to turn away, but Georges Boillot was not cast in that mould. He engaged them – and went down with a bullet in his heart. Curious to think that the engines of those German aeroplanes were almost certainly similar to the one driven by Christian Lautenschlager, winner of the 1914 French Grand Prix.

Taxis into Battle

Wartime England did not see petrol rationing until 1916, although large numbers of 'Do Not Use Your Car for Pleasure' posters were prominently displayed in the metropolitan area. Some private motor cars had been pressed into military service under a scheme started before the war began and, with remarkable foresight, the government had also initiated a plan in 1911 whereby a sum of money was paid anually to owners of petrol-driven lorries to keep them in good running order, on consideration that they too were available for military service if necessary. Some 1300 owners accepted the offer, ensuring at least some mobility for troops at the outbreak of war. The Royal Automobile Club also appealed for car owners to register their vehicles and offer their services for home or foreign duty. The response was overwhelming. Some 13000 made the offer and a small contingent was sent over to France to assist in the movement of troops in the autumn of 1914.

Most European countries had naturally made some technical and tactical researches *vis à vis* motorized mobility before the outbreak of hostilities. Even as far back as the Boer War at the turn of the century, one or two motor vehicles had been used to some effect, and tracked vehicles, armoured conversions of Rolls-Royce cars, Austins and other worthy makes had been built and tested during the year immediately before 1914. Car-mounted mobile searchlights had been used in manoeuvres and camouflage had been tried out on vehicles. One experiment in England helped to educate the War Office in motored mobility – the successful transporting of a battalion of Guards from London to Hastings in 1909 – an early exercise in rapid deployment.

France was in a parlous state in 1914. After only a few weeks of war, a huge German Army was at Meaux, just 45 km (28 miles) from Paris. A detachment of Uhlans had even advanced as far as Luzarches, not 25 km (16 miles) from the cathedral of Notre Dame, and had found little resistance. An injection of a large number of troops into the wavering French front line was essential if the Capital was to be saved. Who first thought of the desperate move is not known, but it was General Gallieni who signed the order to commandeer as many Paris taxis as could be found in the city. The little Renault *'deux-pattes'* (two-cylinder, 8 hp) were scooped up, filled with troops and sent off down the road to Meaux. Von Kluck's troops, assuming that they were presiding over a rout, were taken totally by surprise. Now there were 12000 fresh and furious French troops in front of them. The German army fell back in confusion. Paris was saved.

The Renault *'Taxis de la Marne'* were elevated into legend – and were to be seen around Paris and London for many years after peace had returned. Those taxi drivers, incidentally, were paid the proper fare to Meaux and back, plus a *supplement* of 27 per cent

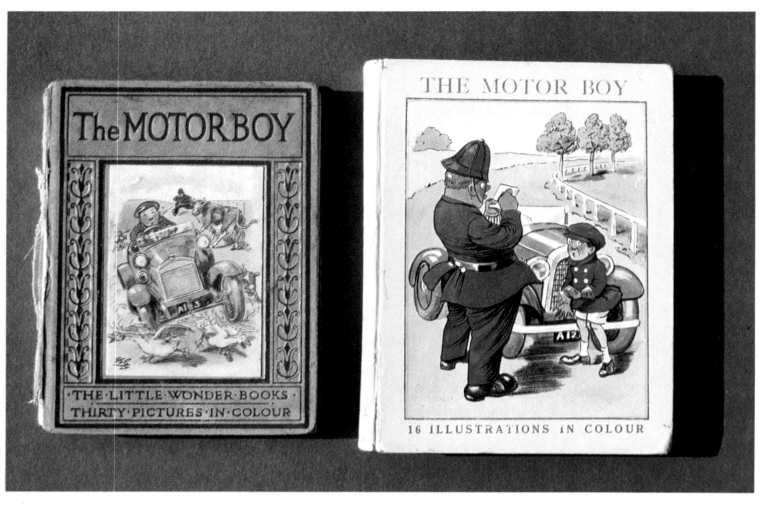

Books from grandfather's boyhood library. Juvenile literature of the 20s had a 'Wind in the Willows' flavour.

on each journey. This incident, the presence of a fleet of double-decker London buses and a large number of British staff cars at the front proved beyond question that the motor vehicle was going to play a vital part in this struggle.

The most dramatic role was that of the heavily armoured vehicle. Rolls-Royce, Minerva, Lanchester, Austin and others were to play parts in the development of mobile armour, but their armoured machines were initially to serve as fast transport with some degree of protection, not as assault vehicles. It was during the terrible battle of the Somme (some say so terrible that it changed the character of the human race for ever) that armoured vehicles of the track-laying type were used. A British invention, the tank was manufactured in 'open' secrecy at Hatfield in Hertfordshire during 1915, the authorities putting out that the mysterious objects were 'mobile water tanks for the Russian front'. The Mark I tank went into action on 15 September 1916 at Cambrai, and proved an enormous success. Said an observer: 'After a hurricane bombardment, through the dust of bursting shells, the great shapes came

lumbering forward in the grey light of dawn ... the enemy emptied their rifles at them ... they turned on their machine guns, and the bullets struck sparks from the great beasts' awful sides. And still the moving horrors came on until they reached the first German trench ....' Not a scene to be forgotten easily. Several French factories quickly converted some of their production lines to manufacturing tracked vehicles and Renault tanks were in action by 1918.

Brave New Market

The lessons of the war and of wartime production were many. Napier, who had learned much from the enforced production of aero-engines, moved into aviation. Sunbeam, too, had made engines for combat aircraft and had reaped rewards from the experience, producing the Sunbeam 2-litre '14' using a wartime-developed alloy engine block and gearbox.

Rolls-Royce, with similar wartime aero-engine work behind it, developed its own aviation engine division rapidly after the war. Austin, on the other hand, was a major producer of vehicles (in addition to shells, munitions and aircraft) between 1914 and 1918, leaving the Longbridge works more easily re-convertible to civilian cars but in dire need of new plant, a fact which considerably retarded its postwar recovery. That plus Herbert Austin's error in producing the Austin 20 (a somewhat transatlantic design based on his own experience of using a Hudson 16 during the war) and the recession that followed the first boom in sales further weakened the company.

The shake-out of war had finally put an end to many of the old car-building practices. Gone was the laborious and painstaking way of coachbuilding, with multi-coated paintwork polished by time-consuming methods. These eliminations (and the vast new knowledge of engineering and metallurgy lately gained) were essential to an industry that if it was to survive in the world of the 1920s – a world which

clamoured for private transport but that had little spare cash in its pockets – had to step-up its competitiveness in the international market place, if not its product quality.

There was a short period when many of the young men returning from war service cared not a fig for the future and compulsively spent on personal transport the small store of cash they had accumulated over the years of enforced saving. However, not all motormakers were yet geared to the growing mass market.

Fiat, for instance, greeted postwar times with Super-Fiat, a V-12 designed, as they said, 'for the prosperous export markets' (they managed to sell five), but brought out several models in the middle-to-modest range. Guy, the lorry people from the English Midlands, brought out a luxury V-8;

After a war spent making military vehicles, shells and aero-engines the British Lanchester company effected a rapid change-over and produced this '40' – which in fact produced 95hp from its six-cylinder overhead camshaft engine.

and French aeroplane pioneer Gabrial Voison offered his first car, a spectacularly bodied 4-litre. Hispano-Suiza capped them all by unveiling a really new modern car, the H6B, from the Paris works. Its six-cylinder overhead-camshaft 6.6-litre engine was the result of aircraft engine development during the war, and now gave 135 hp. The first sight of this superb car at the Paris Salon of 1919 caused quite a stir in the motor world. Hispano-Suiza's superb wartime aircraft engines had been in production since 1915 for the Allied Air Forces and had eventually been made in over 20 factories in England, France, the U.S.A. and Italy. The neat V-8 had powered so many planes that its part in the final victory is acknowledged by all historians. The H6B of 1919 was so endowed with luxury-car virtues – reliability, flexibility in performance, comfort, available power – that in the opinion of many knowledgeable motorists, it rivalled the less powerful Rolls-Royce Silver Ghost of the period, whose only obvious advantage was its silent-travel qualities.

Other manufacturers brought out their postwar offerings remarkably quickly. At the 13th Motor Show in London, the first for six years, a handsome Vauxhall 'Arundel' was shown alongside a new 40/50 'Noiseless' Napier. On show were several new-line torpedo-tourers, a 'Victory' 15.9-hp Arrol-Johnston, a Sunbeam, a Crossley, and what was captioned as 'a Showy Austin at Moderate Price', Herbert Austin's American-inspired 20, to be sold at £395.

A garage and petrol station of the early 1920s, carefully rebuilt from original material and now in London's Heritage Museum at Syon Park. The small two-seater is a 1919 Stellite, an economy model made briefly by Wolseley, the pumps are of course hand-operated.

Those Vintage Years: 1920-1929

The 1920s were turbulent years – the age of jazz and the Charleston and speakeasies, of flappers and bright young things, of the wireless and the talkies, of rampaging inflation in Germany and a general strike in Britain. They were the years in which Hitler, Mussolini and Stalin were accumulating power, but the world was more interested in Valentino, Chaplin and Mickey Mouse.

In motoring it was an era of some of the finest machines ever made, such as Bentleys, Hispano-Suizas, Bugattis. More importantly, it was the decade in which the car finally ceased to be considered a rich man's toy and became an everyday form of transport for ordinary people both in their work and in their leisure time, as smaller and cheaper cars came on the market.

Petrol was never cheaper [1s 0½d (5p) per gallon in Britain]. Roadside petrol pumps came into general use in Britain some 15 years after North America, the most motor-orientated country in the world. Roads improved. Ribbon development began, houses spreading along roads between towns, any gaps being filled by advertisement hoardings for petrol and oil.

In Britain, Winston Churchill, Chancellor of the Exchequer, authorized, for the first time, the diversion of money derived from car taxes to purposes unconnected with roads or

An era of some of the finest machines ever made. Bentleys, Mercedes, Hispano-Suizas were overlords of the road, making their regal progress in silence or accompanied by deep burbling sounds of power. This Red Label Bentley 3 litre is seen here still resplendent some 60 years after it was made.

Above: British Chancellor of the Exchequer Winston Churchill antagonized many motorists by using their Road Fund Licence payments for general purposes. Here he is seen at the wheel of a Wolseley (circa 1925) trying to start the engine – without much success it seems.

Opposite: Back in business rapidly after the war, Mercedes advertising illustrated the far spread of its network. This poster showing a tourist waving 'auf Wiedersehen' to the pyramids has a somewhat formalized Mercedes 2½ litre tourer in the foreground.

Below: Citroen B2 1.5 litre models on an uncomfortable section of the 'Croisiere Noire' the Black Cruise, a 12,000 mile-journey across Africa, mounted to publicize company products.

transport. As the number of cars increased 'Safety First' campaigns began in which pedestrians were warned not to read newspapers while crossing roads. Inconsiderate and reckless drivers were labelled road hogs, a term of abuse used as much by motorists as non-motorists. There was still a gulf between the two classes (unlike today when a pedestrian is simply a motorist whose car is parked) and in once-peaceful villages hatred of the car with its noise and fumes still caused some adults to encourage children to throw stones at motorists and scatter tacks upon the roads.

But the growth of motoring was unstoppable and traffic jams began to be seen, the biggest of the age being on Derby Day in 1928 when 40 000 cars

jammed approaches to Epsom and took police hours to unsnarl.

There were no jams though, in some of the exotic and almost inaccessible places of the world into which cars now penetrated in the search for publicity. In the Black Cruise of 1924, 16 men in eight Citroëns fitted with caterpillar tracks drove through Africa from Algeria in the north to Madagascar, the island off the east coast, over 12 500 miles of desert, bush, savannah, swamp and forest, crossing rivers on tree-trunk rafts. A year later a Renault 'Routier du Desert' car with 12 wheels in six twinned pairs (the rear four pairs driven) travelled the length of Africa from Morocco to Cape Town.

In 1926 a Trojan with solid tyres carried three passengers 12 000 miles through 14 countries between Singapore and London, and in 1927 Francis Birtles made the first overland journey from England to Australia in a 14-hp Bean.

Putting the Brakes On

Engines tended to become smaller and more efficient as the 1920s progressed, though some luxury-car manufacturers compensated for fewer litres by using superchargers – compressors to force the mixture into the cylinders at a pressure greater than that of the atmosphere, and commonly referred to as 'blowers'. They were first seen on racing cars but were available on production Mercedes sports cars early in the decade and, in Britain, appeared on the Alvis 12/80 in 1926.

Brakes came to all four wheels, and

MERCEDES

Fabrikat der
Daimler-Motoren-Gesellschaft
Stuttgart-Untertürkheim
Verkaufstellen und Vertretungen in allen
Hauptplätzen des In- und Auslandes

Mercedes-Benz Publikation um 1920

Above: A British light car of merit was the Belsize Bradshaw from Manchester. This 1922 example had a 1094cc V-twin engine with oil-cooling – resulting in much quieter operation than most of its contemporaries.

Below: Opel, once Germany's leading car-makers, tinkered with rocket propulsion in the twenties. This is Rak 2 after firing its gunpowder rockets to achieve a speed of 125mph. In 1929, the following year, Fritz Opel flew his first rocket aircraft.

were improved considerably when Malcolm Loughhead, an expatriate Scot in the United States of America, developed an efficient system of hydraulic brakes, which were marketed under the easier-to-spell name of Lockheed.

Independent front suspension was introduced in 1923 on the Lancia Lambda, built in Italy by Vincenzo Lancia, a noted racing driver before he became a manufacturer. The Lambda, with a V-4 engine of 2.1 litres and a speed of more than 70 mph, was a remarkably advanced car for its time, with an alloy cylinder block, pump cooling and a unitary body-chassis that was lower than any other of its size. Over 13 000 Lambdas were built before 1931.

Front-wheel drive appeared on some cars, one of the first successful users being the Tracta, an 1100-cc French sports car designed by J.A. Gregoire, though the idea was later to be adopted with more success by Citroën.

Gear changing became simpler (in the United States at least) at the end of the 1920s when Cadillac introduced synchromesh.

There was a vogue for bodies of fabric stretched over wooden frames, the invention of Frenchman Charles Weymann, and first used on Talbot cars in 1922. This was cheaper than using steel and had a 'tailored' look. Then the Budd company in the United States developed a method of mass producing steel bodies by welding them from steel panels, which reduced labour, time and costs considerably. The system was pioneered by Dodge

in 1923 and was adopted in Britain by Morris in 1927.

Cellulose paintwork had been standardized on Oakland cars in the U.S. in 1924 and adopted in Britain by A.C. a year later. Safety glass was developed and introduced in 1926 on Stutz and Rickenbacker cars. One invention that was too far ahead of its time, however, was a 'trafficator' direction indicator system. Arrows appeared on either side of the rear numberplate of Talbot cars in 1926 but the idea failed to catch on then.

Another 'failure' was the idea of rocket propulsion with which Germany's Opel company experimented in 1928. The first car, Rak 1, had eight rockets in its tail which took it to 65 mph in eight seconds in secret trials. Then, in a public demonstration on the Avus track, Fritz Opel drove Rak 2, detonating 24 rockets in stages to achieve a speed of 125 mph. Rak 3 had flanged wheels and 22 rockets and reached 160 mph running on railway lines near Hanover. It was not really a commercial idea at the time – but paved the way for Germany's wartime aircraft rocketry.

The Magnificent Seven

There was a big new market in Europe waiting to be supplied with cars. Thousands had learned to drive in the armed forces and now they wanted cars, but could not afford even the cheapest cars of the time, such as the now-dated Model T Ford, the cost of which in Britain was inflated by the horsepower tax.

This led to a second boom in cyclecars, which were somewhat better than the motorcycle sidecar outfits which had provided transport for lower-earning families in the past, but compared unfavourably with cars.

Usually these second-generation cyclecars carried one or two persons but, like their prewar ancestors, were extremely crude, with little or no weather protection and minimal performance (though some were used in motor sport). Yet there were some 300 different makes, most of them from France where a weight tax encouraged the building of vehicles of less than 350 kg (770 lb).

Typically there was the Amilcar which in 1920 was a two-seater powered by a 903-cc sidevalve engine (though one version could carry a third person in a dickey seat in the boat tail). The Peugeot Quadrilette, introduced originally with a 668-cc engine, was so narrow that the two passengers it could carry had to sit one behind the other, tandem style (a form of seating pioneered by Bedelia in the first cyclecar period before the war).

In Germany there was the Hanomag two-seater, nicknamed the *Kommiss-brot* (army loaf) because of its rotund body; this had a single-cylinder 499-cc rear-mounted engine and chain drive.

However, cyclecars cost about £300 and the 'men on the street' wanted more for their money – real cars at

Many new drivers – (most learned to drive during the war) wanted personal transport, and the now dated Ford T still often offered best value for money.

After the cyclecars – the genuine light car. Sturdy vehicles such as this early Citroen B2 1.5 small family tourer (1921) – very much like the 1919 Type A but with a slightly more horizontal bonnet line – signalled the end of the cyclecar.

affordable prices. One of the first to answer their demand was André Citroën, former chief executive of Mors, who had opened his own factory in Paris where in 1919 he had begun building the first mass-produced French car, the 1.3-litre Citroën A.

In 1922 he brought out the Citroën 5CV with an 855-cc engine and a sturdy duck-tailed two-seat body generally painted lemon yellow. Its colour gave it its name – the *Citron Citroën*. After it acquired a third seat in the centre at the rear, it won another nickname, the Cloverleaf. Some 80 000 were made during the next five years. In Germany, Opel produced a near-copy a year later with a 951-cc engine and a green body, the *Laubfrosch* (Tree Frog). When Citroën sued, Adam Opel remarked philosophically that it was cheaper to settle than to develop an original car. Some 39 000 were sold within four years, but the popularity of both cars was eclipsed by that of the Austin Seven.

Herbert Austin had been finding his Austin 20 difficult to sell and his company was near bankruptcy when he decided to create a car which would cost no more than a motorcycle combination. He summoned a draughtsman to join him at Lickey Grange, his

home near the factory in Birmingham, and there, working on the billiard table every night, they planned the car.

When the Austin Seven prototype was completed the mechanics of the experimental department watched Sir Herbert take his place in the driving seat to make the first test drive, just as he had done 17 years earlier when the first Austin was built. The tiny Austin Seven started first time and moved briskly out of the shop and up the road towards the Lickey Hills with the broad shoulders and bowler hat of its creator silhouetted at the wheel.

In1922 he unveiled the result of his late-night sessions to the Press, a car just 8 feet 9 inches long and 3 feet 10 inches wide, with a 696-cc engine, saying, 'It is a decent car for the man who at present can only afford a motorcycle and sidecar and yet has the ambition to become a motorist.'

Motoring correspondents first dismissed it as a toy, but after trying it out and finding it handled like a real car, reaching 45 mph and giving 50 mpg, and hearing the proposed price, £225, they reported enthusiastically.

The baby Austin went on sale in 1923 with minor amendments including the addition of running boards and a pram-type hood, which had been missing on the prototype. The dashboard had but one dial, a battery charge indicator. There was no speedometer, no petrol gauge, no interior mirror. The lamps used acetylene carbide. It had brakes on all four wheels (the rear operated by pedal, the front by handbrake lever) and lubrication was by 'faith, hope and gravity'. Captain Arthur Waite, Sir Herbert's son-in-law, tuned one and in 1923 won a handicap race at Brooklands and a voiturette race in Italy, the latter at 55.86 mph.

Advertising described it as 'the mighty miniature'. The public called it 'the bedpan', but they bought it and they loved it. The little car, with an engine soon uprated to 747 cc, became affectionately known as the 'Chummy'.

Below top: Herbert Austin's magnificent 'Top Hat' Seven, so-called because of its high roofline, had a tiny four-cylinder water-cooled 747cc 13bhp engine and uncoupled four-wheel brakes. But it was a genuine car – and finally killed off the cyclecar in Britain.

Below bottom: The Austin Chummy. By 1928, 60 000 Sevens had been built. This is a 1926 example.

Petrol in early post-war days was cheap, selling in Britain at just over a shilling (5p) a gallon. Here a smart lady driver in her 1923 Morris Cowley pulls into a station forecourt for a fill from the hand-wound pump.

The car developed steadily; 1926 saw the first Austin Seven saloon. Special bodies were built by coachwork constructors, among them William Lyons, a maker of sidecars in Blackpool (later as Sir William to be the boss of Jaguar cars). There was even a supercharged sports version.

As sales rose the price came down . . . from £210 to £169 to £150 and eventually to £135 which made it the cheapest car in Europe. It was built under licence in France by Rosengart,

in Germany by Dixi (later BMW), in Japan by Datsun and in North America by Bantam. In England extensions were made to the Austin factory and by 1930 Austin was producing a thousand vehicles a week. Many are still on the road and being used in competitions for the marque.

Inevitably there were imitations. By 1928 the rival firm of Morris – the biggest manufacturer in Britain in the mid-1920s, building 20 000 cars a year out of the country's 55 000 – had introduced the 847-cc Morris Minor, which could do 55 mph.

The Austin effectively killed off cyclecars, and the success of Austin and Morris together hastened the end of many small British car companies. Clyno, which had become the third biggest car maker in Britain after Morris and Austin, since building its first car, a 1.4-litre in 1922, made the mistake of cutting prices to match Morris models penny for penny and by 1930, less than two years after opening a new factory in Wolverhampton, the firm was out of business.

Other names vanished too: Swift of Coventry, Calthorpe of Birmingham, Gwynne (London), Arrol-Johnston (Dumfries), Cubitt (Aylesbury), Angus-Sanderson (County Durham), Horstman (Bath). Wolseley went bankrupt and was bought by Morris in 1927. In 1929 Humber, Hillman and Commer merged with Rootes as their distributing agents. Motor manufacturing had always been competitive but it had now entered a more ruthless age in which market shares determined success or failure.

Shrinking the Litres

In racing cars, as in roadsters, the 1920s was a time when designers applied their minds to getting more performance out of fewer litres. There were 11 changes of formulae between 1921 and 1934. These brought the engines of Grand Prix cars down to 3 litres in 1921, to 2 litres a year later

and to 1.5 litres in 1926. Manufacturers offset the limitation by using superchargers.

There were several major changes in motor sport. One was that in 1925 racing cars became single seaters. The role of riding mechanic, always dangerous, had become no longer necessary. Another change was that a clear division emerged between Grand Prix racing and events for touring cars, about to become generally known as sports cars. Along with new circuits there were new names among the manufacturers of racing cars, one of the most distinguished being that of Ettore Bugatti, who was born in Italy but made his cars near Strasbourg in France. Bugatti built cars with the precision of fine watches and they often out-performed much bigger cars. They were also available to all who could afford them, unlike the racers of some factories which were supplied only to works-backed or selected drivers. Bugatti cars, with their distinctive horseshoe radiators, came to dominate sport in the 1920s.

The first significant 'Bug' was the 1.4-litre Type 13 which had made its debut in 1911 when Ernst Friderich had driven one into second place in a French race. Then, in 1921 in the first Italian Grand Prix (a voiturette race), Bugattis came in first, second, third and fourth, with Friderich the winner at 72 mph; as the race was held at Brescia the car became known by that name. Two thousand Brescia racers

In the early 1920s four-wheel brakes were not a standard fitting on all road vehicles although they had been introduced before the war. Here in Rome a cavalcade of the new (four-wheel braked) model Fiat 509 is led by older (two-anchor) 501s.

A recent shot of a Bugatti 35T powering up an incline on the twisting Cadwell Park circuit in Lincolnshire, England. For sheer excitement vintage races outclass even Grand Prix events on these short intimate tracks.

and tourers were eventually made, the later ones with 1.5-litre engines, two of the most famous being Cordon Bleu and Cordon Rouge, which British driver Raymond Mays drove with success in sprints and hillclimbs.

In 1924 Bugatti brought out his first eight-cylinder car, the legendary Type 35 which usually raced under the 2-litre formula, although there were several variants, such as the 35B which had a 2.3-litre supercharged engine and was capable of 125 mph. These cars were the most numerous and successful racers of the late 1920s, winning more than 2 000 awards in all, including Grand Prix victories everywhere.

Another new name in racing was that of Italy's Alfa Romeo. Its first Grand Prix car, the P1 of 1923, never managed to take part in a *grande épreuve*, but the P2 a year later was a winner on its first appearance, an almost unprecedented achievement. By 1925 Alfa had built six of these cars, and running on Elcosine (a mixture of petrol, ethyl alcohol and ether), they swept the board. Antonio Ascari, the winner of the 1924 Italian Grand Prix, renowned as a 'flat-out' driver, was killed while leading the French Grand Prix when he refused to slow down in drizzling rain and ran off the road. The Alfa team withdrew but still won enough points to claim the world championship that year – and added a laurel to their radiator badge.

A long-established name was changed in the 1920s although it did not completely disappear. In 1923 Benz produced a Grand Prix car known as the *Tropfenwagen* (Tear-

drop) that was years ahead of its time. Designed by Edmund Rumpler, it had a six-cylinder 2-litre rear-mounted engine, foreshadowing the Auto-Union, Cooper-Climax and other racing cars of the future. It had an ultra-modern aerodynamic body with a crescent-shaped radiator above the engine and aerofoil 'wings' on bonnet and tail helped hold it on the road at speed – another taste of the future.

The Teardrop appeared only once in a major race, the first Grand Prix de l'Europe at Monza in 1923, when two of the three cars entered finished fourth and fifth. But in 1926 Benz merged with the German Daimler company to become Daimler-Benz, which during the remainder of the 1920s concentrated on sports-car events.

The 'Fast Lorries'

One of the world's greatest series of sports-car races began on 26 May 1923 – the 24 hours race at Le Mans. The race, on the 10.7-mile Sarthe circuit, was to be open to all types of standard touring cars, provided at least 30 of the cars had been built. They had to carry tools and spares and ballast equivalent in weight to a passenger.

There were to be two drivers per car, though only one would be allowed in it at any time, and cars had to maintain a certain average speed – 35 mph in the case of a 3-litre. Failure to maintain this average over a six-hour stretch would mean disqualification.

The race was to start at 4 p.m. so that the night driving would be done while drivers were still fresh, and to augment the headlamps of the cars the

searchlights were placed beside the track with their beams shining along it.

In case a procession of cars going on and on for 24 hours might become boring, the organizers, the Automobile Club of the West of France, had also provided alternative entertainment for spectators in the form of a fireworks display, radio concerts relayed from the Eiffel Tower and dancing to an orchestra and a jazz band, setting a 'Derby Day' atmosphere which has continued to present times.

In this first *Vingt-Quatre Heures du Mans* of 1923 there were 32 starters of 18 makes, all French except for one British Bentley and two Belgian Excelsiors. The night was wet and windy and on a slippery road two Chenard-Walckers with four-cylinder 3-litre engines, (with front brakes but not rear ones!) led throughout, the winning car

covered 1 373 miles at an average speed of 57.2 mph.

The one British entry, John Duff and Frank Clement's 3-litre Bentley (which had only rear brakes), came in fifth, but set a lap record of 66.69 mph. This was W.O. Bentley's first model, massive but elegant, which had gone on sale in 1921. It was a promising debut and Bentley was to fulfil the promise a year later when there was a new rule that hoods had to be provided on open cars and had to be used for at least 20 laps.

Duff and Clement, who were the only overseas entry among the 40 entrants in 1924, took the lead early on Sunday morning and won by over 10 miles at 53.78 mph, though they covered 82 miles fewer than the previous year's winner.

In 1927 Bentley made a big effort

Above: Teardrop racer. In 1923 Benz produced this Grand Prix Tropfenwagen designed by Edmund Rumpler, a designer (he worked for Nesselsdorf, Daimler, Adler) whose brilliant work never received due recognition. The cigar-shaped car had an advanced 80hp overhead camshaft six-cylinder unit.

Below: A 1926 3-litre Bentley in British Racing Green (a colour which can range from almost black to the bright hue seen here).

with a team of three cars, two of 3 litres and one of Bentley's new bigger-engined cars, the 4.5 litre. They met with disaster and turned it into triumph. The disaster came during the night at the White House corner when two of the Bentleys and a number of French cars were involved in a multiple crash. Then the third Bentley, a 3 litre driven by Sammy Davis, rounded the bend and shunted into them.

The first two Bentleys were write-offs; Davis's had a broken wheel, a bent front axle and frame, a broken headlamp and a cracked steering-arm joint. It was patched up as far as

Rolls-Royce after which Bentley cars became Rolls-Royces with different radiators.

What was most surprising about the 1 000-mile Mille Miglia, inaugurated in 1927, was that it spelled a return to the intercity races of the earliest years of the century. The race was to be run on public roads as, indeed, was Le Mans, but for the 24 hours of Le Mans, the roads were closed to non-competitors. During the Mille Miglia, however, the roads were to remain open so that fast racing cars would be mixing with everyday transport such as buses and even peasants with horse-

Le Mans, 1927. Bentley No 3 tails Chantrel's Schneider on the run down to Pontlieu in the early stages of a race that was to be won by the British car.

possible and Davis and his co-driver, Dr. Dudley Benjafield, carried on, running through the night on one headlamp to win the race. Emile Bugatti described the Bentleys dismissively as 'the fastest lorries in the world', but their reign continued and their supremacy at Le Mans became even more convincing in 1929 when the new Speed Six of 6.5 litres, driven by Barnato and Birkin, won at 73.6 mph with 4.5-litre Bentleys in second, third and fourth places.

The French were discouraged and in 1930 there were only 18 starters (including a Bugatti with two women drivers, the first women to compete at Le Mans). In 1930 two Bentley Speed Sixes finished first and second, with the winners, Barnato and Glen Kidston, covering a record 1 821 miles at 75.88 mph.

But that was Bentley's swansong. Despite all the racing success, the company was in financial trouble, aggravated by the worldwide depression. In 1931 it was taken over by

drawn carts. The course of the Mille Miglia was from Brescia to Rome and back over a figure-of-eight course including towns and mountain passes, with the cars starting at intervals. The first race resulted in a win, popular with the home crowd: first, second and third places went to O.M. (Officine Meccaniche) tourers with six-cylinder 2-litre engines, and these were built in Brescia, the starting and finishing point. The winner's speed was 48.27 mph. However, in the next three years the race was to be dominated by Alfa Romeo.

The Road Burners

The cars that ran in sports-car races were also equipped to run on the roads in the 1920s – big machines like great green Bentleys, bizarre Voisins, de luxe Isotta-Fraschinis, as well as small open two-seaters, descendants of the cyclecars.

In Britain the nearest rival of the 4.5-litre Bentley was the Vauxhall 30/98 which had a four-cylinder 4.2-

litre engine beneath its distinctively fluted bonnet. It originated during the year before the war when a wealthy driver had asked Laurence Pomeroy to build a car, capable of winning a hill-climb a few weeks later. Pomeroy bored out the engine of a Prince Henry and installed it in a new body.

The 30/98 won the climb and after the war was put into production as 'a very refined fast touring car capable of high touring speeds and suitable for competition work'. It was the fastest car produced in quantity, guaranteeing 85 mph on the road and 100 mph in Brooklands trim, and 586 were sold before the take-over of Vauxhall by General Motors in 1926. After the

Above: The most famous Bentley of all, the 4½-litre Black Label supercharged car developed 240bhp at 2400rpm in Le Mans tune.

Below: Britain's nearest rival to the legendary Bentley was the 30/98 Vauxhall Velox Fast Touring Car, a distinguished vehicle which between 1920 and 1923 notched up 75 race wins, 52 seconds, and 14 'fastest time' hill-climb records.

This 1926 624cc Mercedes-Benz Type 600 (one of the first products of the new amalgamation of the two German companies) was brought out in an even more powerful version in 1927 known as the 'K', to be followed by the 'S' model. The Type 600 produced 140 hp 'mit kompressor' (supercharged).

take-over the factory was put to work on potentially better-selling but less interesting cars.

Faster and vastly more expensive, and one of the most magnificent cars of the vintage era, was the Mercedes-Benz S series which stemmed from a supercharged 6-litre four-seater designed by Ferdinand Porsche before the 1926 merger with Benz. The S version, with a 6.8-litre engine, appeared in 1927 with a howling supercharger in the nose that could be clutched in or out of the engine by the driver as required.

It was followed a year later by the SS with a 7.1-litre engine, and though it was not designed to be a racing vehicle, it won the 1928 German Grand Prix. This was followed by a competition model with a shorter chassis, the two-seater SSK (the K stood for *kurz*), which won the Irish Grand Prix of 1930 and the German Grand Prix of 1931. The SSKL, the ultimate form of the series, could achieve 145 mph in streamlined form; but it was made available only to works competition drivers.

The Mercedes-Benz was unmistakably Teutonic – big, solid and powerful; Italian Alfa Romeo sports cars were equally Latin in temperament – lighter, more volatile and nimble. Alfa's RL series, built from 1923 to 1927, comprised six-cylinder 3-litre cars of which 2 500 were built. There was also a racing version driven by, among others, 22-year-old Enzo Ferrari (he had abandoned his hope of becoming an opera singer) who later founded his own prestigious marque.

Small two-seaters were a British institution. Although there were many, one of the most distinguished was the Alvis 12/50 of 1924 which came at a time when the Coventry firm, founded in 1919, was near collapse. The four-cylinder 1.5-litre car, with its beetle-back tail, saved the company.

Even more peculiarly British were the 'chain gang' cars of Frazer Nash. After the demise of his cyclecar company, Archie Frazer-Nash began making two-seater open sports cars, driven by a set of chains that needed cleaning and oiling every 500 miles. Most had 1.5-litre engines though a number of

The Mercedes-Benz 'S' was in turn succeeded by the 'SS' with a 7.1 litre unit, and the 'SSK' in 1928 whose power output was by then a shattering 225hp. This is the SSK.

MLI142

Another British eccentricity – the Morgan Super Sport was designed for serious speed work and usually fitted with a 1096cc Blackburne unit if intended for competition.

different power units were used. The cars ran in hillclimbs and races of all kinds, and still do, for although only 350 were built they were so cherished that most of them survive.

Still more eccentric, but also regarded with great affection, were the chain-driven Morgan three-wheelers built at Malvern, Worcestershire, by a

family firm founded in 1910. They were widely known to their owners as 'Moggies'.

The standard three-wheeler could do 70 mph while the Aero or Super Sports model of the late 1920s was 10 mph faster. The Morgan had better roadholding and was much safer than most three-wheelers. The two-seat body was light and was seen in trials, sprints and hillclimbs and raced at Brooklands, though for a number of years it was only allowed in motorcycle events.

Right at the end of the 1920s came a car that was the first of a line that came to epitomize British open two-seaters. It was the MG Midget M. In 1924 Cecil Kimber, who headed the company, began making modifications to the standard Morris cars, starting by rebuilding bullnose Cowleys. In 1929 came first the MG 18/80, a six-cylinder 2.5-litre two- or four-seater, using Morris suspension and engines and, second and far more significantly, the MG Midget. The Midget was based on the 847-cc Morris Minor, with lower suspension, a new ash-framed fabric-covered body, cycle-type wings and a pointed tail. It was capable of 65 mph and 40 mpg, cost £175 and more than 3 200 were sold before it gave way to new models in 1932. The name was to become synonymous with small sports models. Britain's particular contribution to the sports-car market, the marque was to set many speed records.

Fit for Kings

'The finest car in the world' was an accolade hotly contested in the 1920s. The title had, of course, been initially assumed by Rolls-Royce, which in 1922 introduced the Twenty, a comparatively small Rolls with a modest six-cylinder 3.1-litre engine and which was intended for owner drivers.

Meanwhile the Phantom I was introduced in 1925 as the replacement for the Ghost. This had a six-cylinder 7.7-litre engine and servo assistance for its four-wheel brakes. It was built not only in England but in Springfield in the U.S.A. and 3 500 were sold before the Phantom II made its debut in 1929.

The Rolls had its home-bred rivals. Probably the chief competitor was the stately 6.2-litre Lanchester 40 which had some distinguished owners including the Duke of York, later George V. The Daimler Double-Six, the first British 12-cylinder tourer, with a V-12 engine of 7.1 litres created by bringing together two units from the earlier six-cylinder Daimler, was also a contender. King George V also used Hooper-bodied Daimlers.

The Napier, also a challenger for the 'Best Car' title, had a six-cylinder 6.2-litre engine and a speed of up to 70 mph, which was slightly faster than a Rolls.

In France, the Rolls-Royce claim to the crown was contested by the vast Renault 45, used by Presidents of the country, who hired the cars at 1 500 francs a month for official functions. The 45 had a six-cylinder engine of 9.1 litres, huge wooden wheels and 90-mph performance and was a genuine fast rare luxury car, beloved of small boys, many of whom had taken up the popular hobby of car-spotting in those days of highly individual automotive architecture.

In Italy the Isotta-Fraschini, the first straight-eight production car with an eight-cylinder 7.4-litre engine, had customers including Rudolph Valentino (who had two), Clara Bow, Jack Dempsey and William Randolph Hearst, but they did not give it quite the cachet of the Rolls.

The most exclusive limousine of all was the Bugatti Type 41, better known as the Royale, which was, indeed, 'a car fit for kings'. It was around 22 feet long (depending on the coachwork) weighed 2.5 tons, and had an eight-cylinder engine of 12.8 litres, later used in French railcars. It could exceed 100 mph with ease, though at the cost of a gallon of petrol every seven or eight miles. It was the biggest, heaviest, most expensive production car in the world, but no king actually ever bought one. Over a six-year lifespan from 1927 only half a dozen were made, three of which were run by members of the Bugatti family.

French challenger to the Rolls-Royce was the 40CV Renault '45' a 9.21 litre 'iron giant' that was criticized in the press as 'the last chariot of the idle rich' and was often hired out by French presidents of the period for state functions.

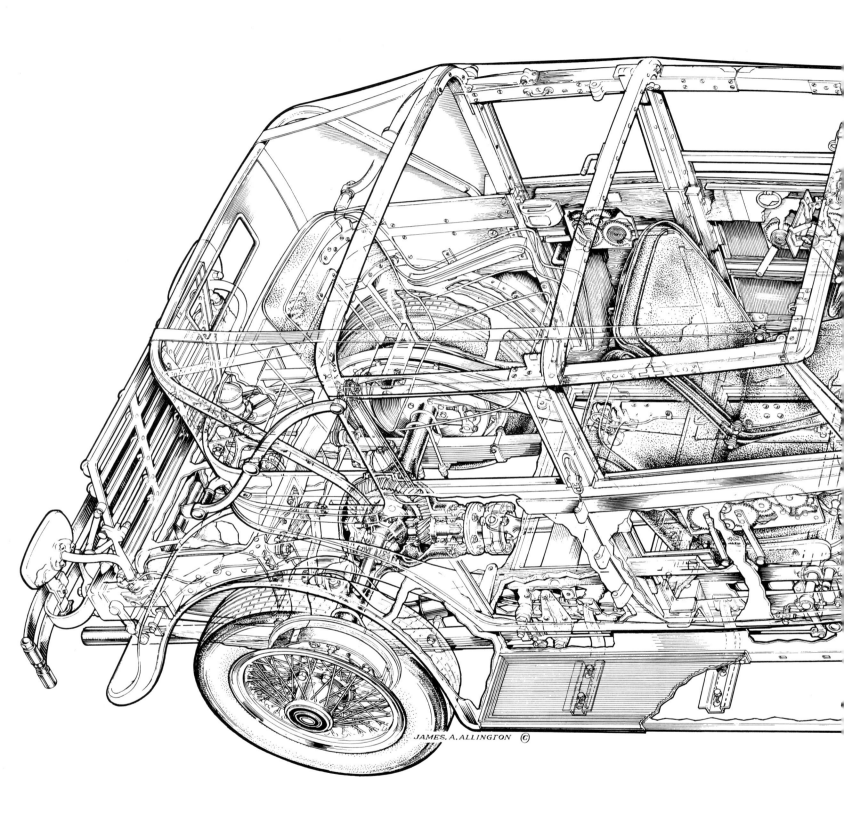

JAMES. A. ALLINGTON ©

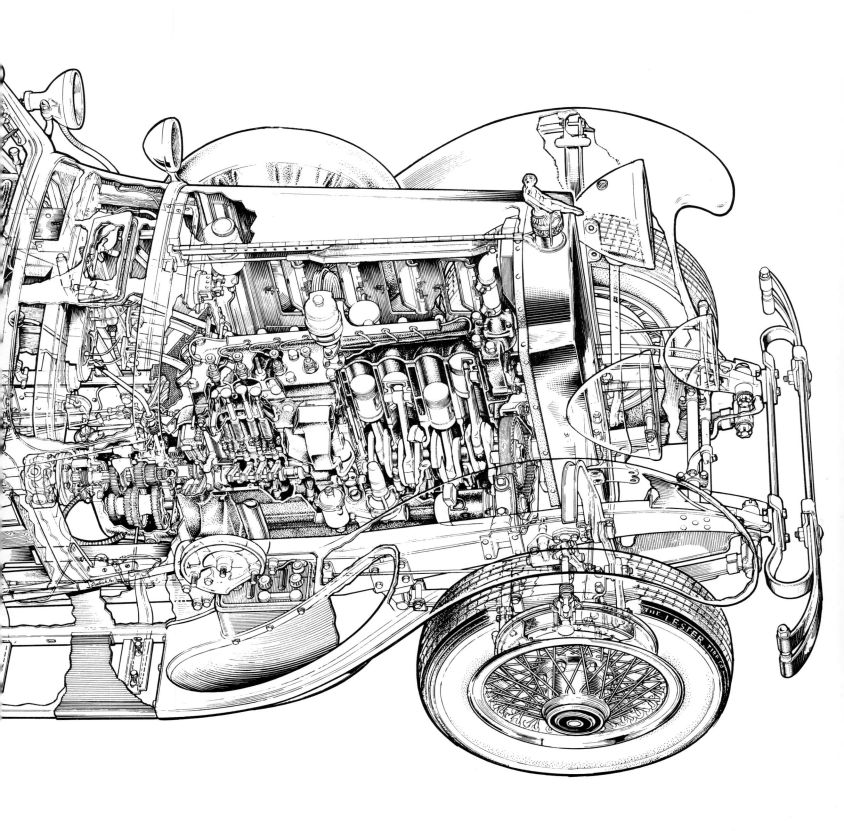

An elegant 1927 Hispano-Suiza Barcelona coupe. Made in Spain the 3.7 litre export model was a small version of the potent French-developed Hispano-Suiza H6B.

The Bubble Bursts

Of prime interest to the rich American with sporting tastes was the Duesenberg. In the first half of the 1920s, the Indianapolis firm marketed the Duesenberg A, which came in the form of open or closed tourers with eight-cylinder 4.3-litre engines, but in 1926 the company was taken over by Errett L. Cord of Auburn who gave Fred Duesenberg the brief to design a car that would out-perform anything on American roads. The result was the Duesenberg J of 1928 with an eight-cylinder 6.9-litre engine and a top speed of 115 mph, for which the company made the same claim as Rolls, 'the world's finest motor car'. It was to be followed in the 1930s by the SJ, a supercharged version capable of 150 mph, which was bought by royalty, sportsmen and film stars.

Cord had taken over Auburn in 1924, a company named after the town in Indiana where the cars were made, and changed a somewhat staid image into something more racy with the two-seat Auburn Speedster of 1928, a high-speed, long-range cruiser with a distinctive boat-style rear, and exhaust pipes emerging through the side of the bonnet. The engine was an eight-cylinder 4.5-litre (though some had a supercharged V-12) and the car was often seen in startling two-tone paint schemes.

A new name on the American scene was that of Walter P. Chrysler, who set up business in Detroit in 1923 and whose first car was a six-cylinder 3.3-litre, the '70' of 1924. This was the first mass-produced American car with four-wheel brakes.

But the American mass sellers were still Ford and Chevrolet. Ford sold more than a million cars in 1922 and more than two million in 1923, while Chevrolet passed the million-a-year mark in 1929. By then Ford had been forced to yield first place in output to Chevrolet's parent group, General Motors, which also incorporated Buick, Cadillac, Oldsmobile and Oakland.

Ford had kept the Model T in production too long, even though when the last one rolled out of the factory in 1927 over *15 million* had been sold. However, the industry still had complete confidence in Henry Ford. During five months while the Ford factories were closed down to prepare for the Model T's succesor, dealers placed orders for 375 000 cars—even though they had no idea what it would be like.

It was in fact a four-cylinder 3.3-litre car, designated the Model A; it had a conventional three-speed gearbox and a top speed of 60 mph. By 1929 its range encompassed taxis and vans and the first-ever volume-production station wagon. Then everything went wrong. Wall Street crashed. Millions were wiped off shares, companies went bankrupt and personal fortunes were lost. General Motors' value was halved. The Depression had begun.

Best U.S. seller with Ford during the 1920s was the Chevrolet range. This 1930 advertisement designed to show the car's economical consumption was part of the campaign that resulted in the company outselling Ford products in 1931.

Buying 5 gallons of gasoline to cover a distance of 100 miles, is a common experience among owners of the Chevrolet Six. Illustrated is the Chevrolet Coach, $565 at the factory.

The Open Road: 1930-1939

Car design in the 1930s was influenced by a number of curious factors; in Britain for example, there was a curious form of so-called horsepower tax, in France an overall fuel tax (1933) and in the U.S.A. a marketing policy that was aimed to attract the woman motorist by developing costly refinements, such as the introduction of synchromesh gears by Cadillac in 1929.

During this period one in 10 Americans owed their jobs to the automobile directly or indirectly, and the industry was a prodigious consumer of oil, iron and steel, and no less than 70 per cent of the country's plate glass. The ratio of population owning a car, or having the use of one, rose to one in 20 in Britain and to one in 24 in Germany, but in the U.S.A. the 'buy-now-pay-later' system had really taken off. This meant that while production had been slashed during the Depression, even in 1932, the darkest year, the United States turned out 1 135 491 automobiles.

But the decade was a great period

New Cadillac and La Salle sedans for 1939. The Fleetwood, Cadillac's flagship, was designed for total luxury. Both had column change, and the La Salle and the Sixty Special foreshadowed later styling by their absence of running boards.

for innovation. It saw the introduction of the front-wheel-drive Cord, Amilcar, BSA, DKW and Citroën. It saw the best years of specialist coachbuilding, and it also saw a number of outstanding cars each based on some amalgam of components from the best mass-produced models. Some of the most famous of these were the MG sports cars, and the S.S. which was based on Standard fundamentals, and which became S.S.-Jaguar before dropping the prefix to become the famous marque it remains today.

There were many other changes in the design of cars, and also in the restrictions governing their use. 'Streamlining', the forerunner of aero-dynamic body shapes, crept in, first with Chrysler's unlovely Airflow. Punitive petrol taxes in France led to the development of more efficient overhead valves (ohv) and alloy cylinder heads in a determined effort to squeeze another kilometre or two out of a measure of *essence*. In the U.K. an outdated power-output tax favoured engines with narrow bores and long strokes – just the opposite of today's high-revving 'square' engine with its bore and stroke measurements very similar. The ultimate was probably the Standard Flying Eight which had the new advantage for a small car of independent front suspension but which, sadly, made a bigger sales

Above: Retractable headlamps, wrapround grille, electric gear selection, independent front suspension, front wheel drive – and a V8 Lycoming motor. With those specifications the Cord 810 was right out of a science fiction book in 1936 when it was first seen in the U.S.A.

Below: On the roads of France the 7CV front-wheel-drive Citroen Traction led the field soon after its introduction in 1934. After the war it was discontinued, but the basic design, with increased sophistication, continued until 1955 when the Citroen DS19 was first seen.

appeal because of its very narrow bore, developed to offset a concurrent increase in horsepower tax.

Drivers in most countries suffered, but sometimes gained concessions from the desk-bound mandarins. In the U.K. the 20-mph blanket speed limit was lifted in 1930. But in 1935 came the 30-mph limit in built-up areas, the mandatory driving test and pedestrian crossings (still called by many older people Belisha Beacons, after Hore-Belisha, the Government Minister in charge of their original installation). At the outbreak of war in Europe fuel rationing arrived within days, and civilian car construction effectively ceased. Contrary to the day's opinion, history shows that the cars built in the late 1930s, particularly, could take wartime rigours without wearing out – a minimum seven-year life, and much longer for some.

Roads and Their Effect on Cars

It is often thought that motorways, expressways, turnpikes – whatever one likes to call them – began in the U.S.A.

but, in fact, the Axis powers, Germany under Hitler and Italy under Mussolini, were the first to introduce the 'purpose-built' major highway. In Italy the first *autostrada* had been built in 1924 using an otherwise unemployed workforce. At first the road structure was mostly three-lane single carriageway. These roads were without entry from side-turnings but the central lane was an invitation to disaster which Italian drivers seem to enjoy to the full. Thus a Lancia or Alfa-Romeo would scorn cars in the 'slow' lanes and when the protagonists approached each other in the central lane it became a game of 'chicken'.

The German *Autobahnen* were also built to absorb unemployed labour, but were dual carriageway. They were constructed essentially for military purposes but they set a new standard of surfacing and safe uninterrupted cruising for the cars of the time. Other countries learned important lessons from the German innovation. The basic autobahn was like a Roman road in England – straight; in contrast, later road builders learned from experience

Germany's autobahn system was planned and started well before the last war. Here, in 1936, the first one is opened near Frankfurt with a blaze of publicity.

The talented Dr. Ferdinand Porsche had been commissioned to design a car for the German people in 1934. He built the first three prototypes in his own garage at home and in this artist's impression is seen discussing the new car with officials in 1936.

that a driver could stay awake more easily when there were fewer straights, and when some mild undulations were incorporated.

The U.S.A., now renowned for its road construction, did not put its programme into full operation until 1940, by which time European countries were otherwise engaged. By 1937 Germany had more than 800 miles of motorway, a fact which has affected German car design for many years. With all those restriction-free roadways being planned and built in the 1930s it was hard on British manufacturers who were forced to produce plainly poor engine designs to conform to what were often absurd taxation and other regulations.

The outstanding example of a German car, built for the new mass-mobility age, was, of course, the Volkswagen, the People's Car, the Strength-Through-Joy car, or simply VW. Hitler had started the project back in 1934 when he commissioned the eminent Dr. Ferdinand Porsche to design a cheap car for mass consumption. By 1938 the Führer had laid the first stone of the VW works and a

scheme had been set up so that savings stamps could be bought by prospective customers until 999 Reichmarks (£50!) had been accumulated. Then the People's Car would be theirs. It never happened; World War Two intervened and when peace returned to a defeated Germany and a wrecked VW factory, there was a great deal of legal hassle as savers claimed their car or their money at current values.

The VW was originally good for about 60 mph, its flat-four short-stroke air-cooled unit buzzing happily away at that speed indefinitely – unusual in that its top speed was also its cruising speed. One might describe the VW as the first car with a built-in overdrive.

The age of the easy-to-drive car had arrived and it flourished during this decade. But just as today drivers look back with affection on the first car they ever owned, so from 1930 onwards those who could play harmonious changes on their 'crash-boxes' felt that their driving skills were being thwarted, and that the more solid, individually built cars of earlier days were worth preserving.

Thus in 1930 the Veteran Car Club of Great Britain was founded, and in 1934 the Vintage Sports Car Club. These have continued, gaining strength and adherents, up to the present. When these British clubs were first formed the rules governing the age of vehicles were somewhat more relaxed than they are today, and it was not impossible to see perhaps a 1908 Alldays or an early Morris Oxford on the Brighton Run in the 1930s. Since then, however, three classes of antique motor cars have been firmly established. Veteran cars are those built before 1905; Edwardians are those built from 1905 to 1918; and Vintage cars are classed as those built from 1919 to the end of 1930. Later cars of excellence, in the opinion of the V.S.C.C., are embraced under the title of Post-vintage Thoroughbreds, are limited to the years between 1931 and 1940, and accepted only on merit.

The 1930s saw only the beginning of built-in obsolescence, which is one of the basic reasons why they lasted so long. This durability was to everyone's benefit during the war which loomed on the horizon for much of the period

and which finally erupted in 1939.

When we look at the cars of the 1930s we have to remember that although the automobile was born in Germany, mass production spread from the U.S.A., giving birth to a proliferation of gadgetry but, more importantly, introducing sophisticated developments which gave cars a wider appeal, enticing those who had never driven before, particularly women drivers (to whom, usually, traditional 'crash' gears were a closed box).

American Greats

Among the best-known of the decade were Buick, La Salle, Cord (now very much a collector's item), Chrysler, Lincoln, De Soto, Terraplane and Chevrolet, plus cars in the upper bracket like Packard and Cadillac, and enormously expensive steam cars like the Doble.

As the 1920s became the 1930s the American quantity-manufacturers left the others behind. Not only was their export record remarkable, having reached one in six by 1931, but in 1940 – cut off from their markets owing to war – they still exported nearly

Above: In Great Britain awareness of the historic value of some cars was beginning to be recognized, and the Veteran Car Club was founded (1930) followed by the Vintage Sports Car Club (1934). Both are doing fine half a century later – as this shot of a Vintage meeting shows.

Opposite: The foundation stone of the Volkswagen factory was laid by Hitler in 1938, and the KdF car – Kraft durch Freude – (Strength through Joy) was born.

Mercedes-Benz 500K, the last word in luxury and engineering in 1936, and the immediate predecessor of the 540K. With supercharger, the 5 litre engine developed 160 horsepower and could reach a speed of 160 km/h.

90 000 cars. But even this was trivial compared with the massive output of their assembly or manufacturing plants in other countries. U.S. companies were firmly settled overseas, particularly in the U.K., France and Germany. Chrysler started production in Kew (London) and introduced 12-Volt electrics to suit the market of 1934. (It was well after the war that designers in the U.S. itself came round to the 12-Volt system which was virtually standard in Europe.)

Companies like Ford in the U.K., France and Germany designed cars specifically for their expatriate 'home markets'. These took into account the taxation systems of the countries concerned and also the road conditions with which they had to contend. It also meant that the models had to cope with the demanding driving techniques of the various nationals at the wheel. It is often said that the most important part of a car is the 'nut' holding the steering wheel. European 'nuts' expected – and up to a point still do – a car which would keep them on the road even when they 'overwound the elastic.' It was tough on the designers. They had learned how to make them big and rugged. Now they had to produce them small and rugged. They managed well with a few doleful exceptions.

There was some opinion that the run-of-the-mill American car had a short life. This was not so, as proved

in World War Two when the life-cycle nearly doubled to more than nine years. What had happened earlier in the decade of the 1930s was that cars were so cheap that it was more economic to junk a car and buy a new one than to repair the old. Thus for the first time came the problem of the disposal of unwanted cars. Britain was to be faced with this problem later when cars were just dumped by the roadside. General Motors devised a clever scheme in which dealers got 25 dollars for each car they could prove to have scrapped. In 1930 this disposal rate was an astonishing two-and-a-half million vehicles and even in 1935 when things were grim and money tight, the 'scrap turnover' was nearly two million.

In the U.S.A. most families owned a car. More than half of these were being paid for on the 'never-never', a system greatly frowned upon by the British at that time as was any form of 'hire-purchase'. While in the U.S.A. housing facilities included provision for a car, in the U.K. there was room for little more than a motorbike and sidecar – and that probably not under cover. Local council house-building was even more rudimentary and, until well after World War Two, council authorities were most reluctant to include a garage in their designs.

European and American approaches to the car itself were also quite different, a fact which can be well-

illustrated by looking at the advertising. For the European, technical details had to be included from which he could narrow down his choice. But what to the European would be called a 'higher compression ratio' was, in American advertising terms, 'Miracle H-power'. To an American the automobile was simply transportation – what went on under the hood was the service station's problem. It is strange, in view of this 'sophisticated' attitude, to find that the Pennsylvania Turnpike, the first road built specifically for motor traffic (converted from a disused railway line), did not open until nearly the end of 1940.

Still Stateside

Some American cars appealed to world 'royalty': Lincolns served for the Norwegian Crown; for the very choosy King Alfonso of Spain, a Duesenberg; for Joseph Stalin – believe it or not – a

Chrysler Imperial 8 Sedan 1932; a 6.3 litre straight-eight with the long road-hugging (for that time) look; automatic clutch and free-wheel, and four-speed transmission were features of the year.

Above: The startling Chrysler Airflow was offered to the public in 1934. Wind tunnel tests had proved that most U.S. cars of the day were better designed, aerodynamically, to go backwards – and the Airflow was the result of building a back-to-front car with a low drag factor way ahead of its time. The public however, did not appreciate it.

Below: The U.S. Prop Set? Two 6 cylinder 3.5 litre De Soto SC6's (made by Chrysler and looked like it, but designed to compete in a cheaper market than its parent) stand by a giant seaplane. The cars look safer transportation than the kite-like plane.

Packard, real capitalist luxury; and for Edward VIII (later Duke of Windsor), a Buick.

As early as 1931, Buick – founded by Scottish immigrant David Dunbar of that name – had settled on a straight-eight with overhead valves. Modern drum brakes were standard and a year later, synchromesh gears became standard also, rather than being an extra. For the rest of the decade Buick followed General Motors practice, with draught-free ventilation in 1933, independent front suspension a year later and hydraulic brakes in 1935, several of these technical advances qualifying for 'first in the field'.

Former steam-locomotive man turned car manufacturer, Walter Chrysler is often unkindly associated more with the publicly rejected Airflow of 1934 than with his successes. Yet the Airflow's main if not sole fault was that it was too far ahead in its outward appearance for the American

buyer, who like most of us, cold-shoulders anything that seems to have skipped a stage in evolution. This car had headlamps flush in the wings, welded unitary construction, all seats within the wheelbase and the luggage compartment neatly incorporated within the overall shape. Although the eight-cylinder Airflow remained in production for three years, in 1935 the company brought out a more conventionally-bodied model, Airstream, but continued with technical innovations including hypoid rear axles (1937), steering column gear-change in 1939, and optional fluid drive.

However Chrysler products generally sold well, and by 1928 Walter Chrysler decided to break into a new market with a cheaper car. Thus the De Soto was created. At first a 21.6-hp six, its price undercut most popular makes and even in Britain, sold for a modest £340. While it had something of an up-and-down career, the most

attractive vehicle during the 1930s was the 3.3-litre Model SC, with a hood which could be erected for the occupants at the front and with the boot lid opening backwards to make a 'rumble seat' for two more. By 1939 the De Soto was offered with the General Motors' improvements mentioned earlier for the group products.

American Austin, who won the contest for the original production of the famous Jeep (often wrongly attributed to Willys Overland or Ford), is known under two names, American Austin

noscenti took their hats off to the models produced by Duesenberg after E.L. Cord took over the company. In 1932 the supercharged SJ version had appeared giving an output of no less than 320 bhp, and at the same time load-bearing components were strengthened to take the extra strain. The result was a maximum speed of 130 mph and a shattering 0-100 mph time of 17 seconds. But a sad aspect of the 1930s was that in 1937 the legend came to an end. The great Duesenberg vanished in 1937 with the Cord col-

Mirror image. This 1939 Buick R0 90L limousine housed a 37.9 hp unit of 3700cc.

from 1930 to 1934 and American Bantam to 1941. Originally American Austin had built, under licence, a mirror image of the famous British Austin Seven, but with body styling in the manner of Chevrolet. The two-seater roadsters were a joy to look at but did not have the size, or clout, to win over the American public. However, Austin captured the Jeep contract in 1940 and was to build it with a Continental engine. However Austin did not have sufficient production capacity and the contract ended up with Willys and later was additionally helped by Ford.

The adventures and progress of Duesenberg have been described in earlier chapters, and by 1929 the *cog-*

lapse, and later attempts to bring it back to life did not succeed.

American cars and their innovations were certainly at a peak during this period when sales were difficult and there had to be added buying incentives, and the country produced so many cars worthy of comment that a wider canvas than this single chapter would be needed to do them justice. However, something must be said of their noteable final 'steamers'.

Steaming Along with the Doble
The famous Stanley steamer had died in the late 1920s, but the Doble made it into the 1930s. The Stanley took a long time to raise steam and thus get

Originally an Austin Seven built under licence, the American Austin (later called Bantam) did not sell well in the United States. However in 1940 the company put together the first successful Jeep prototype. This is a Bantam of 1938.

moving; its deathknell was the introduction of the self-starter. But the Doble, originally from Waltham, Massachusetts, was, without question, the best steam car to date. After the electric ignition switch lit the burner it would start within 90 seconds. In practice (in the cooler climate of England anyway) it took less than a minute. The car had a highly efficient condenser which meant that 1500 miles could be covered on only 24 gallons of water. Fed from the flash boiler, the

horizontal four-cylinder engine developed some 75 bhp with all the flexibility and silence associated with steam engines. Nothing was spared on coachwork and the whole car was guaranteed for three years albeit at a high price tag of 8000 dollars. The Doble's slightly 'laundry' smell as it emerged from its garage in the morning is still evocative to some.

The end of Doble production was typical of many automotive ventures. Abner Doble a brilliant original-

thinking engineer was not equipped to cope with the mundane problems of production. In the later 1930s he moved to England where he became consultant to the Sentinel steam transport firm in Shrewsbury.

As U.S. manufacturers planned the spread of their plants into the major countries, they had not been slow to include Canada, if only because they could then export automobiles to Britain under the guise of 'Empire Made'. However, the proliferation of makes originating in Britain and Continental Europe gave buyers an enormous choice of cars specifically designed for use on European roads.

As far as the all-important roads were concerned it has been mentioned that Italy got in first, albeit with dangerous three-lane single carriageways which were, at least, purpose-built for motor transport. The dreaded overtaking lane in the middle was understandable too, as the density of traffic was so very much less than today. Most newly-built British arterial roads also had the same three-lane single-carriageway characteristic as exemplified by the Oxford by-pass. It was only after World War Two that the 'overtakers lane', thanks to the traffic and average-speed increase, was dubbed 'the undertakers lane'.

Sweden was a noteable exception to all the rules. Cars used were almost without exception American, and with left-hand drive although the rule of the road was to drive on the left, siting the driver nearest to the road verge. The reason was twofold; the soft American suspensions suited the dirt roads (which continued between the towns until well after 1945), the snowfall in winter disguised the road edge, and even when the roads were free of snow the driver when faced with occasional

opposing traffic could see clearly how close he was to the (sometimes precipitous) left-hand verge.

While the U.K. beefed up models to appeal to the so-called 'white Dominions', the U.S. industry did better. Although Morris produced the 15.9-hp 'Empire' Oxford with stiffer and stronger springs and a higher road clearance, it could not compete against American rivals which, in effect, had been designed from the drawing board for similar conditions. Heroes in the popularity stakes at home were the Crossley Ten, Rover 12, Triumph Gloria and some of the Rileys. For the British motorist of the 1930s the important features were fairly small size and de-luxe coachwork – one small model of the exotic Railton even conformed to these requirements. Seats

Above: One of motoring's lost causes, the steam car. However, a solitary make cruised silently into the 1930s – the U.S.-built Doble. This model, circa 1930, was a highly sophisticated machine and could raise enough power to move off from cold in just over a minute.

Below: Ubiquitous, they hoped. A Poster by Terry & Sons of Redditch in Worcestershire. A little like the Renault ad of 30 years earlier it illustrates transport fashion for the mid-1930s in Britain – including the Riley Twelve-Six.

WE STOCK TERRY'S "AERO" VALVE SPRINGS

HERBERT TERRY & SONS LTD. REDDITCH.

Opposite: No more waiting at the bus stop – if you had £100 to spare! The 8 hp 933cc Model Y Ford was first made at Dagenham in 1932. By 1935 its price had been reduced to £100, the first fully equipped car to be sold at that figure in Britain.

Opposite: Family picnic, with 9mm cine-camera. The car is a Crossley six-cylinder 15.7 hp introduced in 1928. It survived until the early 1930s.

Below: A Triumph Dolomite. With the Gloria, this was one of Britain's favourites. With a choice of 1.8 and 2 litre engines it was termed a luxury roadster, its fencing-mask grill (of which various opinions were held) making it an unforgettable model.

were upholstered in leather or similar substitute, unsuitable for tropical areas.

A snag militating against British exports was the nature of roads. While continental roads tended to snake up a hill to keep the gradient low, the British had the peculiarity of having winding roads on the flat, combined with a straight up-and-over approach to steep hills. Arising out of all this the British car generally had an excellent gearbox – but which was sometimes described as having 'three bottom gears and one top'.

In spite of – or perhaps because of – the need for continental gear changing, the British industry can be credited with major advances such as the pre-selection of gears. Armstrong Siddeley had been the early pioneer in 1928, and then in 1930 Daimler introduced its fluid flywheel. By 1933 the self-changing gearbox was widely available even on comparatively cheap cars such as the Standard Big Nine and the 10-hp B.S.A., both costing less than £250. The much-used Wilson epicyclic gearbox was heavy and also costly to make, but it did away with the clutch pedal, which became instead the gear-change pedal. The driver simply had to move a lever with his fingertip from second, say, to third, then press the gear-change pedal when he felt the need arise; Americans visiting Britain, even well after the war, were astonished to find that this gear-change system had been in use for so long.

When in 1930 the blanket speed limit of 20 mph was lifted, there followed five happy years of general mayhem. Sir Henry Segrave, World Speed Record holder, described the safest way to deal with country crossroads was 'flat out, to be in the danger area for the shortest possible time'. But the middle of the decade saw a new 30-mph limit in built-up areas. Just as the 20-mph limit had been largely ignored, so too was the 30-mph, resulting in some of the highest road accident figures ever to be seen.

Closing the Ranks

The main contraction – today it would probably be called rationalization – of the motor industry did not happen until the 1950s, but even in the 1930s there was a lot of it about. Well known marques that fell by the wayside after 1930 included Invicta, Star and Swift, all gone by 1935. Most collapses were due to the understandable inability of small high-grade specialist firms to

It can be yours –

THE £100 FORD SALOON

compete with the larger concerns whose quantity-produced cars suited the new market which preferred appearance to fine engineering. Bentley slid under the protective wing of Rolls-Royce, financial problems plagued Triumph and Lagonda, and in mid-decade Sunbeam and Talbot be-

The Motor Show at Earls Court London, 1935. Cars had to share stands with boats.

PATRON, H.M. The King

TWENTY-NINTH INTERNATIONAL

MOTOR EXHIBITION

CARS & BOATS

OCT. 17-26
1935
OLYMPIA

CATALOGUE ONE SHILLING

came part of the Rootes group. By 1939 Riley had been acquired by Lord Nuffield (formerly William Morris) but managed to retain its individual character.

In spite of these shifts and vanishings the 1930s offered a really wide choice of cars. If a British driver could not find his ideal car at home there were plenty more available from France, Italy or Germany. For the more staid family man, popular choices were the Hillman Minx and the Austin Ten. The former was popular from its introduction in 1932, fitted with an unusually good 1 185-cc side-valve engine. The Minx was quietly developed year by year, and by 1934 had a four-speed gearbox and some luxury extras, including free-wheel and radio. All-synchromesh came in 1935 and integral luggage space a year later. The famous Austin Seven was, of course, too small for the family man with a full quiver, hence the popularity of the next size up – the Ten. In fact, by 1934 Austin offered more than 50 models. Styling was face-lifted in 1937 and also in 1939, and in the latter year the distinctive Seven was given a 900-cc 'Eight' engine. The backbone of Austin's appeal was its solidarity and proven long life in its touring and family versions; no high-speed fun but it would get you there and back.

While the Alvis appeared in a variety of forms, the marque is best remembered during this period for the Speed Twenty, which, in common with the rest of the Alvis range, had pushrod-operated overhead valves. The Speed Twenty (1932) was good looking with its low lines, a four-seater fast tourer (2 511 cc) with exceptionally good handling characteristics, good brakes, reliability and a reasonable price-tag. Another, renowned for its high-speed touring qualities and competitive driving performances, was Aston Martin. Although the car was never made in large numbers its fame was widespread. The 1.5-litre 63-bhp dry-sump overhead-camshaft engine, born in 1928, continued as standard from 1930. In competition its successes were too numerous to list, but included among them was the Biennial Cup at Le Mans in 1932, fifth place at Le Mans in 1933 and third in 1935. In 1935 it also won its class in the 1 000-mile classic, the Mille Miglia. The Ulster model of 1935 developed 80 bhp and could top 100 mph.

For Bentley this was a period of change. It became part of Rolls-Royce who introduced its version at Olympia, London, in 1933. The engine was the Rolls 3.7-litre overhead-valve with pushrods from their '20/25'. It came with a four-speed synchromesh box, Rolls-Royce's famous servo brakes and a top speed of 90 mph. It certainly deserved its title as 'The Silent Sports Car', even though some purists could not see how a saloon could be a sports car. Owing to increasing weight added by specialist coachbuilders, the engine size went up to 4.5 litres in 1936.

While Jaguar did not become a marque in its own right until the mid-1940s, it was really born at Coventry in 1931 as Swallow Coachbuilding, and from 1934 as S.S. Cars Limited.

Above: English sporting elegance. The Lagonda Rapide was the work of W.O. Bentley. Developed from the 1935 Le Mans winning car, it housed a six-cylinder Meadows engine of 4½ litres.

Below: Total exposure to the elements was popular between the wars, this little standard Avon was built in 1933.

William Lyons started building his pretty sidecars in the 1920s; S.S.1, the true Jaguar ancestor appeared in 1931, albeit based entirely on the mechanics of the 16-hp Standard, modified to have an underslung frame. The 2-litre sidevalve engine was not given any extra power, but is *was* housed in a very long bonnet. The styling, as a whole, made the car look far more expensive than it was (a policy that was to continue for some years). What looked like £1 000 to even a practised eye cost in fact just £310. A larger and a smaller engine were then made available and in 1936 the name Jaguar appeared for the first time on a good-looking four-door sports saloon, but now with a 2.7-litre 104-bhp engine, produced by Standard but redesigned by the remarkable auto-engineering team of Harry Weslake and W.M. Heynes. The cars were good for up to 90 mph yet sold for only £385.

The solid success of S.S. Cars Limited was the more remarkable in that it was spread over the period of the Depression. Almost certainly the

Above: Sports car for the impecunious; the Wolseley Hornet appeared in 1932. Its 1.3 litre six-cylinder engine was a departure from tradition and the little car was often seen smartly clothed in special bodywork.

Opposite: Alvis had gained an excellent reputation for building fast robust sports cars and followed this up with a new line in the 1930s headed by the Speed Twenty. The 2762cc Speed Twenty Sports Saloon combined these qualities with comfort.

Below: The 2 litre SS1, ancestor of the Jaguar, first seen in 1931 was based on the mechanics of the 16hp Standard.

Above: The British company headed by Reid Railton, who had designed world speed record vehicles, made hybrid Anglo-American cars in the old Invicta works in Surrey. A U.S. chassis and power unit was bodied in English fashion. This is a 10hp drophead coupe of which just 37 were made.

Opposite bottom: In Germany, after a disastrous war and raging inflation, economy was the keynote of this Mercedes-Benz Type 150H, four-cylinder rear-engined 1½ litre 40 hp oddity – a design influenced by Czech engineer Hans Ledwinka.

best known of the prewar range was the S.S. Jaguar 100. This had a new 125-bhp 3.5-litre engine. Long, low and beautiful, with an impressive pair of headlamps, the two-seater version (£445) was good for a true 100 mph.

MG were competing in a somewhat more spartan sporting field with the J-series, of which the low slab-tanked stylish J2 is still considered the classic British shape of the period.

On the Continent

In the world of motor racing the government-backed Mercedes-Benz and Auto Union swept the field, to Hitler's satisfaction and to the pleasure of most spectators. Their rival successes on the circuit dated from 1934 with first blood to the W25 Mercedes, a supercharged straight-eight 3.36-litre single-seater developing 354 bhp. During the next three years engine size went up to 5.56 litres giving 646 bhp. And for the new 3-litre formula of 1938 and 1939 they built a V-12 supercharged unit finally developing 483 bhp. For the 1939 Tripoli Grand Prix a 1.5-litre unit had to be specially designed. It gave 254 bhp and the result in Tripoli was first and second. The string of

Mercedes-Benz successes was only interrupted from time to time by Auto Union.

Daimler-Benz kept up its good work in the road car market with a string of very fast Mercedes-Benz cars with several alternative engines. The prefix

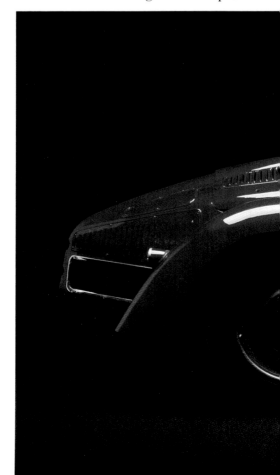

'K', introduced in the late 1920s, was used to denote a short-wheelbase model with superchargers available that could be brought into use only when required, the driver simply pressing down harder on the 'loud' pedal – and loud those blowers certainly were! The range contracted towards the end of the decade. As the blower would mainly be used for brief periods, each engine had two figures for bhp output. Most impressive of the lot was the supercharged Mercedes-Benz 540K sports tourer, a sleek car

Above: Motor sport in the 1930s. Here a Mercedes-Benz W25 (straight-8 345hp) driven by Fagioli, leads into Gasworks Bend during the 1935 Monaco Grand Prix. Italian driver Fagioli won the race.

developing 180 bhp that was given houseroom by many high-ranking Nazi Party members. The chassis of this car later supported the enormous 'Grosser Mercedes' 7.7-litre unit, a version which was also distributed among the political elite of the day.

The end of the 1920s had seen Bugatti with a wide range of models, but as the 1930s arrived so the Type 44 3-litre tourer became the Type 49 with an increased bore size. It proved to be one of his most popular creations. In 1934 came the Type 57, a touring model with two overhead camshafts, a 3.3-litre engine and integral gearbox. This was the last to be built at Molsheim near Strasbourg, and carried on until 1939 by which time 800 had been built.

Citroën intrigued and astonished the motoring public when the company first offered the famous 7CV *Traction Avant* in 1934. Front-wheel drive plus unitary construction, a 1.6-litre over-head-valve engine and torsion-bar suspension all round created a sensation and marked a watershed in automotive thinking as much as did the Austin Mini a quarter of a century later.

Should the 1930s go out on the accepted 'tearing calico' sound of a Bugatti or with the squeak of a mouse? For one special reason perhaps the latter – for who could ignore the Fiat *Topolino* (Little Mouse). Although Fiat built a wide range of cars (and other forms of transport including aircraft) and its famous little Balilla Sport shone in the 1 100-cc class, the baby Topolino 500 was a true ancestor of today's Mini. It was launched in late 1936, with an energetic 570-cc front-mounted engine (with the radiator behind it). It had independent front suspension, hydraulic brakes and a synchromesh gearbox – and a foolproof rolltop for sunny days. What more could a motorist want in the difficult decade of the 1930s?

German leader Adolf Hitler parades before his public in the 150bhp Grosser Mercedez-Benz, a magnificent model that embodied the company's philosophy of never compromising on quality.

War and Peace: 1940-1949

Motoring was one of the first casualties of World War Two. In Britain emergency regulations enforced an instant black-out at night as a precaution against German air raids; street lighting was extinguished and car lamps had to be masked. The immediate effect – despite a 20-mph speed at night – was a doubling in the number of road accidents, killing more Britons than enemy action in the lull before the storm that came to be known as 'the phoney war'.

After three weeks, petrol rationing was introduced, the basic ration so meagre that it could be squandered in one day's motoring, though those deemed 'essential users' of cars had larger allocations. The basic ration was withdrawn completely in March 1942 as the torpedoes of German U-boats sent oil tankers plunging to the sea beds. So-called 'pleasure motoring' was over for the duration of the war.

Gas companies sought to persuade motorists to convert to town gas propulsion, setting up a network of supply points in cities. Cars soon appeared with roof-racks housing gas bags that looked like crumpled feather bedding – and these provided just 25 miles to the bagful. Gas-fuelled cars never achieved general popularity.

Daimler of Coventry, long associated with royal motoring, was to make 6 500 scout cars and 2 500 armoured cars during the war (while Daimler-Benz of Stuttgart was providing aero-

A wartime Daimler production, the MK2 armoured car, with its small 2 pounder gun and smoke mortars. This one was built in 1942.

to a position on top of the driving cab. Hillman and Morris made similar models, and Standard a slightly bigger one based on the prewar Flying Twelve.

Humber, also living in the ill-fated city of Coventry, built four-wheel-drive staff and command cars with six-cylinder 4.1-litre engines; these cars, derived from the prewar Super Snipe, were usually equipped with four individual seats plus two tip-up seats at the back, and some had folding map tables behind the front two seats. General Montgomery, victor at El Alamein in 1942 and Commander of the Allied Armies in northern France in 1944, chose to be driven in a Super Snipe, though some other commanders used the slightly larger Ford V-8.

All over Europe motor manufacturers were similarly supplying the needs of warfare. Only in a few countries like neutral Sweden did private-car production continue through the 1940s, and Sweden was not then a major manufacturer. In Germany, Opel built trucks and 'Wehrmacht buses' for the Afrika Korps; tanks were made by Fiat in Italy, Mitsubishi in Japan and Chrysler in the U.S.A. Car plants turned out not only vehicles but also aircraft engines, steel helmets and other equipment. In the U.S.A., for example, Ford alone produced five billion dollars worth of planes, gliders, Jeeps, trucks, tanks and other engines of war.

The production of civilian cars continued longer in the United States – until 1942, in fact, – because the U.S. did not enter the war until after the Japanese raid on Pearl Harbor in

engines built to stop them). Austin made 100 000 military vehicles (many of which came to be known as 'pick-up' trucks), based on their prewar Austin Ten car, with the spare wheel moved

Opposite top: Daimler's rapid reorganization to peacetime production. By 1947 the Coventry company had this straight-8 DE36 on the market, a pre-war design with the engine enlarged to 5.46 litres. This is a 7-seater landaulette with Hooper coachwork.

Opposite bottom: Opel ranked as top German producer in the 1930s, with a range of stylish small-to-medium engined models. The six-cylinder Opel Admiral was, however, the company's flagship at 3626cc.

Below: The Ford factory at Dagenham in South-east England continued to build transport – this Bren carrier among others, a fast light AFV (armoured fighting vehicle) that with its Czech-designed machine gun was very effective on a rapidly changing battlefield.

Opposite: The go-anywhere carry-anything, low-profile, front-line ¹/₄-ton utility, more popularly known as the Jeep. This carefully preserved example is equipped as for war use, although the vicious-looking roll of barbed-wire at the front is made of rubber.

Below: A 1941 Buick. Buick and others continued to make civilian vehicles into 1942, when the country turned out 222 862 cars. Just 139 non-military automobiles were manufactured in 1943.

December 1941, but factories had begun stepping up the building of military vehicles before then, and such was American capability, that by 1945 its army had one vehicle for every four men. During the war, the U.S. built over three million military vehicles, to be used by the forces of many countries, including the Soviet Union. The United States, the greatest industrial nation in the world, made itself a mighty arsenal, providing for the needs of all the Allies.

The first to be built came from Bantam and incorporated parts from the little Austin Seven, which the company marketed in North America; the others came from Willys-Overland and Ford. Tests were set up to evaluate them and, fittingly, one of the organizers was Colonel (later General) Dwight D. Eisenhower, whose invasion armies were to make much use of Jeeps as they raced across Europe after D-Day.

The Willys model was the one the

Spam-can and Bucket-car

One of the vehicles upon which work began long before the U.S.A. entered the war was to become the war's best known and most-coveted transport. It was, of course, the Jeep, its name derived from the pronunciation of the letters 'GP', which stood for General Purpose. The American services began their quest for a go-anywhere, carry-anything, field car during the interwar years and by the end of 1940 were faced with three separate designs for quarter-ton utilities.

army eventually preferred. It was 11 feet 1 inch long with a four-cylinder 2.2-litre engine that had been fitted in Willys cars of the 1930s. However, it was now linked to four-wheel drive, with a three-speed gearbox giving a choice of upper or lower sets of ratios and of driven or free-wheeling front wheels.

Willys was given an initial order for 16 000, but even before the first were delivered at the end of 1941, the services had decided they wanted many more—far more than the Willys company could hope to make—and so

Above: Many Jeeps were delivered to the British Army. Here, minutes after their glider has landed (somewhat clumsily) in Normandy, troops pile into their Jeep-and-trailer to take up positions.

Below: The new Volkswagen factory in Germany had not started civilian production by the time war broke out. This is the 1.3 litre VW Type 82, known familiarly as the Kubelwagen (bucket car) here seen in North Africa.

Ford, experts in mass production, were also called in to build the Jeep.

By the end of the war, the companies had jointly produced 639245 Jeeps, or 'Spam-cans' as the GIs called them. With a range of engines of up to 4 litres, they served as personnel carriers and light ambulances. Some mounted machine-guns, used to deadly effect by the raiding parties of the Special Air Service and the Long Range Desert Group. Others carried light cranes and towed howitzers. They went to war in gliders and, fitted with flanged wheels, they ran on railway lines in the Far East. There was also an amphibious model.

After the war the Jeep was in demand by farmers and the like and it has continued in production, along with the alternative postwar vehicles it inspired, such as Britain's Land Rover, 12 feet long with a 2.2-litre engine, and launched in 1949. Today wartime Jeeps have become 'cult' cars, eagerly sought by collectors.

Germany had an equivalent wartime vehicle (except that it lacked four-wheel drive) but while the Jeep was a new concept in the U.S. in 1940, the German version was based on a prewar design that was to be even more significant in the future of motoring.

Production of the civilian Volks-

wagen had not got into gear when Hitler sent his troops into Poland, the war began, and the design was switched to a military version.

This was the Volkswagen Type 82, otherwise known as the *Kubelwagen* or 'bucket-car'. It used the same rear-mounted, air-cooled engine of 985 cc (enlarged to 1 131 cc in 1943) as the VW, but the body was basically an open box, made of flat panels for easy manufacture.

Production began in 1940 and the car was first used by Panzer divisions in Poland. Then, as commander of the Afrika Korps in 1941, General Rommel had all his reconnaissance units equipped with them. Later the Kubelwagen served on the Eastern front, where it was perhaps the most successful mud-and-snow vehicle of the Russian campaign, rarely becoming bogged down because it weighed only half a ton and could be manhandled with ease by two men.

Like the Jeep, it served with all three services – as a staff car, an ammunition carrier and a light field ambulance – and it also had an amphibious version, the Type 166 or Schwimmwagen. This had a body like a steel bath; when it entered water an arm with a three-bladed, chain-driven propeller was lowered at the rear. Fourteen thousand of these were made, and some 54 000 Kubelwagens, before production ended in 1944 as Germany's defeat became inevitable.

Postwar Recovery

World War Two finally ended in 1945 after the Japanese surrender, and American plants soon returned to meeting peacetime motoring requirements. Factories were unscathed by war and functioning efficiently. Inevitably there were problems. Petrol was unrationed – the U.S. was the biggest producer in the world – but there were shortages of tyres and steel, causing recurring halts in production because of hiccups in supply. Today there would be a shortage of car doors, the next day of locks for the doors, and the day after of glass for the windows in the doors. Some of these were caused by labour troubles as the unions, patriotic duty done, flexed their muscles in the carefree atmosphere of peacetime bargaining. Even so, by the end of the 1940s, the Americans were making an awesome 6.5 million cars a year, which was then 75 per cent of the world's car production.

In Europe a return to normal manufacturing and motoring took longer. Britain had escaped invasion and foreign armies on its soil, but factories had suffered from the bombings and plant was old and war-weary. Petrol, all of which had to be imported, was scarce and rationing was to continue until 1950. Even then only low-octane 'pool' petrol was available until 1953.

However, motor manufacturers were given official encouragement to make all the cars they could – not for the home market but for export. Bankrupted by the cost of the war, Britain had been given a new slogan: 'Export or Die'. Compelled and encouraged to earn money from overseas, the country was highly successful in doing so in the early postwar years.

There was little competition. Although American production was many times higher, American cars were intended for American roads and

Motoring at home – in Germany a small Russelsheim product overtakes a Hanomag-and-horse, circa 1944. In Germany as in Britain and America petrol for non-essential use was not available – and misuse carried heavy penalties.

American tastes; they were too big for European use – too thirsty, too flaccid in their handling and, above all, too expensive in a world now ruled by the dollar.

The other major European car-producing countries of prewar days – France, Italy and Germany – had all been battlegrounds. The factories of France and Italy had been bombed, in some cases by both the Germans and the Allies. Roads were in an appalling state. Petrol, tyres and steel were all scarce, and their economies were at a low ebb. Germany, having reaped the whirlwind, was devastated, partitioned and occupied by the victors. So Britain became, for a time, supplier of cars to the world.

Britons, however, were not encouraged to buy cars themselves. A purchase tax had been imposed on cars in 1940 when it mattered little, since new cars were not available. By 1947 it was fixed at 33⅓ per cent on small cars, doubling to 66⅔ per cent on cars with a basic price of more than £1 000. (Hence many cars were priced at £990 at that time.)

Demand was still such that waiting lists for some models stretched as long as six years – and even then the buyer had to take whatever was delivered in the way of equipment, fittings and colour. A black market was inevitable. Some motorists ordered new cars of different makes from two or three different dealers, kept the first to be supplied and sold the others at above-list prices.

A new car could be run for several months and still sold at a higher price than it had cost originally. To defeat this, the motor trade imposed a covenant system under which a buyer had to agree to keep the car for six months (later two years) and this restriction was not lifted from all cars until 1953,

Ford of Britain were in the market again rapidly with re-vamped pre-war models Anglia and Prefect using the ubiquitous 1172cc engine. This 1949 Anglia in common with all other British offerings, was the goal of a long queue, and eventually a two-year no-resale covenant.

by which time the only long waits were for the most sought-after models, such as Jaguars, of which only *four* out of every hundred reached the home market.

It was unthinkable in those heady years with the scent of victory still in England's air that Germany—not even allowed to sell cars to its private citizens in 1946—would overtake Britain as a car maker within a decade. Yet this is what happened. Germany made the most astonishing renaissance. It was the view of the occupying powers that they could not indefinitely support a crippled country, and so it was in the general interest to get Germany working and earning again.

So the victors actively aided the rebirth of the German motor industry—and by the mid-1950s it was producing nearly a million cars a year and had moved into second place in the world's car production league, ahead of Britain and all others except the U.S.A.

The People's Car – Again

The car that was the cornerstone of Germany's postwar revival as a motor manufacturer was, of course, the Volkswagen that Hitler and Porsche had planned before the war. Production began again in 1945 at Wolfsburg when the factory—originally almost razed by bombing—was under British control, and the first cars—nearly two thousand that year—were used by members of the British military government and services.

At this point Britain considered transporting the production line to England as war reparations, and it was also offered to the American motor industry, but the VW was considered too ugly to have a future. Henry Ford II described it as 'Not worth a damn'.

In truth it was not beautiful, but it worked. The 13-foot 4-inch body with its drooping bonnet (housing the fuel tank) and its divided rear window

The British-made 3.6 Ford V8, similar to its U.S. twin, had been seen before the war, and was soon on the road again in post-war months, although with a long waiting list of hopeful purchasers.

made the 'Beetle' an obvious nickname for it. The air-cooled 1 131-cc engine at the back reached a maximum power low down at 3 300 rpm and was noisy – but the doors shut with a satisfying clunk. With the high top gear the car needed encouragement to reach 60 mph, but it could then cruise all day at that speed. Passenger and luggage space were as limited as the performance, there was no synchromesh and the brakes were cable-operated, but the car was cheap. Its reliability was to become legendary.

In 1949 the British military government handed back control of VW to the Germans, after appointing Heinz Nordhoff, an engineer formerly with Opel to run it. It was his decision that Volkswagen should stake everything on one car – the Beetle. 'I shall never follow the fashion of bringing out new cars as though I were in the *haute couture* business,' he declared.

Nordhoff's policy worked; exports began in 1950 and the car became a phenomenon, dominating the mass markets of the world. The Beetle went on and on, even after the company was denationalized in 1961, hardly changing in appearance apart from having the divided rear window replaced with a one-piece window in the 1950s. However, there were considerable technical improvements. The car ac-

quired hydraulic brakes and synchromesh, and the engine size was increased progressively, to 1 192 cc in the 1950s and to 1 285 cc in the 1960s. There were also 1.5-litre versions, and numerous derivatives, from sports cars and vans to minibuses.

VW production spread to other factories in Germany and to places as far away as Australia and Brazil. By 1955 a quarter of a million had been sold, by 1961 five million and in 1972 the Beetle passed the record 15 million sale of the Model T Ford. But by now the car was hopelessly dated. Nordhoff had died in 1968, and the one-model policy had gone with him. The German-built Beetle was allowed to make way for a new range of cars with water-cooled engines – the Passat, Golf and Polo.

However, production continued in South Africa, New Zealand and Mexico, where the 20 millionth Beetle was made in 1981.

No other car has approached the sales of the Beetle, but it was far from being the only successful 'people's car' of the 1940s. Another, also rear-engined, was the Renault 4CV, which was being developed when the Germans overran France in 1940. Some work continued on it in secrecy during the occupation.

When liberation came in 1944, Louis Renault was imprisoned for

Volkswagen factories spread over many parts of the globe, particularly in the less-developed regions, where a cheap rugged car would be needed for some years into the future. Here a VW crosses a South American pampas region.

alleged collaboration with the Nazis – he died in jail – and his company was nationalized. Thus the 4CV, like the Beetle, was a state product when production began in 1946.

The 4CV was smaller than the VW, being only 11 feet 10 inches in length and housing a four-cylinder engine of only 760 cc. This was later reduced to 747 cc when the car began to be used in motor sport, to bring it into the smallest competition category. Untuned, it had a top speed in the low sixties and achieved quick popularity as an economical runabout.

The 'Baby' Renault had been unfortunate to meet competition from another French economy car, about which there was nothing conventional. In fact, when it was first shown in 1948 some journalists called it a freak; others thought it was a joke. The Citroën 2CV was no joke.

It also had been conceived before the war and a prototype had been made in 1939. Citroën's aim was to create a cheap, simple runabout for people in the country areas of France who had no hope of buying any existing model – a sort of mechanized pony and trap.

The result came as a shock at first sight. The grey, corrugated body was reminiscent of a garden shed. The roof was a flap of canvas. The seats were

made of webbing which was slung from tubular frames like deck chairs. The engine was a tiny air-cooled flat-twin of only 375 cc and it drove the front wheels. It looked cheap and it *was* cheap, but it was also functional.

The body of simple unitary construction welded to a platform was designed to be taken apart quickly for repairs. The doors lifted out and the bonnet and wings could be stripped in

Above: Fame for the Volkswagen Beetle from Wolfsburg as the star of the 'Herbie' series of feature films

Citroën of France offered its 'minimum' car the 2CV in 1949. Also conceived before the war, its power unit was a tiny 375cc flat-four air-cooled engine.

minutes. The disc wheels were retained by only three bolts instead of the conventional four or five. The seats were surprisingly comfortable and could be adjusted by shifting a peg. An awkward load to be carried – it was simply a matter of removing the rear seat and folding back the canvas roof. The front and rear suspension were interlinked and self-levelling – a property destined to become a traditional Citroën feature. The little engine – with synchromesh on all the forward gears, a refinement unequalled in any cheap car of the time – gave the 2CV a cruising speed in the upper thirties and a top speed of only just over 40 mph, but a gallon of petrol would keep it running for 50 to 60 miles.

'The Citroën is the simplest and most economical instrument yet devised for moving four people and their luggage from place to place with acceptable standards of comfort and weather protection . . . as functional as a bicycle or lawn mower, and it seems to serve as they do, with the minimum of skilled attention', reported *The Autocar* in a 1953 road test.

The car suited the French, who had never been interested in the automobile as a status symbol, or in weekends spent washing and waxing. Demand soon exceeded supply and by 1966 more than 2.5 million had been sold. It is still selling today, though its appeal is now more to youngsters as a fun car than to Burgundian farmers. The engine, increased to 425 cc in 1955, is nowadays 602 cc which has pushed the top speed up to nearly 70 mph, though it is still claimed to give 52 mpg at a constant 56 mph.

In keeping with its modern, cheeky image, later Citroën advertising mocked its own product with slogans such as 'No wonder it's so reliable; there's nothing to go wrong'. And one ad claimed the car had a central locking system ('You can reach all the doors from the driver's seat') and an automatic sunshine roof ('You automatically roll it back when the sun comes out').

Britain's 'people's car' was also launched in 1948. The first new Morris of the postwar period was designed by Alec Issigonis and was eminently respectable and orthodox by comparison. The Morris Minor was 12 feet 4 inches long, of unitary construction and with excellent rack-and-pinion steering; it was a viceless car that set a new standard in handling.

Its initial disadvantage was its aged Morris 918-cc sidevalve engine which made performance leisurely, but in 1952 it was given a livelier 803-cc overhead-valve engine and by the end of the 1950s it had a 948-cc engine which took its top speed into the seventies. The now-classic Minor was

Britain's 'people's car' launched in 1948 was the sturdy 918cc Morris Minor designed by Alec Issigonis. Its unitary construction rack-and-pinion steering and independent suspension gave it good handling and a forgiving nature. The Minor's engine was enlarged later to 948cc.

An unusual post-war 'Woody', this 1948 Chrysler Town and Country convertible was offered with a 4.1 litre six-cylinder unit, or a 5.3 straight-8.

originally available as a two-door saloon or an open tourer – one of the cheapest convertibles on the market – and later as a four-door saloon and a wood-trimmed station wagon.

For many Britons it was their first car. Tolerant of beginners' mistakes, it is affectionately remembered by all who owned one. More than a million had been sold by 1961 and more than 1.5 million by the time the Minor was discontinued at the close of the 1960s. Many cherished examples are still on the roads today.

New Models, New Names

In the United States the European small car was an object of curiosity and amusement. The typical American postwar car had a six-cylinder sidevalve engine of 3.5 to 4 litres. With this went a three-speed gearbox – a rarely-used bottom gear and synchro on the top two ratios. The gear shift was column-mounted to make room for a spacious front bench-seat for three. Automatic transmission had also become common since General Motors introduced its Hydramatic system as an option on Oldsmobiles in 1940.

An upmarket car like the Lincoln Continental, (the Ford flagship) which resumed production in 1946, ran to a V-12 sidevalve engine of 4.8 litres and its two-door body was 17 feet 6 inches long – 4 inches longer than even the Rolls-Royce of the time.

What the Continental had in common with practically every other car of the time was that it had been designed in the 1930s (in this case the Continental had been the brainchild of Edsel Ford, president of the company from 1919 until his death in 1943).

All over the world, the cars that went on sale in the first postwar years were based on prewar designs. Completely new designs did not begin to emerge from the factories until 1947 and 1948.

In North America the main trend was simply to make cars bigger, and cars that were not made larger were made to look larger by the use of masses of chrome and the addition of huge tail fins. These were introduced by Cadillac in 1948, rapidly spread to other American cars, and were then copied in other countries, though never quite as extravagantly.

Engines grew with the bodies. Six-cylinder blocks gave way to V-8 engines of massive horsepower; Cadillac and Oldsmobile adopted 5.4-litre engines delivering up to 160 bhp, which quickly rose to 250 and more in the 1950s.

Less and less was required of the driver. Power-operated hoods came into general use and Lincolns, Cadillacs and Packards added power-operated windows. Warning lights replaced hard-to-read oil pressure and water temperature gauges and dials. Key starting, which did away with the need for a separate starter button, was introduced by Chrysler in 1949. A high proportion of vehicles had automatic gear-change by the early 1950s.

In Europe designers had different

concerns. With fewer long straight highways and with much higher petrol prices, there was no market for 15-mpg engines; the need was to extract the optimum performance from small engines. In Britain, however, an additional constraint on designers was removed when the old horsepower tax was abolished in 1946 and a flat tax of £10, irrespective of engine capacity, was substituted. At the same time France legislated in the other direction, bringing in a horsepower tax!

The big development in Europe was a change to unitary construction – the use of a 'stressed' body shell in place of a separate chassis. This change was resisted in the U.S., partly because rigid unitary bodies were more expensive to repair in the event of damage, but mainly because car makers liked to introduce minor styling changes every year and this was more easily done on a car with a chassis.

One of the most advanced European saloons of the period was the Jowett Javelin, built in Yorkshire. It had been designed during the war, but production did not begin until 1947. It had a unitary body-chassis of an attractive wind-cheating shape, independent suspension all round, and its 1.5-litre flat-four engine gave it a top speed of 80 mph, which was fast by the standards of the day. The gear-change had been moved to the steering column in the American manner, which was to become general practice on British family saloons by the following year.

The car was basically Jowett's sole model, though it was later joined by an open two-seater sports version, the Jupiter, which gained class wins at Le Mans and in Monte Carlo rallies, but in 1954, after 30 000 Javelins had been produced the firm ceased trading. Today the car is regarded as a classic.

The Standard Vanguard, a rather bulbous six-seater costing £544, though not as advanced, was also significant. It foreshadowed how, in the interest of cost efficiency, components were to be used in a number of vehicles, for its 2.1-litre four-cylinder engine was also to power cars from Triumph (which had been bought by Standard at the end of the war), Morgan Plus Four sports cars and even Ferguson tractors. It also foreshadowed how the same cars would be built in different countries, for it was assembled not only in Coventry but under licence by Imperia in Belgium. With several body restylings, the Vanguard went on until 1961.

The most exciting car to be introduced in the late 1940s was undoubtedly the Jaguar XK120 (the prefix 'S.S.' had been dropped for obvious reasons). It was an open two-seater, still stylish and beautiful today as in 1948. Its secret was its first-ever quantity-produced twin-overhead-cam engine, which was originally designed to power Jaguar's still-on-the-stocks Mark 7 saloon. Company chief Sir

William Lyons decided to put it into a sports car, largely to generate publicity. It certainly did that. The 3.4-litre six-cylinder engine developed 160 bhp and it gave the standard car a genuine 120 mph top speed, while a works prototype was timed at 132.6 mph. At £1263 it was a bargain, though one that was impossible to buy in Britain for a number of years as the entire production went for export. In six years, more than 12 000 were sold, and

it led to the XK140 and XK150 of the 1950s, and to a run of international race and rally successes.

In terms of prestige, Rolls-Royce was still the foremost name of course, and the company's first postwar model, built in 1947 at new headquarters at Crewe, was the Silver Wraith, which was also only available for export for some time. It had a six-cylinder 4.2-litre engine and was supplied to coachbuilders of the customer's choice in

One of the most advanced European small saloons of the period, the Jowett Javelin from Yorkshire. A 1½ litre flat-four engine, unitary construction and torsion-bar suspension gave this car (introduced in 1947) a good performance and a top speed of 80mph.

chassis form. At around £4 300, according to the coachwork, it was the most expensive Rolls to date, but it remained in production for 12 years.

Not only were there now new models but there were new names producing them.

In Germany Ferdinand Porsche, designer of the Beetle, began to built cars under his own name, the first being the Porsche 356. It had a VW air-cooled 1 086-cc engine at the rear, VW transmission and suspension. But this was no 'people's car'. Porsche, it is sometimes forgotten, had also designed prewar Mercedes and Auto Unions, and the car to which he gave his name was an upmarket sports car which soon achieved 1 100-cc class wins at Le Mans and in the Mille Miglia. Porsche died in 1951, but under his son, Ferry, the name Porsche has become synonymous with fast, highly prized cars.

In Sweden the Saab aircraft firm unwrapped its first car, the Saab 92, which had been designed and tested during the war. Small, with an aerodynamic body that suggested wind tunnel testing, it had a twin-cylinder two-stroke engine of 746 cc, front-wheel drive and a free-wheeling facility.

In the U.S.S.R. the new name was Moskvitch. Its first model was the 400, an 1 100-cc car that was basically the prewar Opel Kadett, explained by the fact that the Soviets had appropriated

the dies from the German factory as war reparations. The Soviet Union at this time had few garages and pleasure motoring was an almost unknown concept. Cars were trappings of rank, and the Moskvitch 400 was for middle-rank bureaucrats. A cut above it, and intended for government officials, came the Pobieda, which was also a new name, an American-inspired car with a 2.1-litre engine made at the same Gorky works as the Zis (later, Zil), which was the car for chauffeur-driven ambassadors and the like.

In Britain there were many new names, particularly in sports cars. Donald Healey, formerly technical director of Triumph, began building his own cars at Warwick. Using a 2.5-litre Riley engine and transmission on a chassis frame designed by his son Geoff, he made a saloon which was the fastest of its day; one vehicle covered 102 miles in one hour from a standing start. It had successes in club races at Silverstone but production was small – just five a week at first – and in the 1950s production was taken over by Austin.

Sydney Allard, a builder of 'specials' and replicas since the 1930s, also began manufacturing automobiles on an organized basis in 1946, using Ford V-8 engines of 3.6 litres and other Ford components in touring and competition two-seaters, and later in a two-door saloon with distinctive

Opposite top: Standard Vanguard, introduced in 1947. Its 2.1 litre unit was used in the Triumph, Morgan Plus Four, and the Ferguson tractor of its time, a new concept in cost efficiency.

Opposite bottom: The most significant performance car to be made in the 1950s was undoubtedly the Jaguar XK120, with its now-classic six cylinder 160hp 3.4 litre engine. This picture shows rally driver Ian Appleyard putting up the best performance in the 1950 Alpine Rally – an event that was more testing than most.

Below: Sydney Allard had built specials since the thirties. He started commercial manufacturing in 1946, using Ford V8 power units. This is an Allard K1 of 1948.

The Bristol 400 was based on the BMW 328, using its 2 litre engine and chassis. This 401 launched in 1949 was a mechanically similar car but with a more aerodynamically refined body. Strictly a fast touring car.

radiator grilles. In 1952 he was to win the Monte Carlo Rally driving one of his own cars – a 4.4-litre-engined P-Type saloon, but his output was also low, with prices consequently high. Production was discontinued in 1959.

At Bristol airfield, the Bristol Aeroplane Company formed a car division (later Bristol Cars) which began by building the Bristol 400, a superior two-door saloon. It was based on the BMW 328's six-cylinder 2-litre engine and chassis and the bodywork was as sleek and aerodynamic as one would expect from an aircraft firm. With a 94-mph performance and good handling, it was much used in rallies.

Bristol also supplied its engines to the old-established Frazer Nash firm for its sports cars, and to Cooper, a racing-car company founded at Surbiton in 1948 by father and son, Charles and John Cooper. They began by making rear-engined midgets for Formula Three racing, using 500-cc JAP speedway engines and Fiat Topolino parts, with which newcomers Stirling Moss and Peter Collins were early race winners. The Bristol engines were used in the Formula Two cars of 1952 in which Mike Hawthorn made his name.

Racing Returns

The first postwar motor race was held in France in 1945, but it was to be 1947 before Grand Prix racing restarted under the new title of Formula One. A number of prewar venues were no longer available, among them Brooklands, the world's first permanent circuit, which remained in the hands of the aircraft industry. Fortunately, there were many wartime airfields that were happily no longer needed, and one of them – Silverstone in Northamptonshire – opened in 1948 as Britain's new premier circuit.

For the first races the prewar cars were brought out of mothballs. Under Formula One rules, which limited engine size to 1.5 litres supercharged, or 4.5 litres unblown, one car dominated completely – the prewar Alfa Romeo 158 designed by Gioacchino Colombo. This was an eight-cylinder 1.5-litre supercharged car, capable of 180 mph, not significantly less than the top speed of Grand Prix cars nearly 40 years later.

Competition was on the way. In 1947 Enzo Ferrari, who had once raced for Alfa, brought out the first car under his own name. It was a supercharged V-12 of 1.5 litres designed by Gioacchino Colombo. It performed well enough to give Alfa a few frights, but as yet Alfa was too well proven to be beaten.

However, in sports car racing, when the 24 hours race at Le Mans was re-introduced in 1949, Ferraris gained the first of nine victories in the event.

There was also a return to record breaking, again with a prewar car. John Cobb, the big, shy fur broker who had set the last world land speed record before the war at 369.7 mph, brought out his Railton with its two Napier Lion engines and returned to Bonneville Salt Flats, Utah. There, in 1947, he pushed his record up to 394.2 mph which was to stand until 1964. Interest in the record had waned, partly because of the cost and the lack of venues where such high speeds could be achieved, but also due to a waning in public interest in machinery so remote from the everyday family car.

Fast recovery. By October 1945 – MG had brought out the 1250cc TC. By 1948 it was offered with left-hand drive – and became an enormous success in the United States.

Nations on the Move: 1950-1959

Opposite: There was a sense of freedom about motoring in the 1950s after the restrictions of wartime. Introduced in 1946, this Bentley MK VI used the old 4257cc six, first seen in 1937, an engine it shared with the Rolls Royce Silver Wraith.

There was a sense of freedom about motoring in the 1950s. Petrol rationing finally ended after a brief re-imposition in Britain in 1956 following Egypt's nationalization of the Suez Canal. There was a new affluence brought about by full employment. Car owners expected to change their cars regularly and to change them for bigger and better ones, while people who, before the war, had never dreamed of owning a car now found serviceable models within their reach. A Ford Popular, with an 1172-cc sidevalve engine designed in the 1930s and with mechanical brakes, might not be exciting but it was reliable, and could be bought for £391.

The number of cars increased rapidly. At the end of the war there were 45 million in the world; by the mid 1950s there were 100 million.

New and better roads were built. Britain's first stretch of motorway opened near Preston in 1958 and others were begun. That American institution, the motel, where one pays in advance in order to leave when one likes and where space for one's car is guaranteed, began to spread through Europe. Britain's first motel was located at Hythe in Kent in 1953.

Crossing the Channel with a car became easier, for modern drive-on ferries had replaced the last crane-loaders and a car-carrying air ferry service had been established between Lympne and Le Touquet in France.

The popularity of 'woodies' – station wagons with rear doors and space for carrying golf clubs, fishing rods, carry-cots, suitcases and animals – reflected the growing use of cars for leisure pursuits.

Motor sport boomed, both at the top level as a spectacle sport and at club level as a participation sport. There was also a boom in motoring nostalgia, following the success of the 1954 film *Genevieve*, a comedy about the annual London to Brighton veteran car run, which starred Kenneth More and Kay Kendall plus a Darracq and a Spyker of 1905. This film created genuine worldwide interest in early auto-mobiles; motor museums began to flourish, and barns and outbuildings in country districts were ransacked for old cars, many of which had been put away at the outbreak of war and forgotten.

Inevitably there were some curbs on this new universal mobility. In Britain the 1950s brought the first radar speed traps and the first parking meters – some 25 years after the installation of the world's first meters in Oklahoma City, U.S.A. With them came a new cadre of uniformed officials. Traffic wardens could point out truthfully that they existed to help motorists by booking selfish parkers and keeping traffic moving, but in popularity they were doomed to a low rating.

Badge Engineering

This was a time of mergers, not only in industry but in local government, police forces and schools, the belief being that greater size meant greater efficiency and greater economy – a theory which proved to contain some errors. In the motor industry it became accepted wisdom that to remain competitive, firms must keep growing, and in 1951 the empires of Lords Austin and Nuffield (Austin, Morris, Riley, MG and Wolseley) were brought together in the British Motor Corporation.

Models were 'rationalized'; the multiplicity of engines and chassis and bodies were drastically reduced. Morris engines were phased out and Morris cars were given Austin engines, and this led to 'badge engineering' in which virtually the same car appeared under two or more names, little more than the motifs being different. Thus, from 1958 a Wolseley 1500 was virtually identical to a Riley 1.5, while Australian-made models were known as the Austin Lancer and Morris Major.

Five years later there was another British merger when the Rootes Group (Sunbeam and Hillman) acquired Singer and the same process of rationalization was carried out, the Singer Gazelle being essentially a de-luxe version of the Hillman Minx (which celebrated its 25th anniversary in 1957).

In the U.S.A Nash and Hudson merged in 1954 to form American Motors, after which Nash Ramblers were sometimes sold with Hudson badges. However, after only three years the individual names were allowed to die. Similarly the name of Kaiser, a company founded in 1946 by shipbuilding millionaire Henry Kaiser which made only two models, merged with Willys in 1953 but after two years Kaiser cars were no more.

Other countries began to export cars for the first time – the U.S.S.R., for instance, sold its first consignment to Norway in exchange for herrings.

Japan's exports of cars in the mid-1950s were fewer than 50 cars a year, but then its total production was only an annual 32 000. However, a road-building programme was begun in

Japan and the number of cars began to increase, though most of them were European cars made under licence. Hino assembled the Renault 4CV, Nissan the Austin A40, Isuzu the Hillman Minx. Toyota made a two-door sedan of its own design but production was low. Western manufacturers saw no threat from Japan.

Change and Innovation

The shape of cars was changing. Curved glass was developed by Triplex and, used in screens and rear windows, it enabled pillars to be reduced in size and driving visibility to be improved. The 1950 Buick pioneered not only wrap-around screens, but the tinted glass in them.

The general adoption of independent front suspension also affected the

Above: Fewer than fifty cars a year were exported from Japan in the mid-1950s, when total production was some 32 000. In 1983 national production exceeded 7 million. This is a Toyota RHK of 1953.

Opposite: Rising employment encouraged more British motorists to cross the Channel to France. Here holidaymakers drive over the most nerve-racking part of their trip – the ferry ship's gangway.

Below: A sporting overhead-camshaft four, this Mercedes-Benz 190SL introduced in 1955 was in much the same idiom as the renowned 3 litre 300SL which had so shaken the motor world with its racing victories. The 190SL developed 105 hp.

Above: U.S. design improvements during the 1950s included curved glass windshields (some tinted) that allowed slimmer pillars that in turn brought better all-round vision.

Opposite top: The slab-side trend tentatively introduced in the late 1950s is seen here in all its solid state in this 1955 Ford Zephyr. However the car's 2.3 litre six cylinder unit hauled it along in a breezy manner despite its leaden look.

Opposite bottom: Cadillac and Lincoln fitted the first four-headlamp systems during the 1950s. Here a sombre 1959 Cadillac Coupe de Ville tip-toes through the tulips.

shape of cars, as engines were moved forward and down between suspension assemblies which in their turn were moved into the wings. Cars became lower, and bonnets and wings began to merge.

In Britain the influence of American cars was plain. Slab-sided, heavily chromed, steering-column gear-change family cars were built, such as the Ford Consul which had a four-cylinder 1.5-litre engine, and its big brother, the Zephyr, which had a six-cylinder 2.3-litre unit.

Cadillac and Lincoln introduced the

first four-headlamp systems. Chrysler brought in full power steering and an autopilot to maintain a constant throttle setting.

More important was the introduction of better tyres. The shortage of rubber during World War Two had led to experiments with synthetics which resulted in compounds giving better wet-weather adhesion to the road. In 1950 Goodrich introduced tubeless tyres, holding the air inside the case by a soft rubber lining. These reduced the danger of blow-outs, being slower to deflate if punctured, and small holes

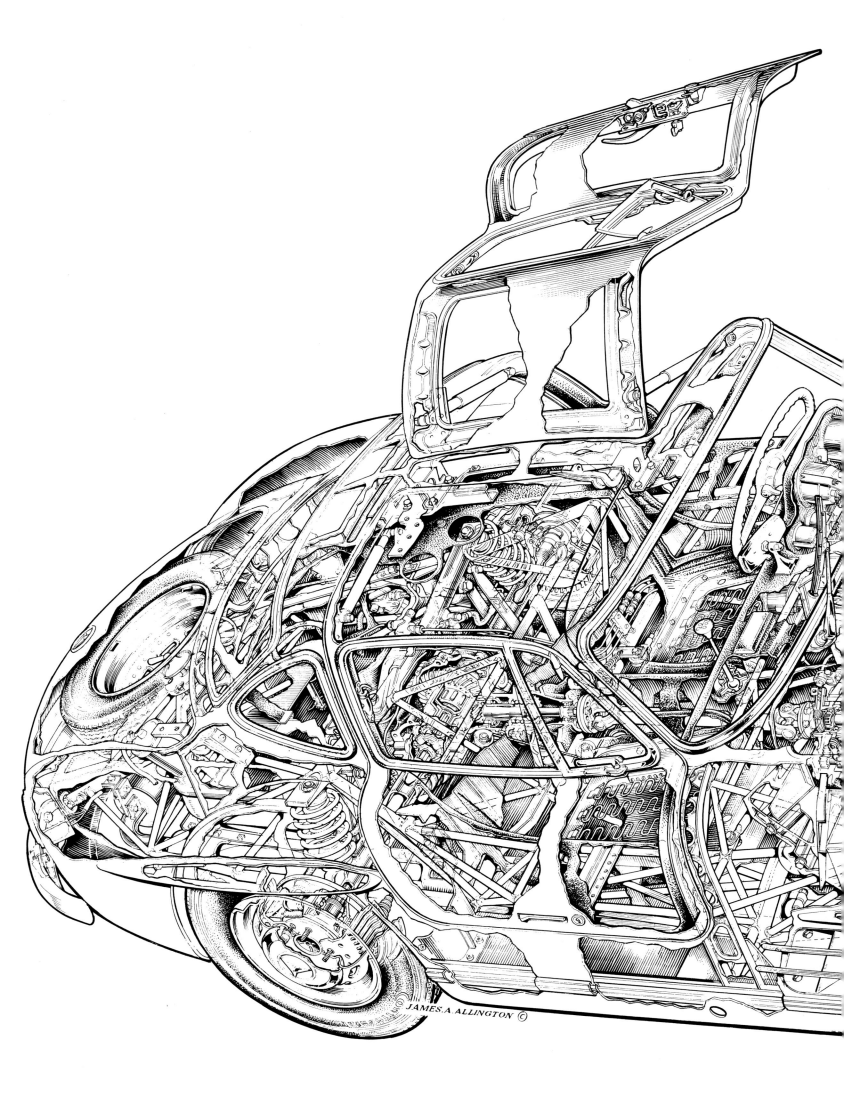

JAMES.A.ALLINGTON ©

MERCEDES-BENZ 300SL 1956

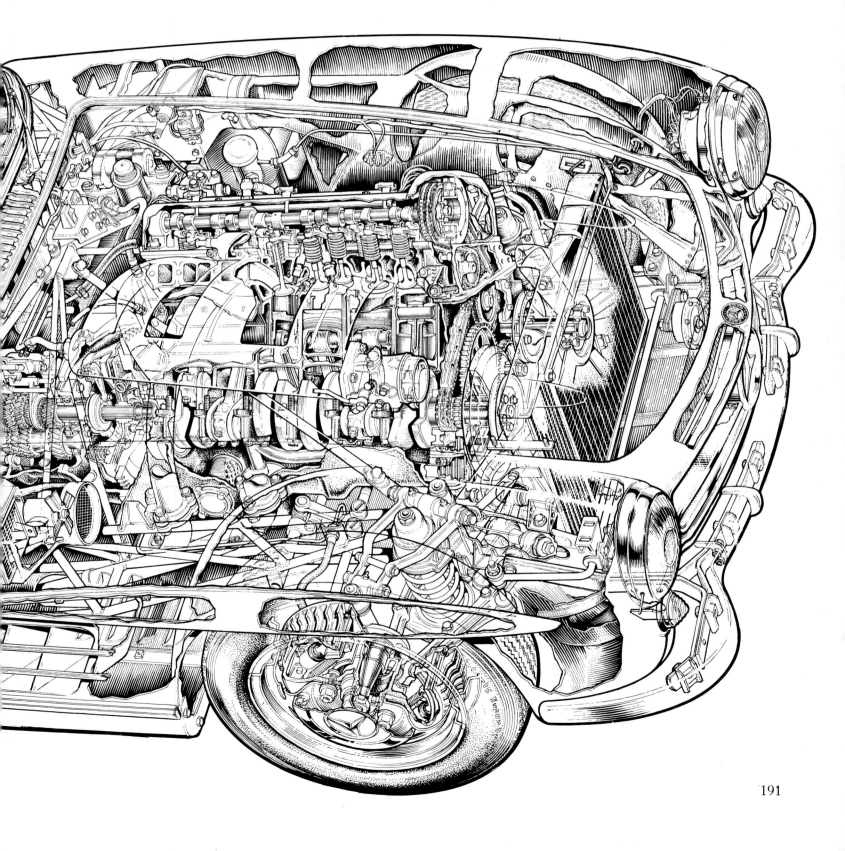

The Rover Jets. Jet 1, T3, T4 and the Rover-BRM that took part (unofficially) in the Le Mans 24 Hours race of 1963 finishing the event at an average speed of 107.84 mph, the first gas-turbine car to complete the race.

could easily be plugged. Manufacturers adopted them swiftly because they were quicker to fit on assembly lines.

A phenomenon of the 1950s was the experimental gas turbine model. The first was built by the Rover company (which, during World War Two had worked with Sir Frank Whittle on the development of the jet aircraft engine). Rover's 1950 car – which bore the apt registration number JET 1 – was essentially a Rover 75 with sports-type bodywork which helped it reach 150 mph in test runs. Renault built the turbined *Etoile Filante*, which was clocked at 191.2 mph, and there were also experiments in the United States, where General Motors made the Firebird. Problems of high construction

costs and high paraffin consumption prevented a gas turbine car ever being put into volume production.

Among production cars, the most advanced car was the shark-like Citroën DS saloon of 1955 with the front-wheel drive which Citroën had pioneered. It had power steering and power braking, and the suspension had hydro-pneumatic units which not only gave automatic self-levelling but by moving a lever the driver could also raise the car to cross rough ground or to change a wheel. (When the lever was moved to the 'high' position the driver could insert a stand on to which the car was lowered by notching back the lever.)

Originally the car had a four-cylinder 2-litre engine, later enlarged to 2.3 litres. The DS, a simpler model, the ID, and a big estate version, the Safari, ran until they were replaced by the CX series in 1975.

Sporting Breed

Nothing illustrated the carefree atmosphere of the first half of the 1950s more than the craze for open sports cars. Young men who, a decade earlier, might have been piloting fighter planes now looked for excitement at the wheel of a two-seater. The cars were made mainly in Britain, but the cult was most noticeable in North America where it began among the extroverts of Hollywood. Americans, accustomed to big, lazy-engined, softly sprung sedans, were delighted by the small size, quick acceleration, taut steering and crisp braking – not to mention the relative economy – of these cars and they were exported to the United States by the shipload. It was actually easier to obtain British sports cars in the U.S.A. than in the land of origin.

The longest established and archetype of these two-seaters was, of course, the MG, traditionally built of steel panels on an ash frame. The first postwar model, the 1.2-litre TC, launched in 1948, was merely an updated version of the prewar TB with a wider cockpit and a synchromesh gearbox. In 1949 the TC was followed by the TD with independent front suspension, and in 1953 came the TF with an engine of 1466 cc. Despite its sporty looks, its top speed was only about 85 mph and although this was quicker than most family cars, owners liked to believe it was faster still.

The TF was, in fact, the last of the traditional, much-loved series. In 1955 MG brought out the sleeker MGA, which could be obtained as an open roadster or a closed coupé, with a 1.5-litre engine that gave it almost 100 mph. (Stirling Moss drove an MG at more than 245 mph in 1957, but that was a supercharged, record-breaking special, the EX181.)

Competition to the MG grew rapidly in the 1950s, the earliest coming from the Morgan family who had been making cars at Malvern in the heart of England since Edwardian days (though in the 1930s they were identified with three-wheelers). In 1950 Morgan produced the Plus Four with a Vanguard 2.1-litre engine (and later with a 1600-cc Cortina engine), an admired car though never a mass-produced model, partly because the firm clung to traditional craftsmanship such as hand-beaten bodies.

New MGs had been seen again in 1948 when the TC was launched, to be followed by the TD with independent front suspension. Then in 1953 came the TF with its 1250cc unit (or optional 1½ litre) the last of the Nuffield units.

Above: The TF was the last of the traditional MG series. The MGA seen here was offered either open or closed, its 1½ litre engine giving it a near-100mph performance.

Below: First and last. In the background the Triumph TR2 of 1953 (using the 2 litre Standard Vanguard engine) and the 2 litre TR7 introduced in 1975, its wedge shape breaking away from the conventional TR lines.

A greater rival of the MG was the Triumph TR2 which went on sale in 1953. Managing director Sir John Black had required that it use, as far as possible, stock parts made for other cars in the Standard organization, so it had the Vanguard engine (modified to 2 litres in competition cars), the Vanguard gearbox and back axle, and the front suspension of the Triumph Mayflower saloon.

It was capable of 110 mph, which was faster than an MG though slower than a Morgan, and it was instantly successful as a club racer. More than 8 000 were sold before it was superseded by the TR3 in 1955. The TR series continued through the 1960s and 1970s, reaching the TR7 before production ended in 1981.

A more powerful car was the Austin-Healey 100. Similarly, Donald Healey had been told to make use of stock BMC parts, and so used a four-cylinder 2.7-litre Austin engine. At the end of the 1950s it was replaced by two models: the 3 000, with a six-cylinder 2.9-litre engine, which came to be

known as 'the big Healey'; and the Sprite, with a 948-cc engine, inevitably known as 'the little Healey'.

Another member of the sporting breed was the Sunbeam Alpine, which had a 1.5-litre engine (later 2.3 litres). It was rallied by Sheila Van Damm, one of the first women to become a name in motor sport. Yet another sporting car was the 105-mph AC Ace, which had a six-cylinder 2-litre engine previously used in the company's saloon cars but now placed on a new chassis by John Tojeiro who, under his own name at Royston, Hertfordshire, made specialized sports cars with MG and Bristol engines.

The Lotus firm, later to have worldwide influence on racing car design, began with kit cars. Colin Chapman, previously a builder and driver of specials such as a tuned and rebodied Austin 7, founded the Lotus marque in 1952 with the Mark 6, sold as a kit. It was followed by Marks 7, 8 and 9, some with 1100-cc and some with 1.5-litre engines. These led, in 1957, to the first enclosed Lotus, the two-

Above: An Austin-Healey 100-6, using the Austin 2.639cc six-cylinder unit, tests its suspension on a corner at Britain's re-opened pre-war circuit, Donington.

Below: This Grenfell special was built by the well-known Brooklands character Granville Grenfell in 1948 and used for hill-climbs and sprints in the post war years. It houses the ubiquitous Ford 3622cc V-8 unit.

One of the English aristocrats, the Daimler Regency MkII – although at 3½ litres its six-cylinder engine was somewhat underpowered.

seater Elite with a Coventry Climax 1.2-litre engine. The Elite pioneered glass-fibre monocoque construction by successfully overcoming the problems inherent in bolting axle and engine units to the shell.

There were some attempts to emulate the British sports car in the United States. One such endeavour was the Crosley Hotshot, a 750-cc two-seater developed by radio pioneer Powell Crosley to give 77 mph (90 mph with a blower) but the car was a rarity and the company folded. Even small specialized concerns in the U.S. normally employed huge engines. For ex-

ample, the Muntz Jet, designed by Frank Kurtis, used a 5.4-litre Cadillac V-8, and the cars built by racing driver Briggs Cunningham had 5.5-litre Chrysler engines.

There was no mass-produced open two-seater made in North America until General Motors introduced the Chevrolet Corvette in 1953.

The Ford Thunderbird which followed was a fine car with a V-8 engine of 4.8 litres – later 5.1 – though it was never sold as a sports car but as what Ford coyly described as 'a personal car'. Even so, every red-blooded American male lusted after the 113-

mph 'T-bird', and 53 000 were sold in its first three years, after which it grew into a five-seater and its glamour faded.

Grand Touring

Not everyone wanted a spartan open two-seater, which in its starkest form could be noisy, draughty and lacking in comfort. For others, particularly men of more mature years with healthy bank balances, the dream cars were the high-performance coupés and saloons made by some of the best-known names in the motor industry.

Many of them acquired the acronym

'GT' for *gran turismo* or 'grand touring' in the 1950s. There was never a precise definition of a GT car; the label meant different things to different manufacturers, though originally it was understood that a GT car was a handsome, long-legged vehicle which could cover vast distances at high speed in supreme comfort, carrying two people, or two adults and two children.

Unfortunately, GT became a much misused term, eventually signifying no more than a slightly tuned version of a family car with trendy wheels and a go-faster stripe on the side.

In the salad days of the GT the most sought-after models came from Italy, which was proper since the Italians invented the name. What has been called the definitive GT was the Ferrari 250 GT Berlinetta of 1953, which had a V-12 3-litre engine with three twin-choke carburettors, and was the car that signified Ferrari's expansion from racing-car manufacturing to production-car manufacturing.

Similarly, the Maserati 3 500 GT was the first true road-going Maserati. Its appearance followed a decision by the Orsi company, which had bought the name from the Maserati brothers, to volume-produce their six-cylinder 3.5-litre racing engine. Alfa Romeo's Giulietta marked a switch from making a few expensive cars to making a great many middle-class thoroughbreds. This four-seat coupé had a four-cylinder 1 290-cc engine and the 1956 Sprint Veloce version was considered by many to be the most handsome of small GT cars.

Italy also produced the Lancia Aurelia, the first postwar Lancia with a V-6 engine of 1.7 litres, later increased to nearly 2.5 litres.

France's Facel Vega, the country's biggest and most expensive car, produced by a firm which had once made cooking equipment, was sadly not a commercial success. It was a two-door, four-seat coupé, with a Chrysler V-8 engine of 6.3 litres, but there were not enough French people with money who wanted one, and in 1964 the company went into liquidation. They are worth a great deal more today, however, as collectors' items.

The American Chrysler 300 of the mid-1950s was even bigger bodied – a two-door coupé 18 feet 2½ inches long – but its V-8 engine of 5.4 litres gave it 130-mph performance, which was

Engineering from Italy. The Lancia Aurelia seen here in competition strip is the 2½ litre B20 of 1952. Aurelias were the first post-war Lancias with a V6 power unit. The model's shape and its unusual engine makes it a coveted classic today.

Aston Martin DB2/4 MkIII 2+2 coupe, housing a 2922cc twin overhead camshaft six developed from W.O. Bentley's 2.6 Lagonda engine. The DB development resulted in some highly successful sports-racing cars.

ahead of any other American car of the day so it, therefore, found a market. Its great power could be used on few roads in the U.S.A., however, with its ever-spreading blanket speed limits.

In Britain the Alvis TC21, a drop-head known as 'the Grey Lady', had a six-cylinder 3-litre engine, and the slightly less costly Daimler Conquest had a six-cylinder engine of 2.4 litres. Both of these cars had 100-mph performance, as did the Aston Martin DB2. The 'DB' came from the initials of tractor magnate David Brown, who had bought both Aston Martin and Lagonda after the war. He married the Aston Martin chassis to a Lagonda six-cylinder 2.5-litre engine in a sleek body, and raced the prototypes at Le Mans to prove them before the car was offered to the public. The DB2 was followed by the DB3 and DB4.

The Baby and the Bubble

Inevitably the GT car was for the discerning, well-heeled few. There was a far greater demand for small, cheap and economical cars, not necessarily from the less-privileged. On the contrary, there was a growing demand from families with one car already in the garage for a second car to use as a runabout.

Among rear-engined 'babies' the most famous name was that of Fiat, whose 600 succeeded the famous Topolino or 'Little Mouse' of prewar days. A new engine of 767 cc was

introduced in 1955. The car was just 10 feet long and 4 feet 6 inches wide, but by 1970 it was a best-seller with more than a million in use, swarming like bees in the big cities of Italy.

In France, the 845-cc Renault Dauphine had a speed of just over 70 mph. It was also made under licence in Italy by Alfa and in Brazil by Willys-Overland, and there were competition models tuned by Amédée Gordini, which helped to make it the first French car to sell more than two million.

In Germany the NSU motorcycle firm produced the Prinz, a small bath-tub with a vertical twin engine of 598 cc.

In Holland, the Daf, built by a firm best known for large commercial vehicles, had to strain to reach 57 mph with its 600-cc air-cooled flat-twin engine, but was remarkable for its ingenious two-pedal Variomatic transmission, a fully automatic system using a belt drive.

Smaller yet were the minicars, like those built by Air Vice Marshal Donald Bennett, known as 'Pathfinder' Bennett for his wartime command of the R.A.F.'s elite first-over-the-target bomber force. His Fairthorpe range began with the Atom, a fibreglass saloon with a rear-mounted BSA engine of 250 cc, followed by a more serious front-engined Electron and Electron Minor (also available in kit form), with 1 098-cc and 948-cc en-

The BMC Mini burst onto the motoring scene in 1960 as the 848cc Austin Seven, or the Mini-Minor, the latter title finally capturing the public imagination. Its extraordinary design brought in a new era of small car motoring and motor sport. Here it crests a hill during an international rally.

gines respectively; both were raced with honours.

There was also the Bond, a three-wheeler with one wheel at the front and two at the back, which had a 122-cc single-cylinder two-stroke Villiers engine, later replaced by a 197-cc unit which gave 43 mph and 80 mpg.

Midgets like these reached their ultimate form in the bubble car, Messerschmitts, Isettas, Heinkels, Friskys and so on which offered the simplicity and economy of a motorcycle with better weather protection. But most buyers wanted 'real' cars – and the bubble burst when the 'Mini' appeared in 1960.

Birth of the Mini

The BMC Mini was the creation of Alec Issigonis, who had designed the Morris Minor a decade earlier. Work

on it was given priority by BMC after the Suez emergency had brought a new concern about fuel economy.

A boxy little car of unitary construction, just 10 feet long but with a surprising amount of room inside, the Mini was new in almost every way. A four-cylinder 848-cc water-cooled engine was mounted transversely in the snub nose to save space, and drove the front wheels. The suspension, developed by Alex Moulton who had revolutionized bicycle design, used rubber cone springs, later superseded by the Hydrolastic system of interconnecting pipes containing a mixture of alcohol and water.

The Mini, priced originally at £466 19s 2d, was an unprecedented success. It was an economical runabout which was easy to park. It also had incredible roadholding and, tuned up, began winning races and rallies at once.

The number of derivatives grew. Originally the car appeared behind the badges of both Austin and Morris, though only the radiator grilles were different; these models were joined by Riley and Wolseley Minis with extended boots, and by 'hotted-up' Cooper and Cooper S versions, the result of collaboration with the Cooper racing company, with twin-carburettor engines ranging up to 1 275 cc.

When Paddy Hopkirk and Henry Liddon drove a Mini to victory in the Monte Carlo rally in 1964, it was the first of a hat-trick of Mini successes in the event.

The Mini was completely classless, driven by impoverished students and by millionaires who spent much money on customized versions. By 1976 sales had passed the four-million mark and the Mini was still selling. Alec Issigonis, born in Smyrna, Turkey, a Greek who became a naturalized Briton, was knighted in 1969 for his contribution to the industry.

Economical in fuel consumption and economical in space, the Mini looked larger inside than outside! The number of derivations multiplied rapidly, and in 1970 the car was given the name Mini in its own right, dropping the Austin/Morris appellations.

Britain's Sporting Breakthrough

The 1950s were years in which British cars and drivers were seen at the front of the starting grid *and* at the chequered finishing flag – English replaced the Latin languages in the hubbub of the pits. None of this had seemed remotely likely at the start of the decade, for the supercharged Alfas were still virtually unbeatable for the first two years of the 1950s and the first two world championships for drivers – the title was first awarded in 1950 – were won by Dr. Giuseppe Farina of Italy and Juan Manuel Fangio of Argentina, both in Alfa Romeos.

The supercharged V-16 BRM, Britain's great hope, arrived on the scene too late. The brainchild of the old ERA team of Raymond Mays and Peter Berthon, it had been built with the backing of a consortium of patriotic British firms and contributions from the general public. The scream of its 16 cylinders was one of the most thrilling sounds ever heard in motor racing and it was hailed as a world-beater – until it actually appeared on the tracks. It was unreliable and when it failed even to start in one early race the public jeered and tossed pennies into the cockpit. The BRM's days of triumph did not arrive until the next decade.

Meanwhile, Enzo Ferrari had engaged Aurelio Lampredi to design an unblown engine, and the Ferrari that made its debut in 1950 was of 3.3 litres, bored out within months to the full permitted 4.5. A tussle with the Alfas was inevitable and at the British Grand Prix at Silverstone in 1951, Ferrari's new car, driven by the Argentine's burly Froilan Gonzales who was known as the 'Wild Bull of the Pampas', defeated the opposition.

There was then so little competition for Ferrari that the formula was brought to a premature end, with world championship events run under Formula Two rules for 2 litres unblown or 500 cc blown. The astonishing Ferrari still triumphed giving Alberto Ascari the world championship in 1952.

The most significant opposition came from Cooper's Bristol-engined car, in which Mike Hawthorn gave the Ferraris such a battle that Ferrari signed the bow-tied Englishman as a driver for the following season, setting the scene for the 1953 French Grand Prix at Reims, which produced motor racing's longest, closest, hardest-fought duel to date.

Hawthorn in the Ferrari and Fangio in a Maserati raced for 150 miles, nearly half the total distance, never more than a length or so apart. Lap after lap they were side by side at 150 mph. Fangio slipstreamed Hawthorn and Hawthorn slipstreamed Fangio until, just a handshake apart on the penultimate lap, Hawthorn fell back into the Maserati slipstream for a final burst. He made it, and beat Fangio across the line by just one second after $2\frac{3}{4}$ hours of racing, the first Englishman to win a *grande épreuve* for 30 years.

In 1954 there was a new Formula One of 2.5 litres which ran for seven years. Mercedes Benz returned to the sport with fuel injection and with Fangio as chief driver, and he took the world championship in 1954 and 1955. He came to dominate the sport whatever car he was driving, for he won again in 1956 with a Lancia-Ferrari (the prancing horse stable having taken over Lancia's racing cars) and in 1957 with a Maserati 250F.

In 1958, when alcohol fuel was outlawed, he retired, much respected, and Mike Hawthorn took the championship in a Ferrari. Sadly, he was to die in a road accident a year later. However, the constructors' championship was won by Britain's Vanwall, built by millionaire bearings-manufacturer Tony Vandervell, who had been one of the original sponsors of the BRM until he left after disagreements to form his own team with Stirling Moss, Tony Brooks and Stuart Lewis-Evans; the latter was tragically killed at the end of the season.

The Vanwall stable disbanded in 1959 due to the illness of Vandervell but Britain was now at the top. The world championship was won by Australia's Jack Brabham in a Cooper with a four-cylinder Coventry Climax engine originally designed for fire pumps. This was mounted at the rear, where Cooper had put the engine in their original 500-cc racers, and was soon to change completely the accepted layout of racing cars.

Britain had already come to dominate sports-car racing in the 24-hour event at Le Mans with the C- and D-type Jaguars of 3.4 and 3.8 litres. In a string of victories comparable with those of the Bentleys in the 1920s, they won in 1951 and 1953 (in which year

Opposite: The 1950s brought a renaissance of British drivers and cars. Here Stirling Moss the uncrowned king of motor racing (he never captured the world championship title although acknowledged as the world's best driver, after Fangio) rounds the hairpin Station Bend in a Cooper-Climax during the 1959 Monaco Grand Prix.

Above: The decade was also the heyday of the Jaguar C and D-types, with wins at Le Mans 1951, 53, 55, 56 and 1957. Here a Jaguar D-type in BRG (British Racing Green) is seen at speed during a recent meeting of historic cars.

Opposite: Mille Miglia 1955; in this Mercedes-Benz 300SLR Stirling Moss won the thousand-mile race around Italy – the first-ever British win, and at an unbeaten record speed of almost 98mph.

they pioneered disc brakes which enabled the drivers to leave braking at the corners until much later) and in 1955, unhappily remembered as the year of motor sport's worst disaster. A Mercedes 300SLR, driven by Pierre Levegh, collided with the Austin-Healey of Lance Macklin and bounced over a safety bank into the crowd, killing the driver and 83 spectators. Jaguars won again in 1956 (with fuel injection in place of carburettors) and 1957.

The 150-mph C-types and the 180-mph D-types, two-seat open racers with minimal screens in Le Mans form, could also be used on the road. Sales were further boosted by publicity stunts such as the one in 1952 when Stirling Moss and three other drivers, working in three-hour spells, averaged 100 mph for a week on France's Montlhéry circuit, which they lapped every 42 seconds. Afterwards they put up a chalked notice: 'For Sale. Jaguar saloon. Carefully run in'.

Le Mans was to continue, despite the 1955 disaster, but the 1950s saw the swansong of long-distance road races such as the Mille Miglia, in which 500 or 600 cars from Topolinos to the latest supercars roared through towns and villages from the northern town of Brescia to Rome and back.

Stirling Moss, with journalist Denis Jenkinson as navigator, won this at a record average speed of nearly 98 mph over 10 hours of non-stop driving in 1955, at the wheel of a Mercedes 300SLR, a version of the 300SL which won Le Mans on its debut in 1952. Over the last 85 miles Moss averaged 123 mph on Italian roads that were *not* (officially at least) closed to the public.

But the 1957 Mille Miglia – won by Piero Taruffi in a 4.1-litre Ferrari at 94.8 mph – was the last. The event was discontinued because of accidents and the dislocation caused to everyday transport.

For the same reasons the classic long-distance rallies which, in the 1950s, included the Monte Carlo, Liège-Rome-Liège, the Acropolis, the Coupe des Alpes and a London-Sydney marathon, began to be curbed, with the results being decided on closed stretches or circuits rather than on roads.

The Balance Changes: 1960-1969

Opposite: The United States now had one car for every five of its population. It seemed the world had too many cars – except in the USSR which had only four cars per thousand. This picture of a Los Angeles freeway shows its normal automotive density.

Below: The Chevrolet Corvair; by 1966 it had grown into a sporting vehicle with options of extremely high powered engines of up to 180hp. A campaign led by Ralph Nader used the Corvair as a peg on which to hang an 'Unsafe at any Speed' slogan.

Suddenly during the early 1960s the automotive industry – in all car-producing countries – was in trouble and under attack from many quarters. Within the industry there were cutbacks in production, lay-offs of workers and strikes. Outside the industry there was increased vocal concern about the despoliation of urban life by motoring, and about the deaths and injuries attributable to it. The root cause of all the problems and concern was the popularity of car ownership.

It seemed the Western world had just too many cars. The United States now had two cars for every five people; the E.E.C. countries averaged a car for every six people. In Europe Sweden had the highest proportion with 240 cars per thousand people. France followed with 198, Britain 172, Belgium 161, the Netherlands 128 and Italy 121. (Incidentally, the U.S. car-owning figure per thousand was 397; in the U.S.S.R. it was four per thousand.)

U.S. production was cut by a quar-

ter as a million new and unsold cars jammed dealers' premises. The effects spread. Many Americans were now forsaking large cars for the 'compacts', introduced at the start of the 1960s, cars such as the Ford Falcon, Plymouth Valiant, Pontiac Tempest and Chevrolet Corvair. These cars were compact only by American standards as they generally were more than 15 feet long with six-cylinder 2+-litre engines

Compacts soon had a quarter of the American market, making it more difficult for European manufacturers to sell in the U.S.A; only VW sales continued almost unabated. Added to this, Japan was now a serious competitor. From fewer than 50 cars a year in the mid-1950s, its exports rose to more than half a million a year.

In old-established firms in Europe, production was cut back and thousands of workers were laid off or put on to short-time working. The problem was exacerbated by government attempts to fight inflation, a mat-

Above: U.S. car production was reduced by over a million in 1961 as unsold cars piled up – and only the German Volkswagen Group continued to maintain its target figures to the U.S.A. This is the final section of two of Wolfsburg's assembly lines.

Below: The 1960s saw a rapid increase in road congestion, but the busy service stations of the Western world 'never had it so good' as the British Prime Minister of the time said.

ter of growing concern in many countries. In Britain there were no less than 17 changes in tax and credit restrictions during the 1960s – and the trend was always harsher. Purchase tax rose to 55 per cent, taxes on fuel and vehicle licensing rose, and a top limit was set on the amount that a company could offset against tax on a new car – a measure that did not help the sales of prestige cars such as Rolls-Royce and Aston Martin.

Car workers, facing their own personal problems in a world of rising prices, became restive and strikes became common in France and in Italy as well as in Britain.

Mergers increased, in hopes of cutting costs; Daimler, with its long 'royal' motoring associations, was

absorbed by Jaguar, which was then itself taken over by BMC. Standard-Triumph was saved from collapse by being taken over by Leyland, the bus and lorry company. Leyland also absorbed Rover, which had already taken over Alvis. Then came Britain's biggest motor merger.

BMC was in difficulties with most of its lines losing money. It, too, merged with Leyland. This brought Austin, Morris, Riley, Wolseley, MG, Austin-Healey, Triumph, Rover, Land Rover, Daimler and Jaguar into what became known as British Leyland. It was organized under one boss, Sir Donald (later Lord) Stokes, regarded as one of Britain's most dynamic export salesmen.

Elsewhere there were other mergers.

Chrysler took over Simca in France and the Rootes Group (Hillman, Sunbeam and Singer) in Britain. Peugeot and Citroën came together in 1964 but parted again in 1966, Peugeot then forming an association with Renault, while Citroën absorbed Panhard, and let the historic name die. Fiat absorbed Lancia and Ferrari, and Volkswagen swallowed NSU and Audi.

Other names vanished to become melancholy subjects of nostalgia; among them were Armstrong-Siddeley, Alvis, Allard, Lea Francis and Frazer Nash in Britain, Borgward in Germany, and Studebaker in the United States.

Living with the Car

This period – an otherwise affluent one in the Western world – saw an increasing number of complaints about the effects of cars and new roads on the environment (a word that not everyone knew existed before the 1960s) – about flyovers that passed close by houses at bedroom-window level, expressways that changed the character of quiet suburbs, concrete 'spaghetti junctions' that sprawled across what had once been fields and, most of all, about the way cars affected town and city centres built in pre-motoring days.

Motorists and non-motorists alike complained about the clogging of town centres by cars. Tradesmen lost trade, commuters were exasperated by delays caused by jams, shoppers were wearied by the problem of finding parking spaces at the end of their journeys. City dwellers began to move out, leaving a depopulated core.

Below: Leyland's takeover of just about every popular marque did not unduly disturb Triumph production. This 2.1 litre TR4 was one of the continuous line of Triumph sports cars starting with the TR of 1955 and ending with the TR7. Here seen in an Alpine village on an international Rally.

The remedies proposed were many and costly. Some advocated accepting the car, demolishing city centres and rebuilding them with walkways at first-floor level, leaving the roads for cars. Others proposed the banning of cars from city centres and providing light railways, electric runabouts or other forms of public transport. Compromisers suggested controlling the entry of cars to towns by licences or punitive tolls, monitoring movements by electronic devices attached to cars and to roads at the points of entry. Solutions proliferated.

Most authorities chose to use gallons of warning paint on kerbs, to ban waiting, to create more one-way traffic flow systems and, sometimes to build new (always inadequate) multi-storey car parks.

The most vociferous campaigner against 'the killer car' was Ralph Nader, an American lawyer. He had begun his campaign for safer cars in 1959 with a magazine article entitled, 'The Safe Car You Can't Buy', and it reached a climax in 1965 with his best-selling book, *Unsafe at Any Speed*.

Statistics were arguable but it was alleged that the car caused 130 000 deaths and 1.7 million injuries in the Western world every year. In the U.S.A. road deaths reached 54 895 in one year in the 1960s, though per head of population the toll was worse in Japan where 16 285 died. The magic carpet had, it seemed, become the killer shark.

Nader accused the motor industry of being more concerned, when designing cars, with style, speed and cost than with safety. His chief target was the Chevrolet Corvair, a rear-engined compact with an air-cooled engine of 2.3 litres, which was said to have dangerous faults, including inadequate brakes and tyres too small for its load.

The safe car Nader sought was, in fact, already in existence — an experimental model built by Cornell Aeronautical Laboratory with a strengthened body that did not collapse into the passenger compartment in a crash, an interior with no sharp or hard surfaces, and a restraining device to hold passengers in their seats. It was claimed that if such safety features were made compulsory they would save 20 000 to 30 000 lives a year.

The motor industry argued that accidents and fatalities were inevitable and blamed the excessive speed or

Opposite top: Britain often found its once-open roads crowded to a standstill, even the new motorways. A major programme of roadbuilding over the next years did little to reduce the problem.

Opposite bottom: Overcrowding, pollution and diminishing energy reserves prompted this Ford electric Commuta city car experiment in 1967. It was just 6 feet long and could take two-plus-child and luggage.

Below: U.S. critic Ralph Nader's condemnation of a number of automobiles caused the industry to look again at its design and safety margins. This model is seen at the moment of a fierce lateral impact during a crash test.

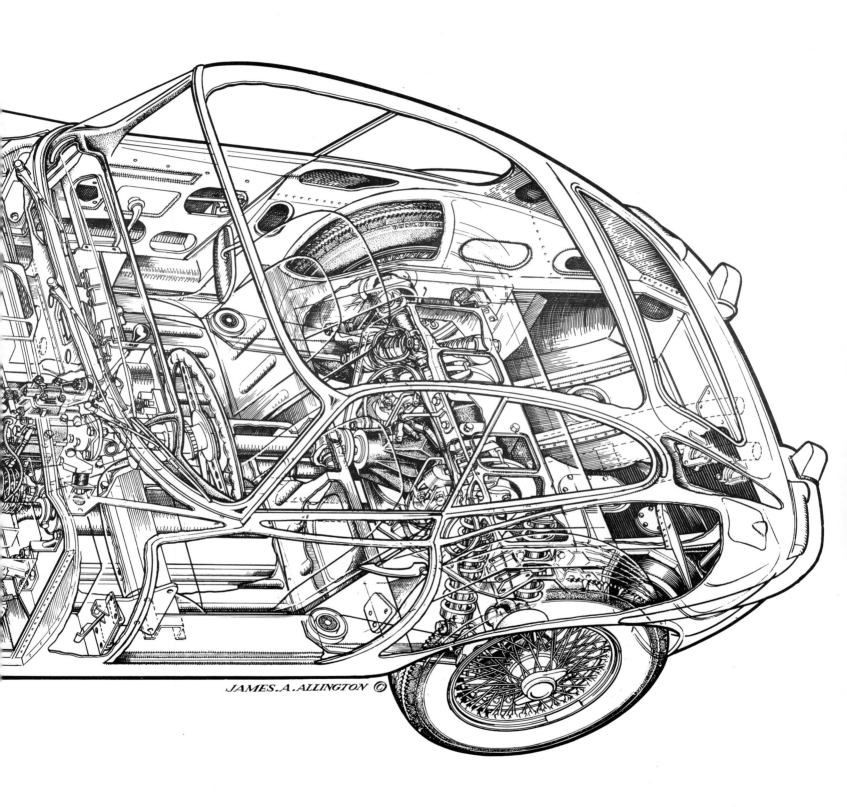

JAMES.A.ALLINGTON ©

carelessness of drivers; a Cornell study claimed that it was poor design rather than speed that killed and that three-quarters of the serious injuries would still occur even if no one exceeded 60 mph.

Nader suggested that the public did not know how safe cars could be because no one told them. His message was that 'Automobiles are so designed as to be dangerous at any speed ... innumerable precedents show that the consumer must be protected at times from his own indiscretion and vanity'.

The campaign by Nader and his supporters – known as 'Nader's Raiders' – was powerful and achieved results. In 1966 Congress passed a Motor Vehicles Safety Act and, as a result, car companies began to incorporate safety features, some mandated by the National Traffic Safety Administration, others voluntarily. Among them were seat belts, energy-absorbing steering columns and instrument panels, better door locks, larger mirrors, warning flashers, high seat backs and head restraints and stronger seat anchorages. More experimental safety vehicles were designed and

exhibited. There were experiments whereby passengers were restrained by means of air bags which inflated instantly in the event of a crash and many others. The Corvair was withdrawn.

The publicity had its shock-effect around the world. In Britain in 1967 it became compulsory to fit seat belts on the front seats of new cars (though not yet to wear them); the annual safety testing of vehicles, which had been begun in 1960 in a modest way (applying only to cars 10 years old or older) was tightened to cover cars only three years old; a 70-mph blanket speed limit was imposed even on motorways; and the breathalyzer was introduced to speed the testing of suspected drunken drivers.

In the U.S.A. the drive for safety was followed closely by a drive to reduce pollution caused by car engines. Following a Clean Air Act, manufacturers were required to reduce noxious emissions from exhaust systems. The most common emission control device involved the installation of a catalytic converter which burned up impurities by passing exhaust gas-

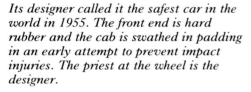

Its designer called it the safest car in the world in 1955. The front end is hard rubber and the cab is swathed in padding in an early attempt to prevent impact injuries. The priest at the wheel is the designer.

This MG 1100 was an attempt by BMC to upgrade its basic front wheel drive 1100 cc car, giving it a couple of carburettors and an MG badge. Here author Peter Roberts is being quizzed by frontier police.

ses over a chemically coated surface. The rules were to be made progressively stricter.

Front-wheel Drive

Front-wheel drive, the new-car trend of the 1960s influenced largely by the BMC Mini, was not, of course, a new concept. Walter Christie of New York City had made 'fwd' cars in the U.S. in 1904 and Citroën had been making them very successfully since 1934, but now almost everyone was introducing at least one fwd model. BMC followed up the Mini with the Morris and Austin 1100, effectively big brothers of the Mini with transverse fwd engine and Hydrolastic suspension. Simca also had an 1100 model. Peugeot introduced the 204, Lancia the Flavia and Fulvia, NSU the Ro80. Renault decided to concentrate on fwd policy and brought out the 4, 6, 12 and 16 models, and when Fiat made its 128 a transverse-engined fwd car, VW and Ford were the only major companies in Europe without fwd models, VW be-

cause it continued to concentrate on rear-engined cars, and Ford because it remained faithful to its conventional front-engined, rear-wheel-drive layouts.

The U.S.A.'s first fwd car of modern times was the Oldsmobile Tornado, a two-door coupé with a V-8 engine of 7.4 litres; this was followed by the similar Cadillac Eldorado.

There was a move back to floor-change gear levers, short, stubby levers that gave a positive feel compared with some of the steering column changes that had been so remote a driver felt like a railway signalman operating a lever that hauled up a signal half a mile down the track.

This was accompanied by a move back to separate front seats, more comfortable and stable than a bench-seat; families had learned that the middle of a front bench was not the safest place to sit a child.

Useless chrome décor was scrapped, saving car owners much work trying to remove or prevent rust. In the U.S.

Above: A 1967 Cadillac Eldorado (foreground) and a De Ville Convertible, the first Cadillacs with front wheel drive. They also had self-levelling suspension, torsion bar i.f.s., front disc brakes, and a 7 litre powerpack.

Below: The NSU Ro80, first seen in 1967. Well in advance of general automotive products, its 2 litre twin-rotor engine drove the front wheels, giving a vibrationless 115 hp.

the Chrysler New Yorker, a 6.7-litre saloon nearly 18 feet long, pioneered cleaner lines, free from excessive trimmings, and the sleek Studebaker Avanti's fibreglass body, housing a V-8 of 4.7 litres, was even more ahead in style.

Some innovative cars employed the rotary engine developed by Germany's Felix Wankel, the rights of which were bought by NSU. First installed in the

Spider, based on the rear-engined two-seat Prinz, as a pilot scheme, its full impact was felt in 1967 when it was put into the Ro80 saloon with fwd.

The twin-rotor engine, equal to a litre in capacity, was small, light and quiet, and would run up to 7 000 rpm without vibration, but there were problems, mainly with the rotor sealing. The engine's 20 mpg thirst was also against it, and NSU was thought to be

selling the car at a loss in the 1960s.

Experiments also continued with another alternative to the conventional piston engine – the gas turbine. In 1963 Rover in association with BRM developed a two-seat racing car in which Graham Hill and Richie Ginther averaged 107.84 mph over 24 hours at Le Mans; however, when it was permitted to compete in the race it could finish no higher than tenth.

Options and Packages

Some cars were immediate winners. The most instantly successful of the decade was the U.S.'s Ford Mustang of 1964 which took the place of the T-bird as a virility symbol. A four-seat compact just over 15 feet long, it used many Falcon components including engines and transmission; the engines included six-cylinder units of 2.8 litres and V-8s of 4.7 litres. There was a

Above: Rover Turbine at Le Mans, 1963.

Below: The Ford Mustang of 1964 was a well-designed compact with a sporting performance. Its 4.7 litre motor could take it up over 108 mph. The young of America took to it avidly and over half a million were sold in the first year and a half.

*ritratto
originale
eseguito da
Pietro Annigoni
in occasione
della Fiat 850*

8 FIAT 850

wide range of choice in other specifications too; the Mustang could be bought with 13-inch or 14-inch wheels, manual or automatic gearbox, disc or drum brakes, manual or power steering and soft or hard top. Options such as these were marketing features in the 1960s.

Four hundred thousand were sold in a year, more than a million in three years. But, like the T-bird, after four years it began to put on weight.

General Motors' competitor for the Mustang was the Chevrolet Camaro (which also sold as the Pontiac Firebird). A two-door with 'almost four' seats, it also came with a range of engines and transmissions from a six-cylinder of 3.8 litres to a V-8 of 6.5 litres.

In Britain similar options were a feature of Fords, particularly the Ford Cortina, introduced in 1962 and destined to be the country's best-seller for nearly all of its 20 years' existence. It became the archetypal fleet car, used by countless sales representatives, and was also the most popular family saloon.

There were four distinct Cortinas during its life span. The Mark 1 was sold until 1966, during which time Colin Chapman worked with Ford to

produce the Lotus Cortina (always painted white with a green flash) which had a twin-cam and lowered suspension – and nerve-shattering acceleration when driven by those who lacked instruction.

The Mark 2 ran until 1970, with the Lotus Cortina becoming the Cortina Lotus. The Mark 3 went on until 1976 and the Mark 4 to 1982.

By now a radio was the least most motorists wanted in the way of what came to be known as 'In-Car Entertainment' or 'ICE' in the 1960s. There were now also tape players and dual units incorporating radio (often with VHF) and players (often with stereo speakers). As traffic delays grew longer the attractions of ICE grew too, and service stations stocked up on soothing,

middle-of-the-road music tapes.

Despite the steeply increasing costs of motoring, there were still those able and willing to pay for speed, and the 1960s brought new machines with a capability far in excess of general speed limits. Iso of Milan, the Italian firm that had made the Isetta bubble cars of the 1950s, brought out the 160-mph Iso Grifo, an Italian-American car with a Chevrolet V-8 engine of 5.3 litres in a two-seat coupé body by Bertone. Also new in Italy was the Lamborghini, created by a company founded in 1963 by Ferruchio Lamborghini, an industrialist who had once been a tuner of Fiat 500s. His first car was a 3.5-litre GT with a V-12 engine, six Weber twin-choke carburettors and a five-speed gearbox.

Above: The Ford Cortina was produced in four successive marks. This is the Mk1, introduced in 1962 in 1.2 litre and 1½ litre form, and soon offered as a startlingly responsive GT with front discs and 83 hp.

Opposite top: Rival to the British Mini was this rear-engined Fiat 850 marketed from 1964 and built in the pre-war 'Topolino' tradition. The girl's portrait is by artist Annigoni.

Opposite bottom: Iso of Milan had manufactured the bean-like Isetta with its 236cc engine during the 1950s. Their second try was in a different mould. The hybrid Rivolta and the later Grifo were up in the 400 bhp range and powered by Chevrolet units.

219

In the face of this competition Ferrari widened its range. It had the world's fastest production car in the 365 GTB4 Daytona, its 4.4-litre V-12 engine developing 86 mph in second gear, 140 in fourth and nearly 180 in top.

This was the last of Ferrari's front-engined coupés; the Dino was its first mid-engined road car, the 2-litre (later 2.4-litre) six-cylinder engine being sited behind the driver as in the firm's racing cars. It was named after Enzo Ferrari's son, Alfredino, who had been

lamps, and designed to give 150 mph.

The U.S.A. produced the Chevrolet Stingray, a two-seat sports car with four choices of engine, its 7-litre unit giving more than 150 mph. In Germany there was the Porsche 911, a two-plus-two closed coupé with a six-cylinder, 2-litre, air-cooled and rear-mounted engine which gave 130 mph.

Rolls-Royce, whose dignified Phantom V gave way in the 1960s (after some 800 were built) to the Phantom VI, with a 6.7-litre engine, four headlamps, and a fitted drinks cupboard as

Opposite top: Ferrari 365 GT. As the GTB4 Daytona it was the fastest production car of its time. This 4.390 litre 1968 Coupé has a body by Pinin Farina and was the largest – and the last – of Ferrari's front-engined touring V12 cars.

Below: At the 1965 Motor Show in London Rolls-Royce revealed an entirely new car, the Silver Shadow. Self-levelling all-round independent suspension and unitary construction made this a very much updated offering.

involved in the engine design but died in 1956, and had 140-mph performance.

Up to this time there had been no Ferrari tourer with more than two seats but Ferrari broke new ground with the 250GT and 330GT which were two-plus-two cars, with four-litre V-12 engines, also capable of 140 mph.

In Britain Colin Chapman produced the 1.5-litre Lotus Europa with a glass-fibre body so low one could almost trip over it. From Jaguar there was the glamorous E Type, with the 3.8-litre XK engine (later 4.2 litres) in a new two-seat body with faired-in head-

standard, was still in prime position. The British Royal family were to have three, made with a higher roof line and extra window area to enable them to be seen. This design was known at Rolls as the 'Canberra style'. The Silver Cloud, first seen in 1955, was still the standard product up to 1965.

More of a departure were the Rolls-Royce Silver Shadow (1965) and Bentley T models with 6.2-litre engines, later enlarged to 6.7 litres. The Shadow was the first of its line to have an integral chassis body, to use disc brakes and to have self-levelling suspension.

Opposite bottom: The Jaguar E-type was first seen on British roads in 1961; it caused a sensation. This at last was a genuine superfast car at a reasonable cost, and housing the already classic 3.8 unit. This is a 1974 V12 E-type.

221

Sporting Sponsorship

Grand Prix racing in the 1960s began amid controversy. A new Formula One called for the fitting of self-starters, the use of pump petrol – and for 1.5-litre unsupercharged engines. British constructors refused to recognize the new formula, claiming it would be totally without interest and thought that, as they were now the main manufacturers of F1 cars, their views would prevail. They did not, and when the new formula began without them they attempted to run 2.5-litre cars in a rival series. This failed and they were forced to concede.

As they had not bothered to develop a 1.5-litre engine, the only power unit available to them was the four-cylinder Coventry-Climax (former fire-appliance) engine that had first appeared in F2 racing in 1957. This

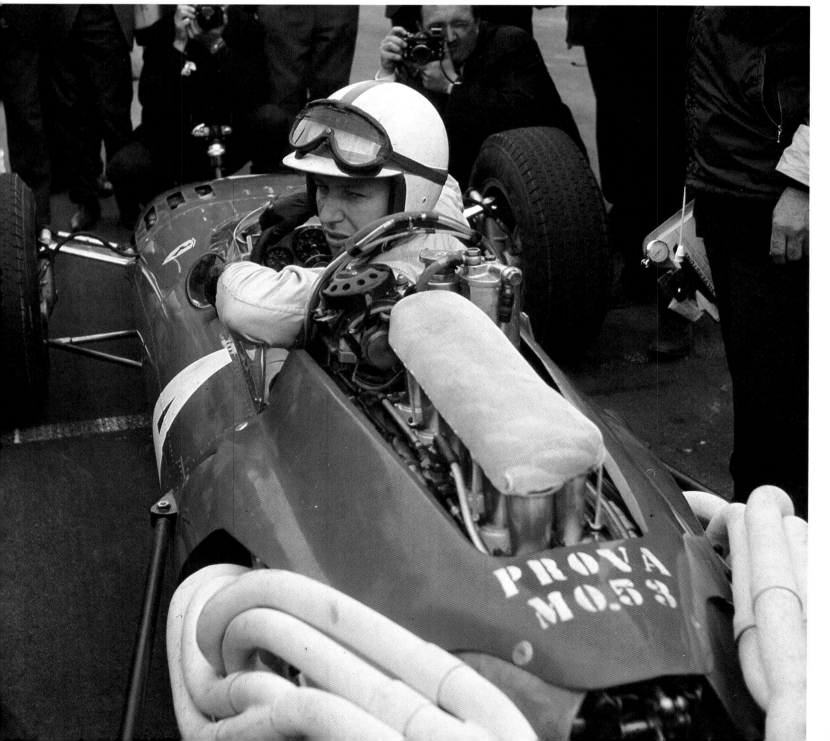

was no match for Ferrari's new V-6, and the first world champion of the 1960s – and the first American to win the title – was Ferrari driver Phil Hill, who had begun his racing in MG sports cars.

A year later the British had caught up and produced their own engines and the 1962 world championship went to Graham Hill, driving a BRM (which had become part of the Owen group). A year later it was the turn of Scotsman Jim Clark in a Lotus, powered by a new Coventry-Climax V-8 converted to fuel injection.

Clark's Lotus changed the design trend of F1 machines yet again. To save weight Lotus manufacturer Colin Chapman had gone over to monocoque construction, using a chassis-less shell in place of the usual multi-tubular cage, and its design called for Clark practically to lie on his back, almost completely hidden from view. Most other constructors were soon using the same engine in similar monocoques with the result that drivers were unrecognizable except for their helmets. No longer could arms and elbows be seen working outside the cockpit as they had in the past, and enthusiasts complained at the absence of spectacle; on the other hand, the cars were now lapping faster than the 2.5-litre cars of a few years earlier.

The 1964 world champion was John Surtees, former motorcycle world champion, in a Ferrari V-8, but in

1965 Clark and Lotus won again, and also found time to take a special Lotus to Indianapolis where the Scot scored Britain's first victory in the 500. Sadly Clark was to die in a crash on the Hockenheim circuit in 1968.

In 1966 Grand Prix racing was run under another new formula, providing for 3-litre engines. Manufacturers built V-12s with which, predictably, there were early problems. Jack Brabham, the Australian world champion of 1959 and 1960, who had begun making his own cars, cashed in on them. He calculated that while his rivals were sorting out their new engines, a reliable old one could win, so he gave his cars a Repco V-8, low on power but high in reliability, which kept going when more sophisticated power mills had stopped. He became the first driver to win the world championship in a car of his own make.

The following year his co-driver, Denny Hulme of New Zealand, took the title. 'Well, I'd shown him how to do it,' joked Brabham, who came second.

Then the mighty Ford organization moved into Grand Prix racing with the same sort of impact it had already created in sports-car racing. It was part of a worldwide Ford master plan to change its image from a maker of comparatively cheap, mass-produced cars to that of a maker of precision machines with successful sporting associations. The first phase of the

Opposite top: From 1960 until the end of 1965 Formula 1 Grand Prix regulations called for a 1.5 litre maximum capacity engine. Here British driver Jim Clark (World Champion Driver in 1963 and 1965) is seen in his Lotus-Climax 1.5 litre V8 at speed.

Opposite bottom: London-born John Surtees won the World Championship title in 1964 driving a Ferrari 158. Here in 1966 he faces the cameras after a test run in F1 Ferrari.

Below: The first British Grand Prix under the new 3-litre rules took place at Brands Hatch. The line-up on the grid included Jack Brabham (No 5), Graham Hill (No 3), Jim Clark (No 1) and Denny Hulme (No 6), all of whom won the title of World Champion during the 1960s.

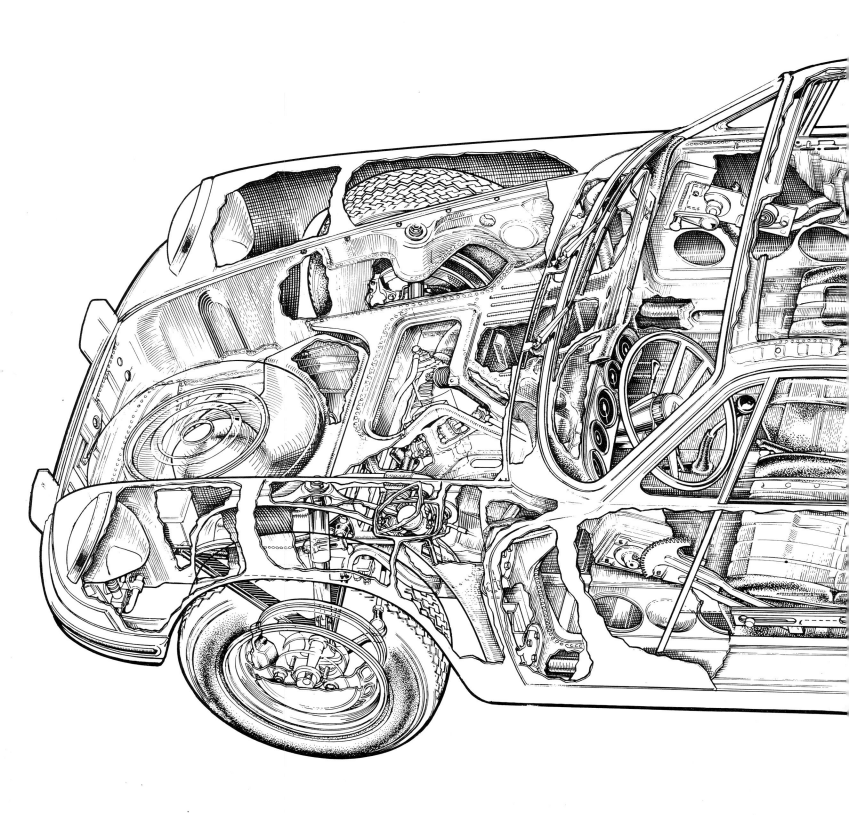

JAMES A ALLINGTON ©

plan was an assault on Le Mans, dominated at this time by Ferrari's mid-engined cars.

Ford's weapon was the GT40, so-called because it was 40 inches high. Built in Britain, it was a mid-engined car with a V-8 of 4.2 litres, and capable of 200 mph on the straight. It made its debut in 1964, without success. Ferraris came first, second and third again at Le Mans, and the same happened in 1965. Ford poured money into its campaign and in 1966 a 7-litre GT40 driven by New Zealanders Bruce McLaren and Chris Amon achieved the victory. The GT40 won again in 1967, 1968 and 1969, its main rival being Porsche. Some 107 of the cars were made, some with detuned and silenced engines for private motorists.

Meanwhile, Ford had turned its attention to F1. In 1967 the Cosworth company, backed by Ford, produced a new 3-litre V-8 all-aluminium engine, which was first made available to Lotus, and in 1968 Graham Hill won

the world championship in a Lotus-Ford.

It later sprouted aerofoils, wings over the tail of a car to help keep it on the ground, which had been pioneered in sports-car racing by American Chaparral cars in 1966, and introduced into F1 racing by Brabham and Ferrari cars in 1968. Aerofoils were banned for a time after those on two Lotus cars collapsed in the 1969 Spanish Grand Prix, but subsequently they were permitted again, subject to regulations regarding size, and all F1 cars adopted them.

By this time the Ford Cosworth engine had been made available to all F1 contenders, as the Coventry Climax engine had been earlier, and most used it. Jackie Stewart won the 1969 championship at the wheel of a Matra-Ford.

At a lower level of the sport Ford also exerted an influence. The 105E Ford Anglia engine came to dominate Formula Junior events and Ford also

The 1964 Twenty-Four Hours of Le Mans saw the formidable Ford GT40 for the first time. The British-built Anglo-American cars had 4.2 litre engines this year, later increased to 7 litres.

initiated Formula Ford for cars using Cortina 1.6-litre engines. This was matched by Formula Renault for Renault 8 engines and Formula Vee for Volkswagen engines.

These formulae helped to make it possible for novices with more ambition than money to break into a sport in which there was now very little room at the top. An even cheaper form of the sport was karting, known as go-karting when it began in California. The karts are fitted with lawn-mower engines of 100 and 250 cc and are so small that they can be hung on a garage wall when not in use, and transported to meetings in a car boot.

At the other end of the spectrum there was a new spate of world land-speed record breaking. In 1964 Donald Campbell, son of Sir Malcolm, went to dried-up Lake Eyre in Australia and pushed the record past 400 mph in his *Bluebird* powered by a Proteus aircraft turbine engine. This was still a conventional car, driven through its wheels, but then record breaking moved into the jet age.

Up to this time pure jet cars had not been eligible for the record because they were not driven through the wheels, but the authorities amended the rules to include any vehicles depending on the ground for support. In 1965 in the Utah desert, Craig Breedlove took the record above 600 mph in his *Spirit of America – Sonic 1*, an aluminium and glass-fibre capsule propelled by a General Electric turbojet.

Above: Aerofoils were first seen in 1968 on Formula 1 Ferrari and Brabham cars. The early designs were too flimsy and some collapsed, and were later banned. Here Belgain driver Jacques Ickx corners in his Ferrari during a 1968 Grand Prix.

Below: American Craig Breedlove raised the Land Speed record four times in his direct-jet Spirit of America. *In 1964 he had lifted the figure to over 500 mph – he is seen here with his 3-wheel version – and in 1965 took the record up to 600.6 mph in the four wheel* Spirit.

One Hundred Years On: 1970 to the Present

As the 1970s opened for business Japanese car imports increased from a trickle to a flood. The first cars were seen by customers in the West as representing good value for money in terms of equipment and fittings, if rather less in suspension and steering engineering. What most other manufacturers offered as optional extras – clocks and radios – the Japanese fitted as standard. However, the cars were conventional, the styling was unexciting and expert drivers considered handling and general performance to be behind the times.

The criticism could not be applied to the Datsun 240Z, made in Yoko-hama and launched on a competition programme that included victory in the gruelling East African Safari rally. The 240Z was an attractive two-seater with a six-cylinder 2.4-litre engine (2.8 litres in the U.S. where it won a Car of the Year award). It was to become the best-selling sports car in automotive history – nearly three quarters of a million were produced.

Other Japanese cars, from Honda, Mitsubishi, Nissan, Toyota, Subaru, Daihatsu and other companies, improved swiftly in appearance and performance. In the 1960s Japanese cars had all been conventional front-engined, rear-wheel-drive models;

Looking a little like an MGB, this Datsun 260Z packed 2.6 litres and 162 hp, giving those who could summon up the courage a top speed of 127 mph. With its immediate precursor the 240Z, it became the world's best-selling sportscar in the 1980s.

now they were seen in all varieties of layout, including front-wheel drive, and Mazda obtained a licence to use the Wankel rotary engine in 100-mph coupés and saloons.

Japanese production rose: four million cars in 1972 . . . six million in 1979 . . . seven million in 1980. Japan had outstripped the U.S.A. as the world's largest maker of cars. It was also the biggest exporter of cars – 3.7 million in 1982. Manufacturers and trade ministers in many countries watched films of cars rolling out of Japanese factories where workers sang company hymns, and shuddered at the prospect of unrestricted exports.

On the principle that 'if you can't beat 'em, join 'em', American manufacturers bought their way into Japanese companies. General Motors acquired shares in Isuzu, Ford in Mazda, Chrysler in Mitsubishi. Some Japanese cars were sold in the U.S. under American names. British Leyland came to an arrangement to assemble an Anglicized version of the Honda Ballade which it sold as the Triumph Acclaim, and Alfa Romeo and Nissan linked to build the Arna.

Production dropped in most of the old established car-making countries.

The U.K.'s was halved – from 1.9 million a year in 1972 to 900 000 in 1981. The U.S.A.'s fell from 8.8 million a year to 6.2 million. In France, Italy, Sweden and Canada, production also fell; only in West Germany did it hold up.

It was not simply the imports from Japan that caused the decrease; an increasing number of mainly low-priced cars were being exported from Eastern Europe – Russia's Lada, Czechoslovakia's Skoda, Poland's FSO and Yugoslavia's Zavasta – and from further east – Korea's Hyundai. By the 1980s imports accounted for more than 55 per cent of car sales in Britain, a country where, in the past, ownership of a foreign car had marked one out either as an enthusiast for a particular marque or as an eccentric.

But imports alone were not entirely responsible for the state of the industry. At the start of the 1970s Rolls-Royce was brought to ruin by losses on an aircraft engine order which was cancelled. The British government mounted a rescue operation, nationalizing the company, but the car division, which was a comparatively small part of the old firm, was hived off and reorganized as Rolls-Royce Motors.

Above: Eastern European countries (now abbreviated to Comecon were beginning to offer the West low-priced cars. This bouncy little Skoda Super Estelle is a later example of a range of Czech cars of around a litre capacity that have improved considerably in recent years.

Overleaf: Not included in a package holiday to the West Indies is this Rolls-Royce Corniche, a Crewe product in the finest tradition. The always-profitable car division became a separate company in 1971; the Corniche was announced a month later.

Opposite top: The Ford Fiesta was built mainly in Spain but was assembled in both Britain and Germany. This cutway shows the Fiesta's general layout and engineering.

Below: A Renault 19GTL with 1.4 or 1.6 litre engine, later to grow into 2 litres or more, and now offered with a fashionable turbo unit that enables the family to cruise at 112 mph. Renault cars were being assembled or produced in some 30 countries by the late 1970s.

Then in the mid-1970s, British Leyland, its size assumed to have ensured its invulnerability, was bedevilled by strikes and came to the verge of collapse. Again the government mounted a rescue operation, acquiring 95 per cent of the shares. However BL lacked new and attractive models, the work force remained restive, and millions of the taxpayers' money was spent in propping up the company before a thrusting new chief executive, Michael Edwardes, brought in from the Chloride battery group, wrung out the major troubles.

He was tough with both management and shop-floor workers, brought forward new models such as the Metro and Maestro, and established stability, before bowing out with a knighthood.

By this time Chrysler was in difficulties, and eventually sold control of all its European companies – in Britain, France and Spain – to Peugeot in France, which had, by this time, also taken over Citroën.

Car makers increasingly moved work from countries where inflation and wage demands were high to less well-developed areas where work was more sought after and labour was cheaper. Ford opened factories in Spain, Renault in Portugal, Chrysler in Iran, Fiat in Brazil and so on.

Cars became more cosmopolitan. The Ford Fiesta was built mainly in Spain but assembly was also carried out in Britain and Germany. Its General Motors rival, sold in Britain as the Vauxhall Nova and elsewhere as the Opel Corsa, was also built in Spain and imported into Britain.

Collaboration between manufacturers grew. Renault made a pact with American Motors which allowed A.M. to build and sell Renaults in the U.S. and Canada (where the Renault 9 became the Alliance) and Renault to import and sell Jeeps in France. In another deal Renault 5s were built in South Africa by Toyota under the same roof as the Japanese company's Corollas, while another factory in the same country made both Mercedes and

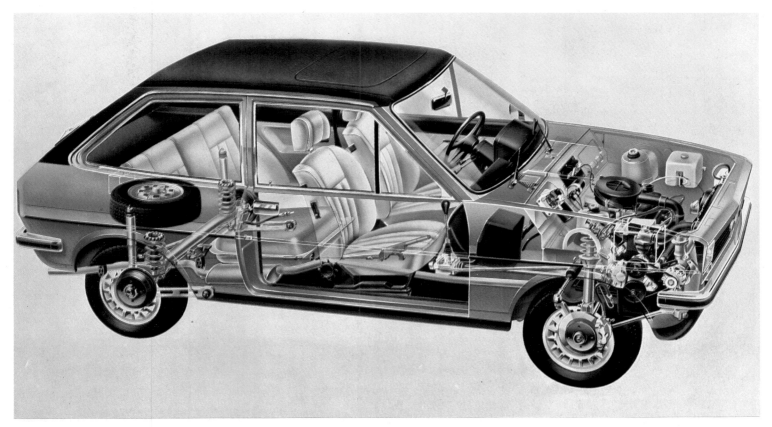

Hondas. This time it all made good commercial sense.

Petrol Pump Blues

In the 1970s the motorist's lot was not a happy one. Car prices rose steeply, largely due to the inflation that affected most countries, and to taxation. Economists claimed that, in real terms, cars were actually cheaper than in the past, citing the number of hours the average person needed to work to buy a car today compared with the higher number necessary in the 1930s. This was small consolation to the motorist who had become accustomed to trading in his car for a new model every two or three years; this had once been comparatively cheap to do but now it required a ransom in ready money.

Running a car was also more expensive. Garage charges rose and motorists began to omit or delay regular servicing, though this was countered by manufacturers redesigning to reduce or abolish greasing points and other components requiring regular attention, and extending the time between services.

Petrol prices shot up, the first big increase coming in the wake of the 1973 Arab-Israeli conflict. The Yom Kippur war at first caused a petrol drought and long queues outside filling stations. Ration coupons were distributed in Britain, though happily

never brought into use. Speed limits were lowered for a time in the interests of fuel economy, and on the Continent there were 'no-motoring' days.

Then, when the conflict was over, the Arab oil producers demanded

Below: In the wake of the Arab-Israeli war these ration coupons appeared in the motorist's morning mail. Scheduled to last for six months they allowed an unspecified but no doubt meagre gallonage per car owner.

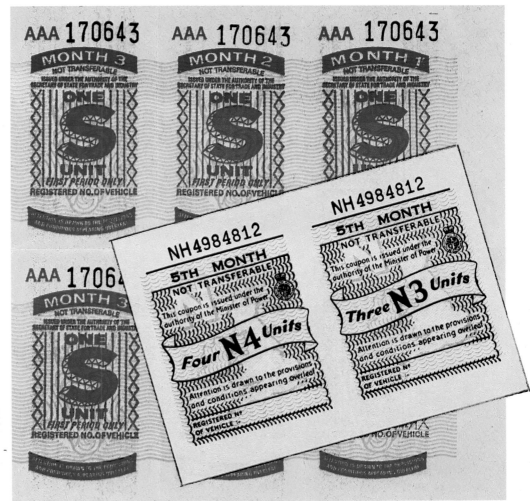

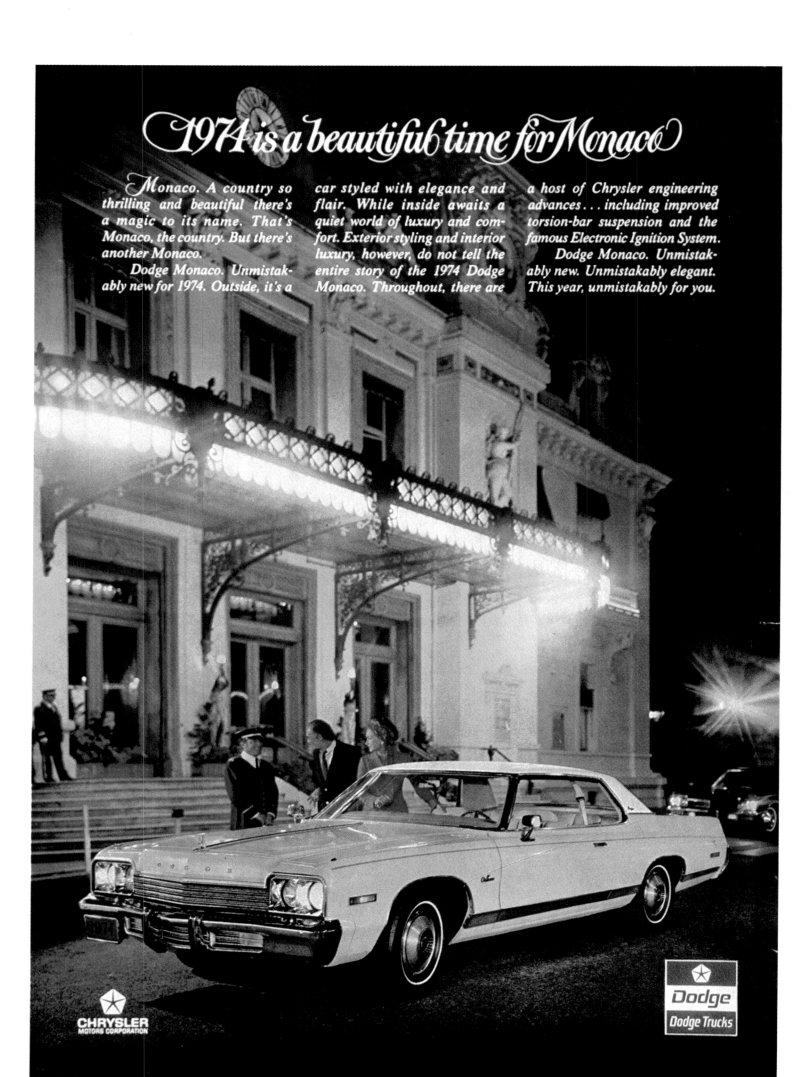

1974 is a beautiful time for Monaco

Monaco. A country so thrilling and beautiful there's a magic to its name. That's Monaco, the country. But there's another Monaco.

Dodge Monaco. Unmistakably new for 1974. Outside, it's a car styled with elegance and flair. While inside awaits a quiet world of luxury and comfort. Exterior styling and interior luxury, however, do not tell the entire story of the 1974 Dodge Monaco. Throughout, there are a host of Chrysler engineering advances... including improved torsion-bar suspension and the famous Electronic Ignition System.

Dodge Monaco. Unmistakably new. Unmistakably elegant. This year, unmistakably for you.

CHRYSLER
MOTORS CORPORATION

Dodge
Dodge Trucks

higher prices. This was not surprising; in the past they had sold oil relatively cheaply and seen governments load the price at the pumps with high taxes. Within months the price of petrol doubled.

Inevitably motorists used their cars less. In the 1930s the Automobile Association had made calculations on the basis of an average annual mileage of 12 000 miles. In 1947 they had revised the average figure to 10 000 miles a year. In 1976 they reduced the figure to 8 000 miles a year.

In Germany the motor industry set itself the task of achieving a 15 per cent improvement in the fuel consumption of new vehicles by 1985. In the U.S., home of appallingly thirsty engines, the government launched a tough campaign to reduce the country's energy dependence, and decreed that the fuel economy of all new cars produced must rise steadily year by year to reach a 100 per cent improvement – and later demanded still more. In 1974 the average American car was giving 12 miles per gallon; this figure must rise by stages said the authorities, to reach 27.5 mpg in 1985.

The most noticeable effect was an acceleration of the move to smaller cars. In the wake of the compacts came super-compacts such as the Buick Skylark, the Ford Pinto, the A.M.C. Gremlin (later the Spirit) and the Chevrolet Chevette. These super-compacts ranged in length from 15 feet down to 13 feet, though most had engines of more than 2 litres. However, the U.S. also began making the VW Rabbit, a three-door hatchback just 13 feet long with a 1.5-litre engine.

Established models were made smaller – 'downsized' in the jargon of the industry. The Cadillac Seville (the first Cadillac to have a unitary body) shrank by 26 inches to 17 feet, and a 5.7-litre engine replaced the giant 8.2-litre unit in use in 1970. Lincoln Continentals became 10 inches shorter, Chrysler downsized its Cordoba and Le Baron, Dodge shortened its Magnum and Diplomat, and Ford decreased its Thunderbird. The U.S.A. quickly learned the lesson which had been forced on European car makers in the 1930s.

Hand in hand with the campaign for energy conservation in the U.S., went

Opposite: Last of the gas-guzzlers? This 1974 Dodge Monaco pictured at the steps of the famous Monte Carlo Casino was offered with a confusing variety of power units – all of them thirsty.

Below: Downsized Diplomat. This Dodge with the distinguished name was chopped front and rear for 'added lightness' and thus less fuel consumption. It was still offered with either a 3.7 litre or a V8 of 5.2 litres.

Opposite: American Motors of Detroit were always unconventional, with designs and engineering usually on a smaller scale than their neighbours. This 1984 Eagle conforms to the current demand for economy, with a 4.2 six and reduced dimensions. It comes with four-wheel drive.

Right: The replacement for the high-selling Jaguar E-type was the XJ-S seen here. With its larger, heavier body and seats for four, power steering, fuel-injection, V12 engine and other sophistications it lost some of the E-type aura.

the campaign against pollution by exhaust emissions. President Nixon, in his 1970 State of the Union message, said, 'The automobile is our worst polluter of air. Adequate control requires further advance in engine design and fuel composition. We shall intensify our research, set increasingly strict standards and strengthen enforcement procedure, and we shall do it now.'

The standards set by Congress called for the amount of carbon monoxide and unburnt hydrocarbons of petrol emitted to be drastically reduced by 1975 and reduced still further by 1980. Manufacturers complained that it was impossible to meet the figures in the time allowed.

In fact, by the second half of the 1970s they were claiming that they had achieved a 70 per cent reduction in carbon monoxide and that pollution by cars had passed its peak and was on the way down, though they were still protesting that the ultimate standards to be achieved were four times more stringent than was necessary to protect public health.

The fight against pollution was being won, but at a cost. There was a reduction in the performance of cars; models that met the emission standards were noticeably more sluggish than similar cars that did not – though with a 55-mph speed limit continuing in force in the U.S.A., the effects of this were minimized.

Curiously, at a time when fuel consumption had become an important factor in the choice of a car for most people, and when most roads were

Opposite: Ferrari 308GTB4; a transversely mounted V8 unit at the rear gave this 2 + 2 coupé a thrusting 255 hp in 1974, a year when most manufacturers were cutting down their power.

Left: The BMW 320i has a six cylinder engine of about the same size as the Mercedes 190, and has a higher top speed and faster acceleration although at the expense of a higher fuel consumption.

Below: The Porsche 911 was launched in 1964, since when the German company has offered half a dozen different model numbers to an admiring public. However, the classic 911 shape has remained a favourite and is still available in a range culminating in the exotic Porsche 911 Turbo.

subject to speed limits, there were still customers for two-seaters, faster than any cars on the roads before.

Fastest of them all was the Lamborghini Countach, a V-12 four-litre car which would reach 196 mph. Its closest rival was the Ferrari Boxer with a Pininfarina body; its 12-cylinder 4.4-litre (later 5-litre) engine gave it a top speed of 175 mph. The Maserati Bora, with a V-8 4.7-litre engine could hit 160 mph.

BMW's six-cylinder Karmann-styled coupés with large boot-lid aerofoils that caused them to be known as Batmobiles reached 140 mph on their 3-litre engines, while the Porsche Turbo, derived from the 911 coupé and looking like a racer though actually built for the road, achieved 155 mph on a similarly sized engine.

Alfa Romeo's Montreal had a V-8 of 2.6 litres and a speed of around 135 mph, and the wedge-shaped Lotus

Above: Lotus's wedge-shaped Esprit and Eclat have been around since 1976 but this turbo-charged 210hp was first seen in 1981. This is the 2174cc 1984 edition.

Opposite: The small Lancashire manufacturer TVR opened for business in 1954 with a single model and moved onto kit cars a couple of years later. Since then their 1600cc coupé has gained respect. The present TVR Tasmin uses a 2 or 2.8 litre unit and the highly sophisticated 350i houses a 3528cc Rover Vitesse engine.

Below: England's most historically distinguished sporting marque is arguably Aston Martin, with its competition activities going back as far as 1919. This is a current V8 Vantage with a 5.3 litre unit and a potential of 150mph.

Esprit, which replaced the Europa, had a four-cylinder 2.2-litre engine but could still get close to 140 mph.

Britain's Aston Martin and the Bristol range are rare birds, seen only occasionally. The Blackpool-made TVR, marketed in various specifications for the past 20 years, is another once-endangered species, although now that the dramatic and swift Tasmin range is offered, we may expect to see TVRs proliferate in the United Kingdom and overseas.

Hatchbacks and Superminis

For explorers and campers and others with equipment to transport over rough terrain, a need was filled in 1970 by the Range Rover, a Jeep-inspired four-wheel-drive, go-anywhere vehicle but more car than truck, with deep carpets, wood door-capping and a speed of 100 mph. It had a V-8 3.5-litre engine, was big, with high seats, and was used by expeditions in every part of the world, and also by police motorway patrols.

For the majority, who need a normal car most of the time but a pick-up or station wagon on occasion, there was another answer. The runaway success of the 1970s – and since – was and is the hatchback – a car with a third (or fifth) door at the rear, and a folding rear seat

which enables large or awkward loads to be carried; it combines the looks and comfort of a saloon with the convenience and adaptability of a station wagon.

It began with the Renault 16 in the 1960s and other manufacturers were forced to follow. The Ford Capri, which had sold a million as a coupé, became a hatchback in 1973. The Citroën GS saloon became the GSA hatchback. The style even came to such an executive-class car as the wedge-shaped Rover 3500.

But the smaller the car, the greater the value of the hatchback style, and this led to the 'superminis', front-wheel-drive hatchbacks of 1 to 1.2 litres, which by the 1980s formed the biggest sector of the European car market for private buyers.

The supermini saga began in 1971 with the Fiat 127, slightly bigger than the Mini but with a similar transversely mounted fwd engine of 903 cc. VW's Polo appeared in 1975, a smaller edition of the fast-selling Golf.

By the 1980s every major European car company offered one or more superminis, even Ford, which finally went over to front-wheel-drive with the Fiesta.

Britain produced the Austin and MG Mini Metro; France, the Talbot Samba, Citroën LNA and Visa, Renault 5 and Peugeot 104; Italy, the Fiat Uno and Panda; Spain, the General Motors Corsa/Nova; Yugoslavia the Zastava Yugo; and from Japan came the Nissan Micra, Daihatsu Charade, Datsun Cherry, Honda Civic and Toyota Starlet – all of them in the supermini bracket.

Duckworth's Wonderful Engine

The 3-litre Grand Prix formula continued through the 1970s and into the 1980s, the longest-lived formula in the history of the sport. It continued to be dominated by the Ford DFV V-8 engine, designed by Keith Duckworth and built by Cosworth of Northampton, England, a firm which had never been involved in Grand Prix racing before it received the Ford contract. However, the 400 bhp it gave when it was introduced in 1967 rose to nearly 500 over the years.

It was the power unit used by all but the few racing teams that made their own engines. In 1970 it powered the Lotus of Austria's Jochen Rindt, the only driver to have been awarded the title of world champion posthumously; he had achieved an unassailable lead in the points table before he was killed during practice for the Italian Grand Prix at Monza that year.

It also powered the Tyrrell of Scotland's Jackie Stewart when he won the

Opposite: Citroën of Paris has been in the small car world for some time, along with their innovative medium-size range. Their 2CV, LN and the ubiquitous Visa gave them a wide appeal when fuel prices increased. Sunning itself on the beach is a Citroën Visa.

Below: Scottish driver Jackie Stewart brings his 3-litre Tyrell-Ford Grand Prix car into Druids Bend at Brands Hatch. Since 1967 Stewart had spent most of his driving F1 life with the Ford DFV V8 engine. Nineteen of the 26 starters at this 1972 British GP were powered by Ford.

Opposite: That other sport – rallying. This is a 1970s scene at Monte Carlo as the survivors arrive after their long drive from multiple-point starts.

Right: Italian-born American citizen Mario Andretti captured the World Championship of Drivers title in 1978 in a Lotus-Ford. Here he receives the trophy that goes to the winner of the German Grand Prix.

Below: The scene, the 1983 British Grand Prix; the car, a Brabham-BMW; and the driver, 31-year old Brazilian Nelson Piquet – on his way to his second World Championship.

world championship in 1971 and 1973, the Lotus of Brazil's Emerson Fittipaldi in 1972 and his McLaren in 1974, the McLaren of England's James Hunt in 1976, the Lotus of the U.S.'s Mario Andretti in 1978, the Williams of Australia's Alan Jones in 1980, the Brabham of Brazil's Nelson Piquet in 1981 and that of Finland's Keke Roseberg in 1982.

The only two world champions of the 1970s to win with other engines both drove the Ferrari, which had its own 12-cylinder unit. The first was Austrian Niki Lauda who won in 1975 and again in 1977, after making an incredibly brave comeback following a crash in the German Grand Prix of 1976 when his face was badly burned. The other was South African Jody Scheckter in 1979.

A new look was given to Grand Prix cars in the 1970s when they acquired skirts like those of a hovercraft. These were first introduced in the Can-Am (Canadian-American) series of races for two-seaters in 1970 when, to help the car hug the road at speed, a Chaparral 2J was equipped with an auxiliary engine, known to drivers as a sucker, to extract underbody air. Skirts were attached at sides and rear to part-seal the vacuum.

Within a year the authorities had

banned the suction device but the skirts—without 'vacuum cleaners'—then appeared in Grand Prix cars with the same object. However, they too were banned later.

At Le Mans, Porsche succeeded in becoming the outstanding car. The Porsche 917, propelled by the most powerful air-cooled engine ever, a 12-cylinder, 4.5-litre unit, won the 24 Hour race in 1970 and 1971. One car in 1971 *lapped* at nearly 152 mph and set records that lasted into the 1980s. For the remainder of the 1970s the main winners were Porsche and France's Matra-Simca, each scoring three victories.

The outstanding driver in this event was Jacky Ickx of Belgium who became the first man to win Le Mans five times. He had won in 1969 in the Ford GT40, in 1975 in the Gulf-Mirage and in 1976, 1977 and 1981 in Porsche cars. The Gulf-Mirage, incidentally, was powered by the same Ford-Cosworth DFV engine used in Grand Prix cars.

Another Cosworth engine, of 1.6 litres, was used in the Ford Escort RS1600 (a sporting version of the family saloon) that won rallies all over the world.

But the sport at its top level grew ever more costly and many firms were forced out of racing in the 1970s.

Even more costly were the world's land speed record attempts. In 1970 Garry Gabelich, an American drag racer who had trained as an astronaut,

went after the record in the *Blue Flame*, a 38-foot-long rocket car, burning liquid gas in an engine used in the space programme. Wearing a T-shirt and 28 strings of beads, and carrying a variety of other talismans, he took the record to 622.41 mph.

Gabelich remained the record holder until 1983 when London businessman Richard Noble raced across Nevada's Black Rock desert in his aluminium-wheeled, parachute-braked *Thrust Two*, powered by the 15 000-hp Rolls-Royce jet engine of a Lightning fighter. He lifted the record to 633.47 mph. But it did not seem to have much to do with motoring any more.

The Road Ahead

It was once fashionable for artists looking ahead to the 21st century to draw a Buck Rogers world of foil-clad people in pencil-slim superfast vehicles capable of both running on roads and taking to the air. Other prophets, the doom-watchers, forecast a return to a primitive way of life in a world which had used up all its modern energy sources.

With the 21st century close at hand —and many current driving licences terminating well into it—forecasts tend to be more mundane. Now it seems probable that a driver of today will still be at home in the vehicle of tomorrow. Although the car has advanced beyond the wildest dreams of its pioneers of the 19th century and many scientists (Volks-

Opposite top: Best rally vehicle? The four-wheel drive Audi Quattro has recorded an impressive fist of rally wins including three Monte Carlo Victories in succession. Here a Quattro makes a short flight during a recent international event.

Opposite below: A past view of the future ... this Buck Rogers-type scene drawn in the 1950s is not as we now envisage the future, at a time when some of our own driving licences are valid until well into the 21st century.

Left: It has been necessary to introduce new disciplines for drivers now that over 17 million vehicles daily crowd the roads of Britain. No, the police officer is not lighting his cigarette—it's the latest 'alcolmeter' breathalyzer.

wagen alone employs 6 000 on research and development) are working on plans for the automobile of the next century, some form of internal combustion engine and some type of fossil fuel will probably be in use well into the next century, while other forms of power are investigated.

Much of the current work is concerned with alternative engines. Even to its most ardent fans, steam now seems unlikely to make a comeback, but electric vehicles still seem desirable on almost every count – clean, quiet and non-polluting. Many electric (or hybrid-electric) vehicles are running today but despite all the work that has been done since the days of Chasseloup-Laubat and Jenatzy, the problems of battery-power storage remain. It is possible to build either a car with a reasonable turn of speed but only a small range between charges, or a car with a viable range but low speed; combining speed and range is a still-unsolved problem.

In the United States many A.M.C. Electrucks are used for postal deliveries in towns – single-seaters just over 11 feet long with a 54V 30-bhp motor giving a speed of up to 40 mph and a range of 30 miles including frequent stops.

At the top end of the scale there is the EAC electric limousine, a six-seater, 18 feet long, based on a Cadillac. It is capable of 70 mph and has a range of 70 to 100 miles – the best yet. Its batteries can be charged on board in eight hours or in 45 minutes with an external fast charge, but it is actually a hybrid with an auxiliary petrol engine to supply air conditioning, heating, power braking, steering and charging.

While the electric car remains a strong hope of the mid-distant future, work continues on the rotary engine. There has also been a more ready acceptance of the diesel engine with its cost-saving advantages in recent years, and in Germany in 1982 diesel cars captured 16 per cent of the market.

The turbocharger, a form of supercharger driven by exhaust gases rather than mechanical means, was also coming into wider use by the late 1970s particularly in Grand Prix racing, where Renault began to take the lead. The turbo was combined with a diesel engine in a number of road cars – for example the Rover SD Turbo housed a four-cylinder 2.4-litre diesel unit

which gave it a top speed of 101 mph and a fuel consumption of 32.7 mpg at a constant 75 mph.

Research into fuels, existing and potential, has been stepped up – the urgency engendered by the U.S.A.'s energy-saving and anti-pollution regulations. After the initial panic of the early 1970s, fears that the world is running out of oil were less frequently expressed, and Henry Ford II, among others, has argued that petrol will be the fuel for decades yet. He said in 1976, 'Nobody knows how much oil is left in the ground and the chances are that we will never find out because we will never get to the bottom of the barrel . . . . More oil is discovered each year than is used, and more has been discovered in recent years than ever before. And we know that most of the world is still untouched by oil geologists . . . . The main reason more oil has not been found is that there has been little incentive to look farther or deeper for still more.'

If oil does run out other fuels are possible. In Brazil more than 700 000 of the country's eight million vehicles are now running on alcohol. They are fuelled by ethanol, which is cheaper in Brazil than petrol and is produced there from surplus sugar cane.

Gas is another option. In 1982 Ford built an alternative fuel vehicle (the AFV) modified to run on methane (natural gas). It was refuelled quickly and easily from domestic gas mains by means of an adaptor. The car's acceleration and cruising range were both claimed to be better than those of an electric car, and it could also be adapted to use ethanol, methanol or liquified petroleum gas (LPG). In Britain a farmer achieved fame by running his car on a gaseous fuel made from chicken droppings. The possibility of further fuel sources for road vehicles derived from nuclear energy or solar power is not as remote as it was a decade ago.

Car shapes will continue to grow more aerodynamic, the outcome of wind-tunnel tests; the first major advances in reducing drag were made in the 1970s, notably by Audi. And new materials – in the 1970s energy-absorbing polypropolene – began to be used for bumpers in place of chromed or polished metal. At the start of the 1980s Citroën introduced its BX cars which were hailed as 'plastic cars' with their bonnets [hoods] and other body

Opposite: Production will become more automated. At this Italian Fiat plant, systems have already progressed well into robotics and much of the small Strada is produced virtually 'untouched by hand'. Here a body shell finds its own way to the next stage of production.

Overleaf: New image from Mercedes-Benz. A smaller car, the 190, was launched by the German company in 1983. It is aimed at the executive company-car market, with a 4 cylinder 2 litre unit.

panels made of a composite polyester and glass-fibre mixture. As a publicity stunt journalists were invited to clout the bonnet with a (smallish) hammer; no dents resulted.

Inside the car, electronics will grow in importance. The 1970s brought electronic digital clocks and electronic ignition. Some Japanese models of the 1980s have digital speedometers, electronic controls for automatic transmission giving the driver a choice of economy or power ranges, and microprocessor-controlled air conditioners and cruise controls.

The trend is highly likely to grow into an onboard computer system monitoring *all* the car's functions. Warning will be given, by means of a digital display, when a door is not shut or washer fluid is low; information will be provided on the elapsed time of the journey, the average speed necessary to complete the journey by a given time, and the like. Not all information will necessarily be revealed visually. An up-range model, the BL Maestro already has a talking warning system, with a synthesized female voice calling attention to such matters as a low-fuel level, and a more urgent male voice calling for an immediate halt in the event of a major malfunction. At present, there is some resistance to these startling innovations, but sooner or later they will undoubtedly become the norm on many vehicles.

Production will become more automated. In the 1970s Fiat based its television advertising for its Strada hatchback on the fact that it was 'Built by robots'. This referred to the Robogate automated production lines at Fiat's Rivalta and Cassino factories where robot machines, including welders, can work on mixed model lines, making different bodyshells consecutively without the need for retooling. As labour costs rise and repetitive assembly-line work becomes even less attractive to workers, the use of robots can only increase.

They will be kept busy. Rising prices and unemployment may make it more difficult for many to afford a new car, but today, one hundred years after Karl Benz drove the first shaky horseless carriage out of his Mannheim workshop, it has become regarded as normal, if not essential, to own a car and enjoy the independence, freedom of movement and ease of travel it brings. No one will willingly surrender that, and whether the motive power is fossil fuel, nuclear energy or sunshine, the automobile is here to stay.

Below: Will this be the shape of things to come? A Ford Ghia prototype that shows a styling exercise coupled with aerodynamics.

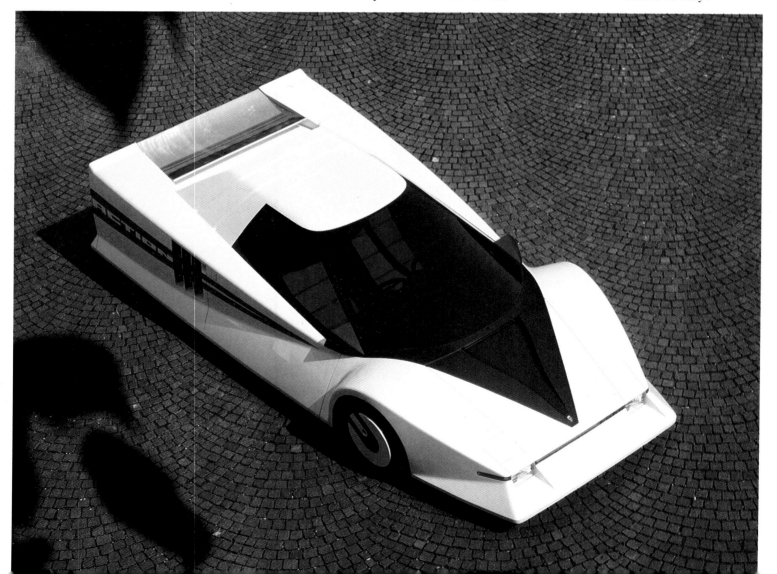

Index